D0746909

IN TRANSIT

In transit

MOVING CONFIDENTLY THROUGH TODAY'S WORLD

A DAILY GUIDE BY DAVID JEREMIAH

EDITED BY MARK L. CARPENTER

TYNDALE HOUSE PUBLISHERS, INC.   WHEATON, ILLINOIS

ACKNOWLEDGMENTS

My appreciation to the young people of the
Haddon Heights Baptist Church, who motivated
me to prepare these studies . . . to Dr. Howard
Hendricks, who taught me how to ask questions
of the Scriptures . . . to Mark L. Carpenter, who
reorganized the material in its present form . . .
and in memory of Donna Miller, who loved these
lessons from the Word of God and never stopped
studying until the day she went to be with Christ.

Photo credits: cover photo, *Tom Rogowski,
courtesy of Huffy Corporation;* January,
H. Armstrong Roberts; February, *Bob Combs;*
March, *Jonathan A. Meyers;* April, *Jonathan A.
Meyers;* May, *Dave DeJong;* June, *Robert Meier;*
July, *Dave DeJong;* August, *P. Gregory Davis;*
September, *United Press International;* October,
AP/Wide World Photo; November, *Dave DeJong;*
December, *United Press International*

Unless otherwise noted, all Scripture quotations
are taken from *The Living Bible,*
and are used by permission.

Second printing, June 1984

TO MY DAUGHTER JAN

WHO WILL SOON BE IN TRANSIT

CONTENTS

INTRODUCTION

As a young person today, you are moving through a stage of life that demands many choices and decisions. You will soon need to make decisions about your future schooling, career, life partner, and Christian service. It's not easy to live as a young Christian in a world affected by changing values, morality, fashions, and technology. The temptation is strong to conform to the world's standards. This is where *In Transit* comes in: As a devotional/Bible study book, it was compiled to help you concentrate on God's Word as you move through this stage of life. It is based on twelve New Testament epistles: eight by the apostle Paul, three by John, and one by James. The daily entries feature:

- Bible readings: Daily Scripture quotes reprinted from the easy-to-read *Living Bible.*

- Text questions: Brief questions that point you to the main theme of the daily Bible readings.

- Applications: Supplementary material (anecdotes, quotes from Christian leaders, and commentaries) that relates the Bible to the specifics of your life.

- A prayer diary: A section at the bottom of each page where you can record daily prayer requests and praises.

IN TRANSIT will help you to make sense of the chaos that surrounds us. It will show you that we *can* move with confidence through today's world.

January ROMANS 1 - 5

Athletes of all nationalities and cultures come together at the world's largest sporting events. Because of their different languages and customs, the athletes seem to have little in common. But then the starting gun sounds, and they're suddenly united with oneness of purpose—the will to win. ■ The first chapters of Romans speak of another, more important factor that unites people of all backgrounds—the gospel. Paul makes it clear that all men need Christ in order to win the largest reward of all—eternal life.

The Corpse in the Saddle

DEAR friends in Rome: This letter is from Paul, Jesus Christ's slave, chosen to be a missionary, and sent out to preach God's Good News. This Good News was promised long ago by God's prophets in the Old Testament. It is the Good News about his Son, Jesus Christ our Lord, who came as a human baby, born into King David's royal family line; and by being raised from the dead he was proved to be the mighty Son of God, with the holy nature of God himself.

And now, through Christ, all the kindness of God has been poured out upon us undeserving sinners; and now he is sending us out around the world to tell all people everywhere the great things God has done for them, so that they, too, will believe and obey him.

And you, dear friends in Rome, are among those he dearly loves; you, too, are invited by Jesus Christ to be God's very own—yes, his holy people. May all God's mercies and peace be yours from God our Father and from Jesus Christ our Lord. (Romans 1:1-7)

Paul is absolutely sure that Jesus Christ is God. What does he believe to be the greatest proof of this fact?

Over one thousand years ago, a Spanish province was under attack by foreign invaders. For many years, a small Spanish garrison withstood the assaults. Their resistance was due to their remarkable leader, Ruy Díaz de Bivar, commonly known as "El Cid." Finally El Cid died of old age. After an initial panic, his lieutenants had an idea. They dressed his body in armor, tied a sword in his hand, and mounted the corpse on his horse. With El Cid's body in the lead, the Spanish forces charged. But they were quickly defeated, for this foolish act fooled neither the foe nor inspired the Spaniards. Christ's resurrection was real. It was not a bold trick by his disciples. His resurrection inspired his followers. And rather than collapsing, as deceptions do, the Good News spread.

P R A I S E :

P E T I T I O N :

Sing a new song to the Lord; sing his praises, all you who live in earth's remotest corners! (Isa. 42:10)

Getting Together

LET me say first of all that wherever I go I hear you being talked about! For your faith in God is becoming known around the world. How I thank God through Jesus Christ for this good report, and for each one of you. God knows how often I pray for you. Day and night I bring you and your needs in prayer to the one I serve with all my might, telling others the Good News about his Son.

And one of the things I keep on praying for is the opportunity, God willing, to come at last to see you and, if possible, that I will have a safe trip. For I long to visit you so that I can impart to you the faith that will help your church grow strong in the Lord. Then, too, I need your help, for I want not only to share my faith with you but to be encouraged by yours: Each of us will be a blessing to the other.

I want you to know, dear brothers, that I planned to come many times before (but was prevented) so that I could work among you and see good results, just as I have among the other Gentile churches. For I owe a great debt to you and to everyone else, both to civilized people and uncivilized alike; yes, to the educated and uneducated alike. So, to the fullest extent of my ability, I am ready to come also to you in Rome to preach God's Good News. (Romans 1:8-15)

What are two reasons Paul wants to visit the Christians in Rome?

Paul is probably the greatest evangelist who ever lived. He has never been surpassed in spiritual stature. Yet here we see that even Paul needed the encouragement that comes in Christian fellowship. Thus we dare not underestimate the importance of Christian fellowship in Christian growth. It is essential for each of us to be part of a group where we can give and receive service and encouragement. This is especially true during life's transitional periods, when we are uncertain of our beliefs and goals.

P R A I S E :

P E T I T I O N :

Love your enemies! Pray for those who persecute you! (Matt. 5:44)

A Shameful Embarrassment

FOR I am not ashamed of this Good News about Christ. It is God's powerful method of bringing all who believe it to heaven. This message was preached first to the Jews alone, but now everyone is invited to come to God in this same way. This Good News tells us that God makes us ready for heaven—makes us right in God's sight—when we put our faith and trust in Christ to save us. This is accomplished from start to finish by faith. As the Scripture says it, "The man who finds life will find it through trusting God." (Romans 1:16, 17)

Why is Paul not ashamed of the Good News?

The secular media are not particularly kind to Christians. Prominent evangelists are often portrayed as money-hungry quacks. Christians of conviction are ridiculed as bigots or fanatics. And Christian morality is often written off as fanaticism. As a result, many of us are embarrassed about showing our faith in public. We don't want to draw undue attention to ourselves by expressing or demonstrating our beliefs. Paul, however, was not ashamed. He had *eternal* values in mind when he stated, "[The Good News] is God's powerful method of bringing all who believe it to heaven." The urgency of that truth obliterates his embarrassment.

PRAISE :

PETITION :

To God, prayer is what incense was to the Jewish temple. It impregnates everything, perfumes everything, and sweetens everything.

The God Instinct

BUT God shows his anger from heaven against all sinful, evil men who push away the truth from them. For the truth about God is known to them instinctively; God has put this knowledge in their hearts. Since earliest times men have seen the earth and sky and all God made, and have known of his existence and great eternal power. So they will have no excuse [when they stand before God at Judgment Day]. (Romans 1:18-20)

What kind of men are the targets of God's wrath? Do you think that any man will escape this wrath?

A favorite saying among several evangelists of the early 1970s was: "Every heart has in it a God-shaped vacuum." The implication, of course, was that man can be complete and fulfilled only with God in his heart. In *Eternity in Their Hearts* (Regal, 1981), Don Richardson tells about countless isolated tribal peoples who have realized the existence of God, then sought to reach him through idolatry and rituals. As Paul stated, "God is known to them instinctively." Their desires for communion with God were honorable, but their efforts at worship were misdirected. How fortunate we are; we know that our "God-shaped vacuums" can be totally filled by the true God, our Creator.

P R A I S E :

P E T I T I O N :

You . . . must build up your lives ever more strongly upon the foundation of our holy faith, learning to pray in the power and strength of the Holy Spirit. (Jude 1:20)

Blind as a Fish

YES, they knew about him all right, but they wouldn't admit it or worship him or even thank him for all his daily care. And after awhile they began to think up silly ideas of what God was like and what he wanted them to do. The result was that their foolish minds became dark and confused. Claiming themselves to be wise without God, they became utter fools instead. And then, instead of worshiping the glorious, ever-living God, they took wood and stone and made idols for themselves, carving them to look like mere birds and animals and snakes and puny men. (Romans 1:21-23)

Here Paul talks about the things men put in place of the living God. Make a list of such substitutes in modern life: What are man's contemporary "idols"?

Mammoth Cave in Kentucky contains many underground streams and rivers. In these waters are fish that at one time had existed outside, where there was light. Scientists have discovered that, because of the total absense of light in the cave, these fish have gradually gone blind. They no longer have eyes. There are only empty sockets. The darkness has robbed them of their vision. This is exactly what the darkness of sin does to people. Prolonged exposure to sin renders us spiritually blind.

P R A I S E :

P E T I T I O N :

He does not ignore the prayers of men in trouble when they call to him for help. (Ps. 9:12)

Musical Sex

SO God let them go ahead into every sort of sex sin, and do whatever they wanted to—yes, vile and sinful things with each other's bodies. Instead of believing what they knew was the truth about God, they deliberately chose to believe lies. So they prayed to the things God made, but wouldn't obey the blessed God who made these things.

That is why God let go of them and let them do all these evil things, so that even their women turned against God's natural plan for them and indulged in sex sin with each other. And the men, instead of having a normal sex relationship with women, burned with lust for each other, men doing shameful things with other men and, as a result, getting paid within their own souls with the penalty they so richly deserved. (Romans 1:24-27)

Paul decries sexual promiscuity, saying it leads to *another* grave offense against God. What is this other sin?

In much of today's popular music, sexual deviance is in vogue. David Bowie and Elton John flaunt their bisexuality. Plasmatics' leader Wendy O. Williams, the first rock/porno star, uses obscenity to draw crowds. Boy George of the Culture Club uses transvestitism to create a "mystique." Prince croons the glories of illicit sex. Though we may be tempted to overlook the sensuality of new music in our desire to "fit in," we should keep in mind Paul's words. In no uncertain terms, he calls sexual deviance "vile and sinful."

P R A I S E :

P E T I T I O N :

Many who cry, "God be merciful" never say, "God be praised."

Poison from the Pulpit

SO it was that when they gave God up and would not even acknowledge him, God gave them up to doing everything their evil minds could think of. Their lives became full of every kind of wickedness and sin, of greed and hate, envy, murder, fighting, lying, bitterness, and gossip.

They were backbiters, haters of God, insolent, proud braggarts, always thinking of new ways of sinning and continually being disobedient to their parents. They tried to misunderstand, broke their promises, and were heartless—without pity. They were fully aware of God's death penalty for these crimes, yet they went right ahead and did them anyway, and encouraged others to do them, too. (Romans 1:28-32)

According to this passage, how does man fall into sin?

Jim Jones, a dynamic young pastor in an evangelical church, allowed sin to creep into his life. But he did not repent of it. Instead, he attempted to justify it. He altered his theology to accommodate it. One sin led to another and before long, he had to leave the church. He persuaded several people to leave with him, then started his own "church." Because of his enthusiasm and intensity, soon he had attracted a large group of followers. Meanwhile, he was succumbing to more and more sin. The ensuing frustration turned him into a moody, thoughtless demagogue. As dictator over his people, he ordered them to sell their belongings and move with him to a "new world" in Guyana. We know the rest of the story: Jones was responsible for the deaths of nearly one thousand people. Jones exemplifies the type of person Paul describes in today's reading. Jones considered sin more important than God; God then "gave him up" to a reprobate mind. Let us always be wary of Satan's deceitfulness. Let us strive to root out sin from our lives, acknowledging God so that, at the end of the age, he will acknowledge us.

P R A I S E :

P E T I T I O N :

O our God, hear your servant's prayer! Listen as I plead! (Dan. 9:17)

Greed Bait

"WELL," you may be saying, "what terrible people you have been talking about!" But wait a minute! You are just as bad. When you say they are wicked and should be punished, you are talking about yourselves, for you do these very same things. And we know that God, in justice, will punish anyone who does such things as these. Do you think that God will judge and condemn others for doing them and overlook you when you do them, too? Don't you realize how patient he is being with you? Or don't you care? Can't you see that he has been waiting all this time without punishing you, to give you time to turn from your sin? His kindness is meant to lead you to repentance. (Romans 2:1-4)

If God detests sin, why is he so kind to sinners?

In certain parts of Africa, monkeys are hunted for their meat. Some hunters use an ingenious method of catching the animals. They take heavy wooden vases into the jungle and fasten them to trees. Each vase has a single opening, just big enough to accommodate the outstretched hand of an adult monkey. Before leaving the scene, hunters drop bits of candy into the vases. Lured by curiosity, monkeys approach the vases, slide their hands through the openings, and grab the candy. But they soon discover that their doubled-up fists are too big to pass back through the openings. Rather than release the candy to escape, most monkeys refuse to drop their treasures even when they see danger—the hunters—approaching. Their greed leads to their death. Likewise, many a man's soul has been trapped because he would not let go of sin or lust.

P R A I S E :

P E T I T I O N :

I am God—I only—and there is no other like me who can tell you what is going to happen. All I say will come to pass, for I do whatever I wish. (Isa. 46:9, 10)

Choose Your Clique

BUT no, you won't listen; and so you are saving up terrible punishment for yourselves because of your stubbornness in refusing to turn from your sin; for there is going to come a day of wrath when God will be the just Judge of all the world. He will give each one whatever his deeds deserve. He will give eternal life to those who patiently do the will of God, seeking for the unseen glory and honor and eternal life that he offers. But he will terribly punish those who fight against the truth of God and walk in evil ways—God's anger will be poured out upon them. There will be sorrow and suffering for Jews and Gentiles alike who keep on sinning. But there will be glory and honor and peace from God for all who obey him, whether they are Jews or Gentiles. For God treats everyone the same. (Romans 2:5-11)

What is the outlook for those who seek honor, glory, and eternal life?

Men have found many ways of dividing and subdividing society. They do it by race, nationality, career, sex, income level, religion, interests, and many other categories. Consider, for example, the typical high school. Most students hang out with their "cliques"—groups that share a common bond. There are the jocks, the intellectuals, the rich kids, the preppies, the musicians, blacks, Hispanics, the burnouts, the car freaks, the computer nerds, the druggies, etc. The old adage is true—birds of a feather flock together. In God's eyes, however, humanity is divided into just two groups—the righteous and the unrighteous. God "treats everyone the same," judging all men according to their faith and works.

P R A I S E :

P E T I T I O N :

He who prays as he ought, will endeavor to live as he prays. (J. Owen)

The Frown in the Suitcase

HE will punish sin wherever it is found. He will punish the heathen when they sin, even though they never had God's written laws, for down in their hearts they know right from wrong. God's laws are written within them; their own conscience accuses them, or sometimes excuses them. And God will punish the Jews for sinning because they have his written laws but don't obey them. They know what is right but don't do it. After all, salvation is not given to those who know what to do, unless they do it. The day will surely come when at God's command Jesus Christ will judge the secret lives of everyone, their inmost thoughts and motives; this is all part of God's great plan which I proclaim. (Romans 2:12-16)

What will God judge in us? What is the basis for that judgment?

Someone once asked Socrates about one of his friends. The friend seemed to be always unhappy, even though he was wise and widely traveled. Socrates explained his friend's situation: "He is unhappy because wherever he goes he takes himself with him." A change of atmosphere or environment can never change the person within. An ancient proverb reads: "Though you sail the seven seas, you cannot escape yourself."

P R A I S E :

P E T I T I O N :

He has given me a new song to sing, of praises to our God. (Ps. 40:3)

The Hollow Boys

YOU Jews think all is well between yourselves and God because he gave his laws to you; you brag that you are his special friends. Yes, you know what he wants; you know right from wrong and favor the right because you have been taught his laws from earliest youth. You are so sure of the way to God that you could point it out to a blind man. You think of yourselves as beacon lights, directing men who are lost in darkness to God. You think that you can guide the simple and teach even children the affairs of God, for you really know his laws, which are full of all knowledge and truth.

Yes, you teach others—then why don't you teach yourselves? You tell others not to steal—do *you* steal? You say it is wrong to commit adultery—do *you* do it? You say, "Don't pray to idols," and then make money your god instead. (Romans 2:17-22)

Paul accuses the Jews of hypocrisy. Make a list of the offenses Paul cites. Are Christians today guilty of any of these?

A headmaster of a school for boys in India found that two of his pupils had cheated by copying essays from a book. The next morning in chapel he announced, "Today we will learn about hypocrisy." He held up a small beam from the roof of a house. Three sides of the beam looked strong and smooth, but the fourth, which had been holding up the roof, was rotten. Ants had eaten up the entire inside. "The beam looks perfect, but it is worthless," he said. Then he read the boys' essays and compared them to an identical essay in a book. After severely reprimanding the boys, he broke the beam over his desk, and gave each boy a piece to serve as a reminder of their transgression.

P R A I S E :

P E T I T I O N :

The glory of the Lord will be seen by all mankind together. (Isa. 40:5)

Looking Good

YOU are so proud of knowing God's laws, *but you dishonor him by breaking them.* No wonder the Scriptures say that the world speaks evil of God because of you.

Being a Jew is worth something if you obey God's laws; but if you don't, then you are no better off than the heathen. And if the heathen obey God's laws, won't God give them all the rights and honors he planned to give the Jews? In fact, those heathen will be much better off than you Jews who know so much about God and have his promises but don't obey his laws.

For you are not real Jews just because you were born of Jewish parents or because you have gone through the Jewish initiation ceremony of circumcision. No, a real Jew is anyone whose heart is right with God. For God is not looking for those who cut their bodies in actual body circumcision, but he is looking for those with changed hearts and minds. Whoever has that kind of change in his life will get his praise from God, even if not from you. (Romans 2:23-29)

Good works often come as a result of our salvation, but they are not the way to everlasting life. What *is* the only way to God?

Jim grew up in a Christian home. While still in high school, he served as a Sunday school teacher. He went on to Bible school, then seminary to prepare for the ministry. While there, he met a beautiful young woman, the daughter of missionaries. They fell in love, and were soon married. After graduation Jim went to work as a youth pastor. He was well-loved, and soon moved to a larger church. He was very successful there, and decided that he should begin an organization to help young people in trouble. His organization grew to world-wide proportions, and thousands of lives were saved. There was only one problem: Jim had never given his life to Christ.   Paul says that it is quite possible for a Jew to undergo the ritual of circumcision, following the Mosaic law to a "T," only to be condemned to eternal damnation. God "is looking for those with changed hearts and minds."

P R A I S E :

P E T I T I O N :

Only those who have struck the deepest note of repentance can reach the highest note of praise.

East by Northwest

THEN what's the use of being a Jew? Are there any special benefits for them from God? Is there any value in the Jewish circumcision ceremony? Yes, being a Jew has many advantages.

First of all, God trusted them with his laws [so that they could know and do his will]. True, some of them were unfaithful, but just because they broke their promises to God, does that mean God will break his promises? Of course not! Though everyone else in the world is a liar, God is not. Do you remember what the book of Psalms says about this? That God's words will always prove true and right, no matter who questions them. (Romans 3:1-4)

If God loves all people equally, and if circumcision is just a symbol, then what's the use of being a Jew? This was the question many believers were asking. Carefully consider Paul's response. Compare man's unfaithfulness to God's faithfulness.

A Chicago businessman wanted to go to New York. He packed his bags and went to the train station. He climbed aboard the first train he saw and paid the conductor. He entered his compartment, prepared for a presentation he'd have to make the next day, then went to sleep. The next morning he awoke just as the train was pulling into a big city. He recognized it as Denver! He had been heading west instead of east. The businessman sincerely believed he was traveling toward New York. But his sincerity was misdirected. He should have taken the time to check the train's destination. We should seek the *truth* (in God's Word) as well as nurture our faithfulness, sincerity, and loyalty. "God's words will always prove true and right."

PRAISE:

PETITION:

I will pour out the spirit of grace and prayer on all the people. (Zech. 12:10)

Two Wrongs

"BUT," some say, "our breaking faith with God is good, our sins serve a good purpose, for people will notice how good God is when they see how bad we are. Is it fair, then, for him to punish us when our sins are helping him?" (That is the way some people talk.) God forbid! Then what kind of God would he be, to overlook sin? How could he ever condemn anyone? For he could not judge and condemn me as a sinner if my dishonesty brought him glory by pointing up his honesty in contrast to my lies. If you follow through with that idea you come to this: the worse we are, the better God likes it! But the damnation of those who say such things is just. Yet some claim that this is what I preach! (Romans 3:5-8)

A question has arisen: "OK, Paul, it is our sin that makes God show his righteousness, right? If we did not sin, then God would not be able to show his righteousness. If we are permitting God to show his righteousness, why are we judged for our sins?" What is Paul's response?

In Manchester, England, Kenneth Simpson went to jail for stealing a lead pipe. He had stolen the pipe in order to raise money to pay a fine for previously stealing another lead pipe. His second crime, instead of helping him pay his fine, landed him in jail—and he was worse off than ever. That is always the consequence when we "do evil, that good may come" (KJV).

P R A I S E :

P E T I T I O N :

I will bless you with incredible blessings. (Gen 22:17)

Race of Sinners

WELL, then, are we Jews *better* than others? No, not at all, for we have already shown that all men alike are sinners, whether Jews or Gentiles. As the Scriptures say,
"No one is good—no one in all the world is innocent."
No one has ever really followed God's paths, or even truly wanted to.
Every one has turned away; all have gone wrong. No one anywhere has kept on doing what is right; not one. (Romans 3:9-12)

According to Paul, what do all men have in common?

A Christian African came to attend an American university. On his first Sunday in this country, he walked into an evangelical church which displayed a large sign reading "All Are Welcome." He was summarily thrown out of the church and told to go to the black chapel down the street. The experience so soured him on American "Christianity" that eventually he abandoned his faith. A few years after returning to his homeland the bright graduate was catapulted into political power. In his new position, his first official action was to expel all American missionaries from his country.   Racism is an abomination to the Lord. To discriminate on the basis of race is to defiantly tell God that some people are indeed better than others. To God, all are equal—all are sinners in need of a Savior.

P R A I S E :

P E T I T I O N :

When you don't get everything you want, think of things you don't get that you don't want.

The Short Story

THEIR talk is foul and filthy like the stench from an open grave. Their tongues are loaded with lies. Everything they say has in it the sting and poison of deadly snakes.

Their mouths are full of cursing and bitterness.

They are quick to kill, hating anyone who disagrees with them.

Wherever they go they leave misery and trouble behind them, and they have never known what it is to feel secure or enjoy God's blessing.

They care nothing about God nor what he thinks of them. (Romans 3:13-18)

Do you know anyone guilty of the undesirable characteristics Paul mentions? What is the only way out of such vile corruption?

A freelance writer once wrote a short story, then prepared it to send to a publisher. He retyped it carefully on expensive paper, included a letter on his beautifully designed stationery, and sent the manuscript in a neatly bound package via overnight mail. Two weeks later he received his manuscript back, along with a rejection slip. The publisher's comment: "Your manuscript *looks* professional, but the writing is substandard." The writer paid more attention to *form* than to *content.* We are often guilty of concentrating on appearance more than essentials. In eternity, the bottom line is salvation; if we are not children of God, nothing else will save us.

P R A I S E :

P E T I T I O N :

I stand silently before the Lord, waiting for him to rescue me. For salvation comes from him alone. (Ps. 62:5)

God's Narrow-Mindedness

SO the judgment of God lies very heavily upon the Jews, for they are responsible to keep God's laws instead of doing all these evil things; not one of them has any excuse; in fact, all the world stands hushed and guilty before Almighty God.

Now do you see it? No one can ever be made right in God's sight by doing what the law commands. For the more we know of God's laws, the clearer it becomes that we aren't obeying them; his laws serve only to make us see that we are sinners.

But now God has shown us a different way to heaven—not by "being good enough" and trying to keep his laws, but by a new way (though not new, really, for the Scriptures told about it long ago). Now God says he will accept and acquit us—declare us "not guilty"— if we trust Jesus Christ to take away our sins. And we all can be saved in this same way, by coming to Christ, no matter who we are or what we have been like. (Romans 3:19-22)

God wants us to follow his laws. But merely following laws will not get us to heaven. What then is the purpose of the law?

A young Christian was talking to an agnostic about the plan of salvation. He said that apart from faith in Christ, no one would get to heaven. "That's the trouble with the world today," replied the agnostic. "People are so narrow-minded. A person has to be born under a certain flag, or have the right kind of blood in his veins. He has to subscribe to one certain religion. There is altogether too much narrow-mindedness." There is some narrow-mindedness in some people, but the gospel excludes no one who wants salvation and is willing to accept it on God's terms.

P R A I S E :

P E T I T I O N :

I, the Lord, will be with you and see you through. (Jer. 1:8)

The Way Out

YES, all have sinned; all fall short of God's glorious ideal; yet now God declares us "not guilty" of offending him if we trust in Jesus Christ, who in his kindness freely takes away our sins.

For God sent Christ Jesus to take the punishment for our sins and to end all God's anger against us. He used Christ's blood and our faith as the means of saving us from his wrath. In this way he was being entirely fair, even though he did not punish those who sinned in former times. For he was looking forward to the time when Christ would come and take away those sins. And now in these days also he can receive sinners in this same way, because Jesus took away their sins.

But isn't this unfair for God to let criminals go free, and say that they are innocent? No, for he does it on the basis of their trust in Jesus who took away their sins. (Romans 3:23-26)

Although God sent his Son to die for us, we are *not* automatically forgiven for all our sins. What action must we take to claim forgiveness and salvation?

Suppose you have been caught speeding. In court, the judge fines you $100 for reckless driving. You tell the judge that you don't have $100, and he then sentences you to jail. But before the officer can haul you away, the judge reaches into his pocket and pulls out his checkbook. He writes a check for $100, and you are free to go. As a judge, it was his responsibility to be just and sentence you. But there was nothing impeding him from paying your fine. In effect, this is what God has done for us on Calvary.

P R A I S E :

P E T I T I O N :

There are moments when, whatever be the position of the body, the soul is on its knees. (V. Hugo)

Pulling Rank

THEN what can we boast about doing, to earn our salvation? Nothing at all. Why? Because our acquittal is not based on our good deeds; it is based on what Christ has done and our faith in him. So it is that we are saved by faith in Christ and not by the good things we do.

And does God save only the Jews in this way? No, the Gentiles, too, may come to him in this same manner. God treats us all the same; all, whether Jews or Gentiles, are acquitted if they have faith. Well then, if we are saved by faith, does this mean that we no longer need obey God's laws? Just the opposite! In fact, only when we trust Jesus can we truly obey him. (Romans 3:27-31)

A work-centered life is a self-centered life. But faith brings about a God-centered life. Does Paul, then, see any value in good works? Explain.

A captain and a private lie wounded on a battlefield. A medical corpsman approaches and says, "You two are suffering from serious wounds, but I can help you." Suppose the captain boasts, "I don't need you. I am a well-trained officer and have been in the army for twenty years. I am a captain. Go take care of that poor private." Such arrogance would be foolish. The captain's rank would not save his life; neither would his seniority or courage. Rank and courage are good things, but in this case, they are no substitute for medical treatment. **O**n earth—God's battlefield—it is important for us to cultivate good works and a godly spirit, but only true faith in Christ will save us.

P R A I S E :

P E T I T I O N :

Keep on asking and you will keep on getting; keep on looking and you will keep on finding; knock and the door will be opened. (Luke 11:9)

The Bank of Heaven

ABRAHAM was, humanly speaking, the founder of our Jewish nation. What were his experiences concerning this question of being saved by faith? Was it because of his good deeds that God accepted him? If so, then he would have something to boast about. But from God's point of view Abraham had no basis at all for pride. For the Scriptures tell us Abraham *believed God*, and that is why God canceled his sins and declared him "not guilty."

But didn't he earn his right to heaven by all the good things he did? No, for being saved is a gift; if a person could earn it by being good, then it wouldn't be free—but it is! It is *given* to those who do *not* work for it. For God declares sinners to be good in his sight if they have faith in Christ to save them from God's wrath. (Romans 4:1-5)

Abraham was not justified by the law. He was not justified by good works. And Christ did not die until centuries later. How then was Abraham justified?

Bill Dollar was a crisp, new five-dollar bill. Everyone praised him for the many fine deeds he performed. Bill paraded before the public as a great philanthropist and benefactor of mankind. He was used to buy a week's supply of groceries for a poor family. Then he became payment for a badly-needed pair of shoes for a little girl. Once he was given as a tip to a needy waitress. He went around making people happy and satisfied. One Sunday Bill even found himself in the collection plate of a rescue mission. But then it happened: Bill was taken to the bank and a teller detected a serious problem. Bill was counterfeit! All the good Bill had done could not change that fact. He was a fraud. So, too, the sinner cannot expect to be admitted to the Bank of Heaven by good works alone.

P R A I S E :

P E T I T I O N :

The people who know their God shall be strong and do great things. (Dan. 11:32)

The Great Pardon

KING David spoke of this, describing the happiness of an undeserving sinner who is declared "not guilty" by God. "Blessed, and to be envied," he said, "are those whose sins are forgiven and put out of sight. Yes, what joy there is for anyone whose sins are no longer counted against him by the Lord." (Romans 4:6-8)

David had great insight into the nature of fallen man. In light of David's own great sins, reflect on his words in this reading.

Because of his implication in the Watergate scandal, Richard Nixon felt compelled to resign from the office of President of the United States. But after the resignation he still faced serious charges and possible imprisonment. When Vice-President Gerald Ford succeeded him, though, one of his first actions was to grant Nixon a pardon. The ex-President was then legally absolved of all wrong-doing in office. He was still guilty, but was spared the agony of punishment. How much greater is "the happiness of an undeserving sinner who is declared 'not guilty' by God."

P R A I S E :

P E T I T I O N :

In the great events and crowning periods of the life of Jesus, we always find him in prayer—at the beginning of his ministry, at the Jordan River, when the Holy Spirit descended upon him, just prior to the transfiguration, and in the Garden of Gethsemane.

Multiple Choice

IS this blessing given only to those who have faith in Christ but also keep the Jewish laws, or is the blessing also given to those who do not keep the Jewish rules, but only trust in Christ? Well, what about Abraham? We say that he received these blessings through his faith. Was it by faith alone? Or because he also kept the Jewish rules?

For the answer to that question, answer this one: *When* did God give this blessing to Abraham? It was *before he became a Jew*—before he went through the Jewish initiation ceremony of circumcision.

It wasn't until later on, *after* God had promised to bless him *because of his faith,* that he was circumcised. The circumcision ceremony was a sign that Abraham already had faith. (Romans 4:9-11)

Once again Paul discredits the notion that circumcision is necessary to find favor in God's eyes. Paul insists that faith is the essential element, and that circumcision is merely a ritual, a sign. According to Paul, what was the purpose of Abraham's circumcision?

Circle the best description of a Christian:

A Christian is someone who
  a. obeys each of the Ten Commandments.
  b. is a Protestant evangelical.
  c. trusts and obeys Christ as Savior.
  d. attends church regularly.

If you circled item c, you probably have a good grasp of what Christianity is all about. To become a Christian, it is essential for man to repent of his sins, and to trust and obey Jesus as his Savior. The other items listed above characterize most true Christians, but they are not absolutely essential to one's salvation.

P R A I S E :

P E T I T I O N :

I bless the holy name of God with all my heart. Yes, I will bless the Lord and not forget the glorious things he does for me. (Ps. 103:1, 2)

Limit of the Law

IT is clear, then, that God's promise to give the whole earth to Abraham and his descendants was not because Abraham obeyed God's laws but because he trusted God to keep his promise. So if you still claim that God's blessings go to those who are "good enough," then you are saying that God's promises to those who have faith are meaningless, and faith is foolish. But the fact of the matter is this: when we try to gain God's blessing and salvation by keeping his laws we always end up under his anger, for we always fail to keep them. The only way we can keep from breaking laws is not to have any to break! (Romans 4:13-15)

Is it possible to always obey the law? Why or why not?

At the end of the reading above, Paul makes an interesting statement: "The only way we can keep from breaking laws is not to have any to break!" At first this statement sounds like a denouncement of legislation. But if we examine it in the proper context, here's what is evident: We need laws. Without them, sin would run rampant, and society would fall into anarchy and chaos. So we should try to keep the law, although most of us will occasionally break it, inadvertently or otherwise. But we should also remember that laws exist to keep us from sinning and from evil consequences. *They are not meant to lead us to God!* Adherence to the law protects us from sin; faith in God protects us from hell.

P R A I S E :

P E T I T I O N :

All glory to him who alone is God, who saves us through Jesus Christ our Lord. (Jude 1:24, 25)

God, Unlimited

SO God's blessings are given to us by faith, as a free gift; we are certain to get them whether or not we follow Jewish customs if we have faith like Abraham's, for Abraham is the father of us all when it comes to these matters of faith. That is what the Scriptures mean when they say that God made Abraham the father of many nations. God will accept all people in every nation who trust God as Abraham did. And this promise is from God himself, who makes the dead live again and speaks of future events with as much certainty as though they were already past.

So, when God told Abraham that he would give him a son who would have many descendants and become a great nation, Abraham believed God even though such a promise just couldn't come to pass! (Romans 4:16-18)

"God will accept all people in every nation who trust God as Abraham did." What is the one condition of this acceptance?

Paul refers to God "who makes the dead live again and speaks of future events with . . . certainty." This reminds us once again of God's absolute power over the universe. He created not only the material universe, but also the laws of science which govern it. No mortal can comprehend the divine creative power. God's activity includes the creation and maintenance of animate and inanimate objects. The nature of the objects may be discussed—minds, matter, energy— but the whys and hows of their existence can be known accurately only to the extent that God reveals them.

P R A I S E :

P E T I T I O N :

True prayer is not asking God for what we want, but for what he wants.

Engineering Faith

AND because his faith was strong, he didn't worry about the fact that he was too old to be a father, at the age of one hundred, and that Sarah his wife, at ninety, was also much too old to have a baby.

But Abraham never doubted. He believed God, for his faith and trust grew ever stronger, and he praised God for this blessing even before it happened. He was completely sure that God was well able to do anything he promised. (Romans 4:19-21)

Reread the passage above, paying close attention to the great faith of Abraham. This is the brand of faith for which all of us should strive.

A man drives his car at fifty-five miles per hour across a bridge that is strong and well built. It is not his faith that carries him across the stream—it is the bridge. If he has the same faith on a stormy night when a flood has swept away the foundations, and comes down the road as usual, he will soon find himself in the middle of a raging river. Faith, to be worth anything, must have the proper foundations under it. That is why true faith can be in none other than the living God.

PRAISE:

PETITION:

The Lord is far from the wicked, but he hears the prayers of the righteous. (Prov. 15:29)

Love Story

AND because of Abraham's faith God forgave his sins and declared him "not guilty."

Now this wonderful statement—that he was accepted and approved through his faith—wasn't just for Abraham's benefit. It was for us, too, assuring us that God will accept us in the same way he accepted Abraham—when we believe the promises of God who brought back Jesus our Lord from the dead. He died for our sins and rose again to make us right with God, filling us with God's goodness. (Romans 4:22-25)

Why is Christ's resurrection central to Christian theology? Isn't it enough that he died for us?

Because of Abraham's faith, God forgave his sins and regenerated him. Paul says that if we have similar faith, we too will be accepted and approved. There is a basic difference, however, between Abraham and the Christian. Abraham believed, or trusted in God. The Christian trusts the same God, but he is now known as the God who raised Jesus Christ from the dead. Whereas in the Old Testament we see that God often demonstrated his love for man, in the New Testament that love is manifested in an incomparable manner—the sacrifice of a beloved Son on behalf of man. There can be no doubt that God deeply loves each of us.

_P R A I S E :_

_P E T I T I O N :_

God . . . will show compassion . . . according to the greatness of his lovingkindness. (Lam. 3:32)

Rough Riding

SO now, since we have been made right in God's sight by faith in his promises, we can have real peace with him because of what Jesus Christ our Lord has done for us. For because of our faith, he has brought us into this place of highest privilege where we now stand, and we confidently and joyfully look forward to actually becoming all that God has had in mind for us to be.

We can rejoice, too, when we run into problems and trials for we know that they are good for us—they help us learn to be patient. And patience develops strength of character in us and helps us trust God more each time we use it until finally our hope and faith are strong and steady. Then, when that happens, we are able to hold our heads high no matter what happens and know that all is well, for we know how dearly God loves us, and we feel this warm love everywhere within us because God has given us the Holy Spirit to fill our hearts with his love. (Romans 5:1-5)

Why should we rejoice when we experience problems and trials?

The Boeing 707 jet has a line of small blades midway down the wing surface and on the tail. These blades are called "vortex generators." Their function is to cause the airflow to swirl as it passes over the rear wing area. The rear assembly of the 707 does not steer accurately when the air current is too smooth, so the vortexes must be generated. The element of roughness must be added to attain directional accuracy. This is also true of the Christian life. God sometimes causes trials to cross our paths so that we can experience his purpose in our lives.

P R A I S E :

P E T I T I O N :

Prayer is not a device for getting our wills done through heaven, but a desire that God's will may be done on earth through us.

The Gift of Death

WHEN we were utterly helpless with no way of escape, Christ came at just the right time and died for us sinners who had no use for him. Even if we were good, we really wouldn't expect anyone to die for us, though, of course, that might be barely possible. But God showed his great love for us by sending Christ to die for us while we were still sinners. (Romans 5:6-8)

Why was it necessary for Christ to die for us?

A young couple was strolling through a park in early evening. Suddenly a gun-wielding man jumped out in front of them, demanding their money. "But we left everything back at the apartment," blurted the young husband. "Oh, yeah? Well, somebody's gonna have to die then," sneered the drug-crazed mugger, and pointed the gun at the woman. Without hesitation, the husband bravely stepped in front of his wife, ready to die for her. It is conceivable that a person would give his life for a loved one. Even so, this is a rare trait among men. But Christ gave his life to save not only those who love him, but those who hate and despise him as well. He died for the young couple, the mugger, and for you and me. We are all equally sinful in his eyes.

P R A I S E :

P E T I T I O N :

O Lord, thank you so much for answering my prayer and saving me. (Ps. 118:21)

Robin Hood and Little John

AND since by his blood he did all this for us as sinners, how much more will he do for us now that he has declared us not guilty? Now he will save us from all of God's wrath to come. And since, when we were his enemies, we were brought back to God by the death of his Son, what blessings he must have for us now that we are his friends, and he is living within us!

Now we rejoice in our wonderful new relationship with God—all because of what our Lord Jesus Christ has done in dying for our sins—making us friends of God. (Romans 5:9-11)

What did Jesus die to save us from?

Anyone who knows the story of Robin Hood will recall the first time the celebrated thief encountered Little John. Both men were traveling through the forest heading toward each other. They first saw each other at the opposite ends of a bridge which was designed to hold just one man at a time. Each was too proud to let the other pass first, so they both started across. They met at the middle, exchanged insults, and began to fight. As the story goes, both men fell into the waters below. Later, as they recovered on the banks of the river, they began to laugh at themselves. Subsequently, they became the best of friends. Not only had these adversaries settled their differences; they had gone a step further, becoming good friends. Before we became Christians, we were in effect opposed to God. Our surrender to him didn't lead to a mere master-slave relationship. As Paul says in today's reading, Jesus Christ's act of love has made us friends of God.

PRAISE:

PETITION:

Christ . . . is a mighty power within you. (2 Cor. 13:3)

A Joyful Noise

WHEN Adam sinned, sin entered the entire human race. His sin spread death throughout all the world, so everything began to grow old and die, for all sinned. [We know that it was Adam's sin that caused this] because although, of course, people were sinning from the time of Adam until Moses, God did not in those days judge them guilty of death for breaking his laws—because he had not yet given his laws to them, nor told them what he wanted them to do. So when their bodies died it was not for their own sins since they themselves had never disobeyed God's special law against eating the forbidden fruit, as Adam had.

What a contrast between Adam and Christ who was yet to come! And what a difference between man's sin and God's forgiveness!

For this one man, Adam, brought death to many through his *sin.* But this one man, Jesus Christ, brought forgiveness to many through God's *mercy.*

Adam's *one* sin brought the penalty of death to many, while Christ freely takes away *many* sins and gives glorious life instead. The sin of this one man, Adam, caused *death to be king over all,* but all who will take God's gift of forgiveness and acquittal are *kings of life* because of this one man, Jesus Christ. (Romans 5:12-17)

What did Adam bring to mankind? What did Christ bring to mankind?

One of Joseph Haydn's friends once asked him why his church music was almost always of an animating, cheerful, and even festive quality. "Shouldn't worship music be more . . . sedate?" the friend asked. The composer replied, "I cannot make it otherwise. I write according to my thoughts. When I think upon God, my heart is so full of joy that notes dance and leap, as it were, from my pen. Since God has given me a cheerful heart, it will be easily forgiven me that I serve him with a cheerful spirit."

P R A I S E :

P E T I T I O N :

Prayer should be the key of the day and the lock of the night.

The Danger Within

YES, Adam's *sin* brought *punishment* to all, but Christ's *righteousness* makes men *right with God,* so that they can live. Adam caused many to be sinners because he *disobeyed* God, and Christ caused many to be made acceptable to God because he *obeyed.*

The Ten Commandments were given so that all could see the extent of their failure to obey God's laws. But the more we see our sinfulness, the more we see God's abounding grace forgiving us. Before, sin ruled over all men and brought them to death, but now God's kindness rules instead, giving us right standing with God and resulting in eternal life through Jesus Christ our Lord. (Romans 5:18-21)

Explain the true purpose of the Ten Commandments.

In Victor Hugo's *Ninety-Three,* a sailing ship is flailed by a heavy storm. Everyone aboard is concerned about the powerful seas and tremendous winds. Suddenly a thundering noise deep in the ship is heard. A heavy gun has broken loose from its moorings and is careening wildly on a lower deck. In a matter of minutes, this moving monster will hurl itself through the ship's side, unless it is secured. The real danger is within, not without. So it is with us—sin inside our lives poses the greatest threat to our eternal lives.

P R A I S E :

P E T I T I O N :

Even when walking through the dark valley of death I will not be afraid, for you are close beside me, guarding, guiding all the way. (Ps. 23:4)

February *ROMANS 6-10*

Through drugs, evil influences, and uncontrolled desires, many young people wind up on the wrong side of the law. They soon learn what society will—and will not—tolerate. But they learn it the hard way. ■ This section of Romans says Christ came to deliver people from the law. Does that mean we no longer have to obey it? Of course not, says Paul. In this life, we need the law to show us the difference between right and wrong. But in the life to come, law will be replaced with love.

Killing the Spider

WELL then, shall we keep on sinning so that God can keep on showing us more and more kindness and forgiveness?

Of course not! Should we keep on sinning when we don't have to? For sin's power over us was broken when we became Christians and were baptized to become a part of Jesus Christ; through his death the power of your sinful nature was shattered. Your old sin-loving nature was buried with him by baptism when he died, and when God the Father, with glorious power, brought him back to life again, you were given his wonderful new life to enjoy.

For you have become a part of him, and so you died with him, so to speak, when he died; and now you share his new life, and shall rise as he did. Your old evil desires were nailed to the cross with him; that part of you that loves to sin was crushed and fatally wounded, so that your sin-loving body is no longer under sin's control, no longer needs to be a slave to sin. (Romans 6:1-6)

What does it mean to "die with Christ"?

I recently read of a man who always had the same thing to confess at his weekly prayer meeting. His prayer seldom varied. It went something like this: "O Lord, since we last met, the cobwebs have come between us. Clear them away once again so that I can see your face." One week when the man began the same prayer again, an exasperated brother said aloud, "O Lord, kill that spider!" Sweeping away the cobwebs will be a never-ending chore if we don't kill the spider. When Christ died for us, he dealt not only with the side-effects of sin; he dealt sin itself the death blow.

PRAISE:

PETITION:

Let us come boldly to the very throne of God and stay there to receive his mercy and to find grace to help us in our times of need. (Heb. 4:16)

The Defaced Mirror

FOR when you are deadened to sin you are freed from all its allure and its power over you. And since your old sin-loving nature "died" with Christ, we know that you will share his new life. Christ rose from the dead and will never die again. Death no longer has any power over him. He died once for all to end sin's power, but now he lives forever in unbroken fellowship with God. (Romans 6:7-10)

Paul says Christ "died once for all to end sin's power." Is this the only reason he died? Explain (see 2 Corinthians 5:15, if necessary).

A young boy found a discarded mirror in a vacant lot. He looked into it, saw his reflection, and entertained himself by making funny faces. Then he turned the mirror over, and with a sharp rock, scraped off the quicksilvering. Later he flipped it back over to look at himself again. To his surprise, he could not see his reflection. Without the quicksilvering, the mirror was now just an ordinary piece of glass.   When we allow sin to deface our lives, we become incapable of properly reflecting Jesus.

PRAISE :

PETITION :

And I will give you a new heart—I will give you new and right desires—and put a new spirit within you. I will take out your stony hearts of sin and give you new hearts of love. (Ezek. 36:26)

The Rod of Justice

SO look upon your old sin nature as dead and unresponsive to sin, and instead be alive to God, alert to him, through Jesus Christ our Lord. Do not let sin control your puny body any longer; do not give in to its sinful desires. Do not let any part of your bodies become tools of wickedness, to be used for sinning; but give yourselves completely to God—every part of you—for you are back from death and you want to be tools in the hands of God, to be used for his good purposes. (Romans 6:11-13)

We should not give ourselves to our bodies' sinful desires. What then should we give ourselves to?

In Islam, penalties for transgressing against the law are often quite harsh. The punishment for stealing, for example, is the amputation of the hand. Other penalties include castration and public flogging. Maiming, disfiguring, executions, and public embarrassment are all a regular part of the judicial systems of countries such as Iran, where Muslims hold all political power. Christianity, however, does not demand severe earthly penalties for yielding to sin. But if we allow our bodies to become "tools of wickedness," and if we are not repentant, we will be sentenced to the greatest of all punishments—eternity in hell. In today's reading, Paul reminds us that we should strive "to be tools in the hands of God, to be used for his good purposes."

P R A I S E :

P E T I T I O N :

God is concerned about our prayer. He wills it, he commands it, he inspires it.

Bye-Bye Bahai

SIN need never again be your master, for now you are no longer tied to the law where sin enslaves you, but you are free under God's favor and mercy.

Does this mean that now we can go ahead and sin and not worry about it? (For our salvation does not depend on keeping the law, but on receiving God's grace!) Of course not!

Don't you realize that you can choose your own master? You can choose sin (with death) or else obedience (with acquittal). The one to whom you offer yourself—he will take you and be your master and you will be his slave. (Romans 6:14-16)

According to this passage, what frees us from sin's enslavement?

Bahaism is a cult comprised of people working toward equality for all and the establishment of world peace. One of its basic tenets is the oneness of all religions. According to Bahaullah, the cult's founder, followers of any religion may become Bahais without renouncing their original faiths. True Christians, of course, would have a problem with this, for Jesus says he is the only way to God. How could we join in spiritual fellowship with people who do not accept this fundamental principle of Christian faith?   Paul says we can choose one master only: "You can choose sin (with death) or else obedience (with acquittal)."

PRAISE:

PETITION:

I want men everywhere to pray with holy hands lifted up to God, free from sin and anger and resentment. (1 Tim. 2:8)

The Wages of Porn

THANK God that though you once chose to be slaves of sin, now you have obeyed with all your heart the teaching to which God has committed you. And now you are free from your old master, sin; and you have become slaves to your new master, righteousness.

I speak this way, using the illustration of slaves and masters, because it is easy to understand: just as you used to be slaves to all kinds of sin, so now you must let yourselves be slaves to all that is right and holy.

In those days when you were slaves of sin you didn't bother much with goodness. And what was the result? Evidently not good, since you are ashamed now even to think about those things you used to do, for all of them end in eternal doom. But now you are free from the power of sin and are slaves of God, and his benefits to you include holiness and everlasting life. For the wages of sin is death, but the free gift of God is eternal life through Jesus Christ our Lord. (Romans 6:17-23)

Compare the two servitudes mentioned in the reading. What is the difference between the fruits they bear?

A few years ago *Time* magazine published a story about an elderly writer who had been well known in the early days of his life. He had become famous by writing obscene novels and indecent verse. The magazine reported that now, in his old age, "he flaps through Greenwich Village eating and drinking when he can beg a handout or peddle a bit of verse. Mostly he lives on gin and the memory of the time when the life brought him greater rewards." He is now reaping the sort of "wages" that sin pays its servants—often in this life, always in eternity.

P R A I S E :

P E T I T I O N :

He has removed our sins as far away from us as the east is from the west. (Ps. 103:12)

Slaves of Christ

DON'T you understand yet, dear Jewish brothers in Christ, that when a person dies the law no longer holds him in its power?

Let me illustrate: when a woman marries, the law binds her to her husband as long as he is alive. But if he dies, she is no longer bound to him; the laws of marriage no longer apply to her. Then she can marry someone else if she wants to. That would be wrong while he was alive, but it is perfectly all right after he dies.

Your "husband," your master, used to be the Jewish law; but you "died," as it were, with Christ on the cross; and since you are "dead," you are no longer "married to the law," and it has no more control over you. Then you came back to life again when Christ did, and are a new person. And now you are "married," so to speak, to the one who rose from the dead, so that you can produce good fruit, that is, good deeds for God. When your old nature was still active, sinful desires were at work within you, making you want to do whatever God said not to, and producing sinful deeds, the rotting fruit of death. But now you need no longer worry about the Jewish laws and customs because you "died" while in their captivity, and now you can really serve God; not in the old way, mechanically obeying a set of rules, but in the new way, [with all of your hearts and minds]. (Romans 7:1-6)

What is the difference between service under the law and service under God's grace?

Here we learn about how Christ has saved all believers from eternal damnation. The law—God's universal principles of right and wrong—demanded that, as sinners, all humans be put to death in punishment for their transgressions. However, Christ came to deliver mankind from the law's claim requiring condemnation (see Gal. 2:19). This deliverance is certainly one of the greatest evidences of God's love for man. Being discharged from the law means we are free to pursue a relationship with our Creator. We are no longer slaves to the law; we are now servants of Christ, free to obey him and do his will.

P R A I S E :

P E T I T I O N :

When prayer is answered, don't forget praise. The apparently conquered enemy steals in again at the door of an ungrateful heart.

In Full View

WELL then, am I suggesting that these laws of God are evil? Of course not! No, the law is not sinful but it was the law that showed me my sin. I would never have known the sin in my heart—the evil desires that are hidden there—if the law had not said, "You must not have evil desires in your heart." But sin used this law against evil desires by reminding me that such desires are wrong and arousing all kinds of forbidden desires within me! Only if there were no laws to break would there be no sinning.

That is why I felt fine so long as I did not understand what the law really demanded. But when I learned the truth, I realized that I had broken the law and was a sinner, doomed to die. So as far as I was concerned, the good law which was supposed to show me the way of life resulted instead in my being given the death penalty. Sin fooled me by taking the good laws of God and using them to make me guilty of death. But still, you see, the law itself was wholly right and good.

But how can that be? Didn't the law cause my doom? How then can it be good? No, it was sin, devilish stuff that it is, that used what was good to bring about my condemnation. So you can see how cunning and deadly and damnable it is. For it uses God's good laws for its own evil purposes.

The law is good, then, and the trouble is not there but with *me,* because I am sold into slavery with Sin as my owner. (Romans 7:7-14)

Does the law cause man to be separated from God? How does Paul define the purpose of the law?

When the snow of winter melts, the ground of an empty lot is brown and bare. But when the sun has shone upon it for a while, the lot soon becomes full of weeds. The sun does not create the weeds. It merely causes them to show themselves.   Like the sun, the law is not evil. It is not sinful, but it does reveal sin in the lives of the disobedient. As the weeds cannot be killed before they are revealed, so sin cannot be wiped away before it is exposed.

PRAISE:

PETITION:

Please be with me in all that I do, and keep me from all evil and disaster! (1 Chron. 4:10)

Prisoner of a Prisoner

I don't understand myself at all, for I really want to do what is right, but I can't. I do what I don't want to—what I hate. I know perfectly well that what I am doing is wrong, and my bad conscience proves that I agree with these laws I am breaking. But I can't help myself, because I'm no longer doing it. It is sin inside me that is stronger than I am that makes me do these evil things.

I know I am rotten through and through so far as my old sinful nature is concerned. No matter which way I turn I can't make myself do right. I want to but I can't. (Romans 7:15-18)

Examine today's reading once again, then describe what happens when we attempt to single-handedly defeat sin.

During a fierce battle, a soldier valiantly took a prisoner. He radioed his commanding officer with the news. The captain ordered that the prisoner be brought to him. After a few minutes, the soldier replied, "He won't come." "Then leave him alone and come yourself," shouted the captain into the radio. "He won't let me," whined the soldier. If we think we have sin under control, but do not live in light of the truth, the tables are soon turned, and once again we are held as prisoners in the clutches of sin.

PRAISE:

PETITION:

Sing to him; yes, sing his praises and tell of his marvelous works. (1 Chron. 16:9)

The Expanding Vice

WHEN I want to do good, I don't; and when I try not to do wrong, I do it anyway. Now if I am doing what I don't want to, it is plain where the trouble is: sin still has me in its evil grasp.

It seems to be a fact of life that when I want to do what is right, I inevitably do what is wrong. I love to do God's will so far as my new nature is concerned; but there is something else deep within me, in my lower nature, that is at war with my mind and wins the fight and makes me a slave to the sin that is still within me. In my mind I want to be God's willing servant but instead I find myself still enslaved to sin.

So you see how it is: my new life tells me to do right, but the old nature that is still inside me loves to sin. Oh, what a terrible predicament I'm in! Who will free me from my slavery to this deadly lower nature? Thank God! It has been done by Jesus Christ our Lord. He has set me free. (Romans 7:19-25)

By what is Paul held captive here? What does he see as his only means of escape?

Nobody takes his first sip of beer expecting to become an alcoholic. And a first joint is usually laughed off as just a bit of innocent fun. But many a young person finds that the first indulgence soon leads to the second, the third. . . . And if he is going through problems with family, friends, the authorities, or his own insecurities, the temporary escapes provided by these drugs are welcomed and sought out in larger and larger doses. Soon these substances hold him firmly in their evil grasp. Such is sin. The tiniest sin, nurtured into adulthood, can become a monster which controls our lives. On our own strength, we cannot overcome the awesome power of what Paul calls the "deadly lower nature." But, as Christians, we know the way to freedom.

PRAISE:

PETITION:

Speech distinguishes men from animals, but prayer distinguishes the children of God from the children of this world.

Eternal Protection

SO there is now no condemnation awaiting those who belong to Christ Jesus. For the power of the life-giving Spirit—and this power is mine through Christ Jesus—has freed me from the vicious circle of sin and death. We aren't saved from sin's grasp by knowing the commandments of God, because we can't and don't keep them, but God put into effect a different plan to save us. He sent his own Son in a human body like ours—except that ours are sinful—and destroyed sin's control over us by giving himself as a sacrifice for our sins. So now we can obey God's laws if we follow after the Holy Spirit and no longer obey the old evil nature within us. (Romans 8:1-4)

What is the power that frees us from sin and death?

The story is told of a man who had been condemned by a Spanish court to be shot. Because he was an American citizen and of English birth, the consuls of the United States and England decided to intervene. They declared that the Spanish authorities had no power to put him to death. Their protest went unheeded, and the Spaniards proceeded to prepare the firing squad. At the time the execution was scheduled to take place, the consuls boldly approached the accused man, already tied and blindfolded, and wrapped him up in their flags—the Stars and Stripes and the Union Jack. Then they shouted, "Fire a shot if you dare! If you do so, you will bring the powers of our two great empires upon you." There stood the prisoner, unharmed. One bullet could have ended his life, but protected by those flags and the governments they represented, he was invulnerable.   The Lord Jesus takes the soul of the sinner who believes in him and covers the guilty one with his blood. Thus wrapped and sheltered by the Savior, he is safe.

P R A I S E :

P E T I T I O N :

Oh, sing to him you saints of his; give thanks to his holy name. (Ps. 30:4)

Lost and Found

THOSE who let themselves be controlled by their lower natures live only to please themselves, but those who follow after the Holy Spirit find themselves doing those things that please God. Following after the Holy Spirit leads to life and peace, but following after the old nature leads to death. (Romans 8:5, 6)

What happens when we follow the Holy Spirit instead of the old nature?

In the sixties and seventies, "finding yourself" was a popular concept. Many people dropped everything under the guise of discovering "who I really am." Marriages were abandoned, academics and careers were relinquished, personal goals were forgotten, relationships were neglected—all due to the elusive search for self. And what did these people find? Exactly what they set out to discover—themselves. Sinful, guilt-ridden, godless, cynical lives that were held captive by the lower nature. Rather than attempting to find ourselves, we should strive to lose ourselves in the freedom and love of Christ. We were created to please him only.

PRAISE:

PETITION:

I am for you, and I will come and help you. (Ezek. 36:9)

Hollow Applause

BECAUSE the old sinful nature within us is against God. It never did obey God's laws and it never will. That's why those who are still under the control of their old sinful selves, bent on following their old evil desires, can never please God.

But you are not like that. You are controlled by your new nature if you have the Spirit of God living in you. (And remember that if anyone doesn't have the Spirit of Christ living in him, he is not a Christian at all.) Yet, even though Christ lives within you, your body will die because of sin; but your spirit will live, for Christ has pardoned it. And if the Spirit of God, who raised up Jesus from the dead, lives in you, he will make your dying bodies live again after you die, by means of this same Holy Spirit living within you. (Romans 8:7-11)

As Christians, Christ lives within us. Does that mean we will never die? Explain.

The experts tell us that Verdi's early operas were really nothing to write home about. But when one of his earliest works was produced in Florence, Italy, the enthusiastic but indiscriminating audience went wild. There were unwarranted raptures and extended cheering and applause. Verdi, though, paid little heed. He slowly raised his eyes to where the musical genius Rossini sat in silence. That was the opinion that mattered most. Unless he satisfied the maestro, the plaudits of the crowd meant nothing.   May we learn to scorn the praise of men to gain the approval of heaven.

P R A I S E :

P E T I T I O N :

True thanksgiving is thanksliving. (J. Newton)

The Dove Man

SO, dear brothers, you have no obligations whatever to your old sinful nature to do what it begs you to do. For if you keep on following it you are lost and will perish, but if through the power of the Holy Spirit you crush it and its evil deeds, you shall live. For all who are led by the Spirit of God are sons of God.

And so we should not be like cringing, fearful slaves, but we should behave like God's very own children, adopted into the bosom of his family, and calling to him, "Father, Father." For his Holy Spirit speaks to us deep in our hearts, and tells us that we really are God's children. And since we are his children, we will share his treasures—for all God gives to his Son Jesus is now ours too. But if we are to share his glory, we must also share his suffering. (Romans 8:12-17)

How can we crush our sinful nature? Examine this passage carefully, then describe what we can gain through the Holy Spirit.

In the deserts of Saudi Arabia there is a certain guide who never loses his way. He is known as the "Dove Man." He carries with him a homing pigeon with a very fine cord attached to one of its legs. The other end of the cord is tied to the guide's wrist. When in doubt as to which direction to take, the guide throws the bird into the air. The pigeon quickly strains at the cord to fly in the direction of home, and in this manner leads his master unerringly. The Holy Spirit, the heavenly Dove, is willing and able to lead us if we will only allow him to do so. In humble self-denial and submission, we should follow his unerring guidance.

PRAISE:

PETITION:

I will give to the thirsty the springs of the Water of Life—as a gift! (Rev. 21:6)

The Curse

YET what we suffer now is nothing compared to the glory he will give us later. For all creation is waiting patiently and hopefully for that future day when God will resurrect his children. For on that day thorns and thistles, sin, death, and decay—the things that overcame the world against its will at God's command—will all disappear, and the world around us will share in the glorious freedom from sin which God's children enjoy. (Romans 8:18-21)

What sort of freedom does Paul label as "glorious"?

When Eve and Adam disobeyed God, and ate the fruit of the forbidden tree, a curse settled over the earth. God's creation was no longer quite so beautiful. Weeds grew up among flowers, vegetarian animals turned into carnivorous predators, destructive insects and rodents appeared, and great natural disasters began to occur. The human condition was altered—pain, anguish, suffering, hatred, and death came into existence. Human life was reduced to a struggle for survival. The curse still has the universe in its grasp, "yet what we suffer now is nothing compared to the glory he will give us later." We must remember to remain faithful to God and our beliefs, even through the storms of pain, persecution, and death. God plans to restore our earth to its original condition, granting his children "glorious freedom."

P R A I S E :

P E T I T I O N :

I am the Lord your God, who . . . leads you along the paths that you should follow. (Isa. 48:17)

Fish Nets

FOR we know that even the things of nature, like animals and plants, suffer in sickness and death as they await this great event. And even we Christians, although we have the Holy Spirit within us as a fore-taste of future glory, also groan to be released from pain and suffer-ing. We, too, wait anxiously for that day when God will give us our full rights as his children, including the new bodies he has promised us—bodies that will never be sick again and will never die.

We are saved by trusting. And trusting means looking forward to getting something we don't yet have—for a man who already has something doesn't need to hope and trust that he will get it. But if we must keep trusting God for something that hasn't happened yet, it teaches us to wait patiently and confidently. (Romans 8:22-25)

According to this passage, what saves us from pain and death?

Large nets are used for mackerel fishing off the coast of New England. So that the nets will float, fishermen attach large corks to each end. The middle part of the nets are held under water by lead beads. Without the cork, the net would sink to the bottom of the ocean. But without the weights, the nets would ineffectively float on the surface. We have problems, trials, and weights in our lives, and without God we would sink to the depths of despair. But God gives us hope to make us buoyant. Our trust in God works against our human tribulations, making us into mature, effective servants.

PRAISE:

PETITION:

Cold prayers, like cold suitors, never make much headway.

Rock and a Hard Place

AND in the same way—by our faith—the Holy Spirit helps us with our daily problems and in our praying. For we don't even know what we should pray for, nor how to pray as we should; but the Holy Spirit prays for us with such feeling that it cannot be expressed in words. And the Father who knows all hearts knows, of course, what the Spirit is saying as he pleads for us in harmony with God's own will. And we know that all that happens to us is working for our good if we love God and are fitting into his plans.

For from the very beginning God decided that those who came to him—and all along he knew who would—should become like his Son, so that his Son would be the First, with many brothers. (Romans 8:26-29)

What should we do when we're not sure how to pray?

A woman had two grown sons. One of them was a gardener; the other was a potter. One day they came to their godly mother with prayer requests. The gardener said, "Mother, please pray for rain so that my garden will grow." The potter said, "Mother, please pray for sunshine so that my pots will harden." She loved them equally—what should she do? She realized that there are times when we are not sure how to pray. At these times, it is best to leave things in the hands of the Lord.

PRAISE:

PETITION:

O God, my heart is ready to praise you! I will sing and rejoice before you. (Ps. 108:1)

Dead End

AND having chosen us, he called us to come to him; and when we came, he declared us "not guilty," filled us with Christ's goodness, gave us right standing with himself, and promised us his glory. What can we ever say to such wonderful things as these? If God is on our side, who can ever be against us? Since he did not spare even his own Son for us but gave him up for us all, won't he also surely give us everything else?

Who dares accuse us whom God has chosen for his own? Will God? No! He is the one who has forgiven us and given us right standing with himself.

Who then will condemn us? Will Christ? *No!* For he is the one who died for us and came back to life again for us and is sitting at the place of highest honor next to God, pleading for us there in heaven. (Romans 8:30-34)

If we are true believers, will God ever accuse us of sin or condemn us to damnation?

For many years George and Mary had lived in a big house at the end of a dead-end street. Their children had grown up there, and had since gotten married and moved away. One winter night, after a hard day's work, George and Mary settled in front of their favorite spot, the fireplace. They quietly sipped hot chocolate and chatted about their future. Suddenly a tremendous noise surrounded them and they thought the house was falling apart. George whipped around and saw, to his amazement, a pickup truck lying on its side *in the living room!* A drunk had been racing down the street and, not realizing there was a dead end, sped up the lawn and crashed through the front wall of the house. We are never more vulnerable than when we feel safe from the cares of the world. As believers, we should feel total security only in the salvation Christ has granted us.

P R A I S E :

P E T I T I O N :

He will deliver you again and again, so that no evil can touch you. (Job 5:19)

Did God Goof?

WHO then can ever keep Christ's love from us? When we have trouble or calamity, when we are hunted down or destroyed, is it because he doesn't love us anymore? And if we are hungry, or penniless, or in danger, or threatened with death, has God deserted us? (Romans 8:35)

Read today's passage once again, and answer Paul's questions. Explain your answers.

If God is good, why do people suffer? This is a question millions are asking. Their desire to know the answer accounts for the success of such books as *When Bad Things Happen to Good People*, by Rabbi Harold S. Kushner (Schocken, 1981). Many people cannot conceive of a benevolent God who would create a world plagued with sin, suffering, injustice, and death. Many Christians are wondering the same thing: Did God goof? Christian theologians have attempted to rationalize the problem. Some say God causes suffering in order to punish his children. Others believe God holds no sovereignty over his creation, and that "accidents will happen." Certainly the answer lies somewhere between. We must accept the question as one of the unrevealed mysteries. Nevertheless, of one thing we can be certain: God loves each of us. He takes no pleasure in the suffering of his children. In fact, there is reason to believe that God feels our pain and suffers with us. He is anxious to restore us to glory, where suffering and death will cease forever.

PRAISE :

PETITION :

Prayer requires more of the heart than of the tongue. (A. Clarke)

Son of God/Son of Sam

NO, for the Scriptures tell us that for his sake we must be ready to face death at every moment of the day—we are like sheep awaiting slaughter; but despite all this, overwhelming victory is ours through Christ who loved us enough to die for us. For I am convinced that nothing can ever separate us from his love. Death can't, and life can't. The angels won't, and all the powers of hell itself cannot keep God's love away. Our fears for today, our worries about tomorrow, or where we are—high above the sky, or in the deepest ocean—nothing will ever be able to separate us from the love of God demonstrated by our Lord Jesus Christ when he died for us. (Romans 8:36-39)

All of us are mortal. We must be ready to face death at every moment of the day. But for Christians, death is not the end. How can we triumph over death?

Son of Sam. Adolf Eichmann. Charles Manson. Nero. John Gacy, Jr. Jack the Ripper. Adolf Hitler. These are just a few of the kind of people we consider to be among the greatest enemies of mankind: cold-blooded mass murderers. Because of their heinous crimes, many of us have a hard time even thinking of them as human. They seem to be evil, satanic agents motivated by dark forces few of us could ever understand. But though these people appear to be the very embodiment of evil and destruction, they are human. And because of their humanity, in God's eyes we are equal to them. All of us, from the most offensive criminal to the sweetest, most innocent grandmother, are sinners in need of a Savior. And, as Paul writes to the Romans here, nothing can ever separate us from Christ's love. All that stands between man and God is man's acceptance of God.

PRAISE:

PETITION:

Come to me and I will give you rest—all of you who work so hard beneath a heavy yoke. (Matt. 11:28)

The Mission Next Door

OH, Israel, my people! Oh, my Jewish brothers! How I long for you to come to Christ. My heart is heavy within me and I grieve bitterly day and night because of you. Christ knows and the Holy Spirit knows that it is no mere pretense when I say that I would be willing to be forever damned if that would save you. God has given you so much, but still you will not listen to him. He took you as his own special, chosen people and led you along with a bright cloud of glory and told you how very much he wanted to bless you. He gave you his rules for daily life so you would know what he wanted you to do. He let you worship him, and gave you mighty promises. Great men of God were your fathers, and Christ himself was one of you, a Jew so far as his human nature is concerned, he who now rules over all things. Praise God forever! (Romans 9:1-5)

In this passage, what is Paul's greatest declaration of love for his Jewish brothers?

A locomotive engineer was deeply moved one night while listening to the great Charles Spurgeon preach about missions and Christian service. He went to see Spurgeon after the service, introduced himself, and said that he wanted to become a missionary. Spurgeon asked the man if the fireman on his locomotive was converted. **"N**o," replied the engineer, "he isn't." **"M**y dear fellow," said Spurgeon, "that, then, is your mission."

P R A I S E :

P E T I T I O N :

A man who walks with God reverently will walk with men reverently.

Tender Delusions

WELL then, has God failed to fulfill his promises to the Jews? No! [For these promises are only to those who are truly Jews!] And not everyone born into a Jewish family is truly a Jew! Just the fact that they come from Abraham doesn't make them truly Abraham's children. For the Scriptures say that the promises apply only to Abraham's son Isaac, and Isaac's descendants, though Abraham had other children too. This means that not all of Abraham's children are children of God, but only those who believe the promise of salvation which he made to Abraham.

For God had promised, "Next year I will give you and Sarah a son." (Romans 9:6-9)

How does this passage about Abraham and his descendants apply to modern Christians?

In the movie *Tender Mercies,* Robert Duvall plays a retired country-western singer who has recently remarried. His new wife is an avid churchgoer who sings in the choir and recites her prayers every night. Near the end of the film Duvall and his small son decide to be baptized. Clearly uncertain about what baptism means, but anxious for the approval of their wife and mother, they are baptized during a morning worship service. On the way home, the boy turns to his father and asks, "Do you feel any different?"   **"N**aw, not really," replies Duvall, "Do you?" The boy shakes his head, then looks into the rearview mirror to see if his *looks* have changed at all.   **P**aul says that "not all of Abraham's children are children of God." In a contemporary context, he may have said, "Not all who go to church are Christians."

P R A I S E :

P E T I T I O N :

He protects all those who love him. (Ps. 145:20)

Love and Hate

AND years later, when this son, Isaac, was grown up and married, and Rebecca his wife was about to bear him twin children, God told her that Esau, the child born first, would be a servant to Jacob, his twin brother. In the words of the Scripture, "I chose to bless Jacob, but not Esau." And God said this before the children were even born, before they had done anything either good or bad. This proves that God was doing what he had decided from the beginning; it was not because of what the children did but because of what God wanted and chose. (Romans 9:10-13)

It seems as though God arbitrarily chose to bless Jacob but not Esau. How do you explain this?

A woman once approached Spurgeon and said, "I cannot understand how God could hate Esau."   **"T**hat is not my difficulty," Spurgeon replied. "My difficulty is understanding how God could love Jacob."   **W**hen we consider man's defiant transgressions against a benevolent God, it is difficult to understand God's loving tolerance of man. How can he love a created being that chooses to thumb his nose at the Creator? Christ's death on Calvary was the greatest, most extraordinary expression of love ever demonstrated. Through God's grace and infinite love, we can be reconciled to him.

P R A I S E :

P E T I T I O N :

May people all over the earth know that the Lord is God, and that there is no other god at all. (1 Kings 8:60)

Choices of Destiny

WAS God being unfair? Of course not. For God had said to Moses, "If I want to be kind to someone, I will. And I will take pity on anyone I want to." And so God's blessings are not given just because someone decides to have them or works hard to get them. They are given because God takes pity on those he wants to.

Pharaoh, king of Egypt, was an example of this fact. For God told him he had given him the kingdom of Egypt for the very purpose of displaying the awesome power of God against him: so that all the world would hear about God's glorious name. So you see, God is kind to some just because he wants to be, and he makes some refuse to listen. (Romans 9:14-18)

According to today's reading, upon whom does our salvation depend?

In light of man-made ethics and judicial systems, it seems as though God's choosing of who and who not to bless is quite unfair. (Such choices of God are generally referred to as "predestination.") But since God is good, anything and everything he does is inherently good. God does not need to explain his acts to anyone. Here's how A. W. Tozer deals with this question: "God will not hold us responsible to understand the mysteries of predestination and the divine sovereignty. The best and safest way to deal with these perils is to raise our eyes to God and in deepest reverence say, 'O Lord, thou knowest.' Those things belong to the deep and mysterious depths of God's omniscience. Prying into them may make theologians, but it will never make saints."

PRAISE:

PETITION:

What can a man do but pray? He is here—helpless—and his origin, the breath of his soul, his God must be somewhere. And what else should he pray about but the thing that troubles him? (G. MacDonald)

Self-Exam

WELL then, why does God blame them for not listening? Haven't they done what he made them do?

No, don't say that. Who are you to criticize God? Should the thing made say to the one who made it, "Why have you made me like this?" When a man makes a jar out of clay, doesn't he have a right to use the same lump of clay to make one jar beautiful, to be used for holding flowers, and another to throw garbage into? Does not God have a perfect right to show his fury and power against those who are fit only for destruction, those he has been patient with for all this time? And he has a right to take others such as ourselves, who have been made for pouring the riches of his glory into, whether we are Jews or Gentiles, and to be kind to us so that everyone can see how very great his glory is. (Romans 9:19-24)

Do you think the analogy of the two jars is appropriate? In the world of today, who are the "beautiful jars" and the "garbage jars"?

This is a good time for you to assess your spiritual condition. Complete the appropriate sentence below (be honest!):

1. I am sure of my salvation because _____
_____ .

2. I am not sure of my salvation. Here's why: _____
_____ .

If you don't know how to answer, or if you are troubled by what you have written, read through the rest of Romans in your Bible. Then read the Gospel of John. These books explicitly outline what is necessary for salvation in Christ.

P R A I S E :

P E T I T I O N :

You must worship only the Lord; he will save you from all your enemies. (2 Kings 17:39)

Sinners' Rights

AND Isaiah says in another place that except for God's mercy all the Jews would be destroyed—all of them—just as everyone in the cities of Sodom and Gomorrah perished.

Well then, what shall we say about these things? Just this, that God has given the Gentiles the opportunity to be acquitted by faith, even though they had not been really seeking God. But the Jews, who tried so hard to get right with God by keeping his laws, never succeeded. Why not? Because they were trying to be saved by keeping the law and being good instead of by depending on faith. They have stumbled over the great stumbling stone. God warned them of this in the Scriptures when he said, "I have put a Rock in the path of the Jews, and many will stumble over him (Jesus). Those who believe in him will never be disappointed." (Romans 9:29-33)

What prevented the destruction of all the Jews?

It is estimated that over one-eighth of San Francisco's population is homosexual. The California city has unofficially become the principal center for the American "gay rights" movement. Homosexuals are seeking to attain minority status so that discrimination against them would be considered unlawful. They believe their lifestyle is neither sin nor psychological ailment. To them, homosexuality is simply an "alternative way of life." Incredible as it may seem, there are even homosexual churches operating under the guise of Christianity. The churches are comprised of people patting each other's backs, assuring each other that they too are children of God. As Billy Graham has said, if God is to bless such churches, he must first apologize to Sodom and Gomorrah.

P R A I S E :

P E T I T I O N :

Prayer opens our eyes that we may see ourselves and others as God sees us. (C. Palmer)

God's Superheroes

DEAR brothers, the longing of my heart and my prayer is that the Jewish people might be saved. I know what enthusiasm they have for the honor of God, but it is misdirected zeal. For they don't understand that Christ has died to make them right with God. Instead they are trying to make themselves good enough to gain God's favor by keeping the Jewish laws and customs, but that is not God's way of salvation. They don't understand that Christ gives to those who trust in him everything they are trying to get by keeping his laws. He ends all of that.

For Moses wrote that if a person could be perfectly good and hold out against temptation all his life and never sin once, only then could he be pardoned and saved. But the salvation that comes through faith says, "You don't need to search the heavens to find Christ and bring him down to help you," and "You don't need to go among the dead to bring Christ back to life again." (Romans 10:1-7)

What is the "misdirected zeal" of the Jews?

Contrary to what many Christians believe, missionaries are not saints or superheroes of the faith. Most are simply people who have a strong desire to let others know about Christ. In today's Scripture reading, we see in Paul this kind of desire: "The longing of my heart and my prayer is that the Jewish people might be saved." Elsewhere he states, without presumption, that if his own condemnation would bring about the salvation of the Jews, he would gladly descend to hell and eternal damnation. The desire to see others saved is the missionary's strongest characteristic. Christian leaders often say one must be "called" into missions. But a "call" need not be an audible voice from heaven. The mere recognition of a need usually constitutes a call to service.

P R A I S E :

P E T I T I O N :

Thank the Lord for all the glorious things he does; proclaim them to the nations. (Ps. 105:1)

Hearts and Mouths

FOR salvation that comes from trusting Christ—which is what we preach—is already within easy reach of each of us; in fact, it is as near as our own hearts and mouths. For if you tell others with your own mouth that Jesus Christ is your Lord, and believe in your own heart that God has raised him from the dead, you will be saved. For it is by believing in his heart that a man becomes right with God; and with his mouth he tells others of his faith, confirming his salvation.

For the Scriptures tell us that no one who believes in Christ will ever be disappointed. Jew and Gentile are the same in this respect: they all have the same Lord who generously gives his riches to all those who ask him for them. Anyone who calls upon the name of the Lord will be saved. (Romans 10:8-13)

Jews and Gentiles have the same Lord. Who will be saved?

The United States prides itself on permitting religious freedom for all. Freedom of religion is one of the basic tenets of the American constitution. But although religious freedom is tolerated, proselytizing (attempting to convert people to another faith) is generally looked upon with contempt. The unwritten rule goes something like this: "You can believe anything you want. So can I. But don't try to talk me into anything." We are a rights-oriented culture, and many of us are nervous about infringing on someone else's rights or freedom. And because proselytizing is so unpopular, many Christians shy away from evangelizing. But we should not be afraid to proclaim the truth of the gospel. After all, it is a universal truth meant for all men. Paul says salvation is as near as our own hearts and mouths. Our hearts believe, our mouths proclaim.

PRAISE :

PETITION :

In most cases prayer consists more in groaning than in speaking, in tears rather than in words. (St. Augustine)

Roll-Your-Own Salvation

BUT how shall they ask him to save them unless they believe in him? And how can they believe in him if they have never heard about him? And how can they hear about him unless someone tells them? And how will anyone go and tell them unless someone sends him? That is what the Scriptures are talking about when they say, "How beautiful are the feet of those who preach the Gospel of peace with God and bring glad tidings of good things." In other words, how welcome are those who come preaching God's Good News!

But not everyone who hears the Good News has welcomed it, for Isaiah the prophet said, "Lord, who has believed me when I told them?" Yet faith comes from listening to this Good News—the Good News about Christ. (Romans 10:14-17)

The first paragraph of today's reading is one of the New Testament's most urgent challenges to service. Read the first four questions again. What is your commitment to the proclamation of the Good News?

The power of God's Word should never be underestimated. An old man once received a pocket New Testament from a preacher. He beamed with happiness, and the pastor felt he had done a good deed. However, the old man's happiness was due to the fact that the thin pages from the small book were just right for rolling homemade cigarettes! He smoked his way through Matthew, Mark, Luke, and part of John. When he reached the tenth chapter of John, he ran out of tobacco. To pass the time, he began to read. Soon he became convicted of sin in his life, and surrendered his life to the Lord. The old man had smoked his way right into the kingdom of God!

P R A I S E :

P E T I T I O N :

Why am I praying like this? Because I know you will answer me, O God! (Ps. 17:6)

Jesus for Jews

BUT what about the Jews? Have they heard God's Word? Yes, for it has gone wherever they are; the Good News has been told to the ends of the earth. And did they understand [that God would give his salvation to others if they refused to take it]? Yes, for even back in the time of Moses, God had said that he would make his people jealous and try to wake them up by giving his salvation to the foolish heathen nations. And later on Isaiah said boldly that God would be found by people who weren't even looking for him. In the meantime, he keeps on reaching out his hands to the Jews, but they keep arguing and refusing to come. (Romans 10:18-21)

Why have so many Jews refused to accept the gospel? Does Paul believe it is because they haven't heard of Jesus? Are the Jews alone in their rejection of Christ?

Nearly two thousand years after Paul wrote to the Romans, there are still millions of Jews worldwide who refuse to recognize Christ as the promised Messiah. They cling to their old ways, following only the law of the Old Testament, still waiting for the coming of a messiah. But there are thousands of Jews who *have* discovered and accepted the Good News. Among these is Moshe Rosen, a Jewish intellectual who has since founded an organization called Jews for Jesus. As its name implies, the purpose of the organization is to show Jews that accepting Jesus as Savior makes sense in light of the Old Testament teachings. Jews for Jesus has shown remarkable growth in recent years as hundreds of Jews have learned that Jesus is not a fraud, but indeed the Son of God.   There are many other Christian organizations committed to evangelism. We should take an active interest in them, supporting them through participation, prayer, and financial giving.

P R A I S E :

P E T I T I O N :

If [a man] confesses and forsakes [his mistakes], he gets another chance. (Prov. 28:13)

March ROMANS 11-16

Moving into a career can be one of the most exciting times of life. It is a time filled with plans, dreams, and ambitions. For the Christian, it can provide new opportunities for witnessing. The final chapters of Romans contain instructions about how to live the Christian life. These teachings make it clear that Christianity should be lived in public—among friends, business acquaintances, and the world at large.

Holdouts of the Faith

I ask then, has God rejected and deserted his people the Jews? Oh no, not at all. Remember that I myself am a Jew, a descendant of Abraham and a member of Benjamin's family.

No, God has not discarded his own people whom he chose from the very beginning. Do you remember what the Scriptures say about this? Elijah the prophet was complaining to God about the Jews, telling God how they had killed the prophets and torn down God's altars; Elijah claimed that he was the only one left in all the land who still loved God, and now they were trying to kill him too.

And do you remember how God replied? God said, "No, you are not the only one left. I have seven thousand others besides you who still love me and have not bowed down to idols!"

It is the same today. Not all the Jews have turned away from God; there are a few being saved as a result of God's kindness in choosing them. And if it is by God's kindness, then it is not by their being good enough. For in that case the free gift would no longer be free—it isn't free when it is earned. (Romans 11:1-6)

After all the charges brought against unbelieving Israel in chapter 10, Paul anticipates the question that many may ask: "Has God rejected and deserted all the Jews?" Paul's answer is, "Oh no, not at all." How does Paul use himself as proof that God has not cast away or given up on the Jews?

The truth of God's Word has never died out; it has never been completely lost, abandoned, or destroyed. From the beginning of man, there have been groups of people, often quite small, who have faithfully upheld it. The Bible calls these small holdouts of the faith "remnants" (KJV). Noah and his family were a remnant in the days of the flood. Lot and his family were a remnant in Sodom. Paul and other believing Jews were a remnant in the first century. God's remnant today is composed of all those who have become his children through faith in Christ. It is our responsibility to pass on the Word to our families, friends, and acquaintances.

PRAISE:

PETITION:

If a wicked person turns away from all his sins and begins to obey my laws and do what is just and right, he shall surely live and not die. (Ezek. 18:22)

Melt/Harden

SO this is the situation: Most of the Jews have not found the favor of God they are looking for. A few have—the ones God has picked out—but the eyes of the others have been blinded. This is what our Scriptures refer to when they say that God has put them to sleep, shutting their eyes and ears so that they do not understand what we are talking about when we tell them of Christ. And so it is to this very day.

King David spoke of this same thing when he said, "Let their good food and other blessings trap them into thinking all is well between themselves and God. Let these good things boomerang on them and fall back upon their heads to justly crush them. Let their eyes be dim," he said, "so that they cannot see, and let them walk bent-backed forever with a heavy load." (Romans 11:7-10)

According to this passage, what portion of the Jews have found favor in God's eyes?

A sculptor was fashioning a new work from clay and wax. Over a weekend, he inadvertently left two lumps—one of wax and one of clay—on an outdoor slab of cement. On the following Monday when he came to retrieve the materials, he discovered that the hot summer sun had altered them. The lump of wax had melted thoroughly; all that was left of it was a dark stain on the slab. The lump of clay, however, had hardened into a rocklike mass. The same sun that melts wax hardens clay. Whenever the light of the gospel is proclaimed, some people are saved and strengthened in their faith; others are confirmed in their unbelief.

PRAISE:

PETITION:

You can never please God without faith, without depending on him. (Heb. 11:6)

Jealous Desires

DOES this mean that God has rejected his Jewish people forever? Of course not! His purpose was to make his salvation available to the Gentiles, and then the Jews would be jealous and begin to want God's salvation for themselves. Now if the whole world became rich as a result of God's offer of salvation, when the Jews stumbled over it and turned it down, think how much greater a blessing the world will share in later on when the Jews, too, come to Christ. (Romans 11:11, 12)

Again Paul anticipates a question: "Does this mean that God has rejected his Jewish people forever?" What is his answer?

Two-year-old Barbara was being unusually boisterous. Her young mother, trying to quiet her, offered her a book to look at. But the child pouted and pushed the book away. Her mother shrugged, walked away, and handed the book to Barbara's six-month-old brother. When Barbara saw this, she screamed in displeasure. The book she had rejected had now become desirable, because someone else had it.   God knew the rebellious Jews would react in much the same manner. If his offer of salvation to them were extended to the Gentiles, he knew the jealous Jews would suddenly be keenly interested.

PRAISE :

PETITION :

Talking to men for God is a great thing; talking to God for men is the first thing.

Augustine's Conversion

AS you know, God has appointed me as a special messenger to you Gentiles. I lay great stress on this and remind the Jews about it as often as I can, so that if possible I can make them want what you Gentiles have and in that way save some of them. And how wonderful it will be when they become Christians! When God turned away from them it meant that he turned to the rest of the world to offer his salvation; and now it is even more wonderful when the Jews come to Christ. It will be like dead people coming back to life. (Romans 11:13-15)

What is the analogy Paul uses to dramatize the coming of the Jews to Christ? Why is this analogy appropriate?

In early life, Augustine was interested more in humanistic philosophy than in Christianity. He was determined to leave home and go to Rome. This was in opposition to the wishes of his godly mother, who prayed constantly for his salvation. He deceived his mother and sailed for Italy. No doubt this seemed to his mother a refusal of her prayers. But in the providence of God, Augustine was later brought to the faith, and went on to become one of the greatest Christian thinkers. God often takes human failure and transgression and transforms it for his own glory.

P R A I S E :

P E T I T I O N :

You are all children of the light and of the day. (1 Thess. 5:5)

A Hand for the Queen

AND since Abraham and the prophets are God's people, their children will be too. For if the roots of the tree are holy, the branches will be too.

But some of these branches from Abraham's tree, some of the Jews, have been broken off. And you Gentiles who were branches from, we might say, a wild olive tree, were grafted in. So now you, too, receive the blessing God has promised Abraham and his children, sharing in God's rich nourishment of his own special olive tree.

But you must be careful not to brag about being put in to replace the branches that were broken off. Remember that you are important only because you are now a part of God's tree; you are just a branch, not a root.

If the Jews leave their unbelief behind them and come back to God, God will graft them back into the tree again. He has the power to do it. (Romans 11:16-18, 23)

The Gentiles have been offered the right to salvation, just as the Jews have. What should be the attitude of the Gentiles in light of this unexpected blessing?

In the "Ethics" column of a recent issue of *Esquire*, Anthony Brandt sets forth an astounding story of devotion and forgiveness: "I cherish the story of John Stubbs, a Puritan divine of Queen Elizabeth's time who strongly opposed her projected marriage to the Duke of Alençon, a French Catholic. Stubbs knew the penalty for doing so, which was the loss of a hand; nevertheless he published a pamphlet against the marriage. He was accordingly tried, convicted, and led out for public execution of the sentence. Stubbs laid his right hand on the block, the ax fell, and he rose to his feet, lifted the bloody stump high in the air, and cried to the crowd, 'Long live the queen!' " Paul says that after all Israel has done, God will still forgive her. He will not respond to Israel's iniquities with bitterness and revenge; he will accept his repentant, errant people with open arms.

PRAISE:

PETITION:

Give your burdens to the Lord. He will carry them. He will not permit the godly to slip or fall. (Ps. 55:22)

The Boot of Love

AND then all Israel will be saved.

Do you remember what the prophets said about this? "There shall come out of Zion a Deliverer, and he shall turn the Jews from all ungodliness. At that time I will take away their sins, just as I promised."

Now many of the Jews are enemies of the Gospel. They hate it. But this has been a benefit to you, for it has resulted in God's giving his gifts to you Gentiles. Yet the Jews are still beloved of God because of his promises to Abraham, Isaac, and Jacob. For God's gifts and his call can never be withdrawn; he will never go back on his promises. Once you were rebels against God, but when the Jews refused his gifts God was merciful to you instead. And now the Jews are the rebels, but some day they, too, will share in God's mercy upon you. For God has given them all up to sin so that he could have mercy upon all alike. (Romans 11:26-32)

God has promised to be just but merciful. What could possibly drive him to break one of his promises to man?

In the barracks where the sergeant slept was a deeply spiritual private who got down on his knees and prayed every night before piling into his bunk. The sergeant didn't like this. One night he picked up his muddy boot and hurled it at the praying soldier, striking him on the head and stunning him. The private finished his prayer without a word. The next morning when the sergeant reached for his boots, he found them cleaned and polished. Later he found out that the praying private had shined them. The sergeant just couldn't take it— he was driven to look for the One who could make a man act like that.

_P R A I S E :_

_P E T I T I O N :_

It is not the body's posture, but the heart's attitude that counts when we pray. (B. Graham)

Describing God

OH, what a wonderful God we have! How great are his wisdom and knowledge and riches! How impossible it is for us to understand his decisions and his methods! For who among us can know the mind of the Lord? Who knows enough to be his counselor and guide? And who could ever offer to the Lord enough to induce him to act? For everything comes from God alone. Everything lives by his power, and everything is for his glory. To him be glory evermore. (Romans 11:33-36)

Today's reading is a beautiful expression of praise and admiration to God. Though we can know God, how much of his greatness can we truly understand?

Thales, the great philosopher, was once asked to describe God. He agreed to try, and retreated to his home. After weeks of study, he finally emerged and confessed that he had been unable to do it. Tertullian, one of the fathers of the early church, seized upon the incident, saying that it was an example of the world's ignorance of God outside of Christ. "There is the wisest man in the world," he said. "He does not know Christ, so he cannot tell you who God is. But even the most ignorant mechanic among Christians knows God intimately and is able to make him known to others."

P R A I S E :

P E T I T I O N :

In response to all he has done for us, let us outdo each other in being helpful and kind to each other and in doing good. (Heb. 10:24)

Father to Child

AND so, dear brothers, I plead with you to give your bodies to God. Let them be a living sacrifice, holy—the kind he can accept. When you think of what he has done for you, is this too much to ask? Don't copy the behavior and customs of this world, but be a new and different person with a fresh newness in all you do and think. Then you will learn from your own experience how his ways will really satisfy you. (Romans 12:1, 2)

What is Paul asking the Romans to do? Should we take his requests seriously today? Explain.

Imagine the following scenario: A boy approaches his father, a big smile on his face, and says, "Daddy, I've decided that I want to do everything that you want me to." The father grabs the boy by the collar, slaps his face, and snarls, "Boy, I am going to make you the most miserable kid in town. I'm going to break all your toys and make you eat spinach three times a day. You're not going to have any more fun." No decent father would treat his son that way. Yet many Christians think that if they submit their lives to the Lord, he will delight in making them miserable. But if human fathers desire the best in life for their children, how much more will the heavenly Father take pleasure in showing us the way to true happiness.

P R A I S E : _____

P E T I T I O N : _____

If two of you agree down here on earth concerning anything you ask for, my Father in heaven will do it for you. (Matt. 18:19)

Halfway Conceited

AS God's messenger I give each of you God's warning: Be honest in your estimate of yourselves, measuring your value by how much faith God has given you. Just as there are many parts to our bodies, so it is with Christ's body. We are all parts of it, and it takes every one of us to make it complete, for we each have different work to do. So we belong to each other, and each needs all the others. (Romans 12:3-5)

What does this passage have to say about the differences that Christians have between themselves?

A husband, finding his wife brushing her hair for the seventh time that day, remarked, "You certainly are conceited! All you do is look at yourself in the mirror." The wife, annoyed, shot back, "That's not true. I am not conceited. Actually, I don't think I'm half as beautiful as I really am!" **G**ood personal appearance is important to our self-esteem. But being overly concerned about how we look can lead to unhealthy vanity and self-centeredness. Paul's advice is: "Be honest in your estimate of yourselves."

PRAISE:

PETITION:

Prayer is the strong wall and fortress of the church. (M. Luther)

To Each His Own

GOD has given each of us the ability to do certain things well. So if God has given you the ability to prophesy, then prophesy whenever you can—as often as your faith is strong enough to receive a message from God. If your gift is that of serving others, serve them well. If you are a teacher, do a good job of teaching. If you are a preacher, see to it that your sermons are strong and helpful. If God has given you money, be generous in helping others with it. If God has given you administrative ability and put you in charge of the work of others, take the responsibility seriously. Those who offer comfort to the sorrowing should do so with Christian cheer. (Romans 12:6-8)

According to this passage, what does God desire from us?

Reexamine today's reading. In the spirit of this passage, complete the sentences below as you believe Paul would have filled them in.

If you are a welder, _____

_____

If you are a housewife, _____

_____

If you are a student, _____

_____

If you work in a restaurant, _____

_____

If you are a writer, _____

_____

P R A I S E : _____

P E T I T I O N : _____

May he answer all your prayers! (Ps. 20:5)

Extra Love

DON'T just pretend that you love others: really love them. Hate what is wrong. Stand on the side of the good. Love each other with brotherly affection and take delight in honoring each other. Never be lazy in your work but serve the Lord enthusiastically.

Be glad for all God is planning for you. Be patient in trouble, and prayerful always. When God's children are in need, you be the one to help them out. And get into the habit of inviting guests home for dinner or, if they need lodging, for the night. (Romans 12:9-13)

Does the "work" Paul talks about refer to all work, or just to Christian work?

When early printers, using handset type, received an order to print an anthology of Alfred Tennyson's poems, they at once bought hundreds of additional letters "L" and "V" for their presses. They realized that Tennyson used the word "love" so much in his poetry that the average set of type could not possibly supply all the needed letters. As Tennyson's poetry was saturated with "love," so the life of a Christian should overflow with it.

PRAISE:

PETITION:

May he be given glory forever and ever through endless ages because of his master plan of salvation for the church through Jesus Christ. (Eph. 3:21)

The Return of George Lucas

IF someone mistreats you because you are a Christian, don't curse him; pray that God will bless him. When others are happy, be happy with them. If they are sad, share their sorrow. Work happily together. Don't try to act big. Don't try to get into the good graces of important people, but enjoy the company of ordinary folks. And don't think you know it all!

Never pay back evil for evil. Do things in such a way that everyone can see you are honest clear through. Don't quarrel with anyone. Be at peace with everyone, just as much as possible.

Dear friends, never avenge yourselves. Leave that to God, for he has said that he will repay those who deserve it. [Don't take the law into your own hands.] Instead, feed your enemy if he is hungry. If he is thirsty give him something to drink and you will be "heaping coals of fire on his head." In other words, he will feel ashamed of himself for what he has done to you. Don't let evil get the upper hand but conquer evil by doing good. (Romans 12:14-21)

How should a Christian fight evil?

The third movie in the *Star Wars* series was originally titled *Revenge of the Jedi*. Several months prior to the release of the film, many promotional materials were sent to movie theaters and chains across the country. Then someone suggested to director George Lucas that if the Jedi knights were indeed agents of goodness and peace, they would not be motivated by revenge. Lucas thought about it, then agreed. Even though a title change would mean a substantial cost in redesigning film titles and replacing promotional materials, Lucas retitled the film *Return of the Jedi*. In our culture, vengeance is not an uncommon concept. When someone does us wrong, our immediate reaction is to want to get back at them. If we are to be Christlike, though, we must give up our vengefulness: "Dear friends, never avenge yourselves. Leave that to God, for he has said that he will repay those who deserve it."

P R A I S E :

P E T I T I O N :

Prayer puts us in the proper attitude to discern the will of God. (B. Graham)

The Escape of Surrender

OBEY the government, for God is the one who has put it there. There is no government anywhere that God has not placed in power. So those who refuse to obey the laws of the land are refusing to obey God, and punishment will follow. For the policeman does not frighten people who are doing right; but those doing evil will always fear him. So if you don't want to be afraid, keep the laws and you will get along well. The policeman is sent by God to help you. But if you are doing something wrong, of course you should be afraid, for he will have you punished. He is sent by God for that very purpose. (Romans 13:1-4)

How can a man destroy his fear of the authorities?

Occasionally we hear about an undetained thief or murderer who one day walks into a police station and gives himself up. We always wonder about his motivation—if he has safely escaped detection, why would he surrender? Today's Scripture reading gives us some insight: "those doing evil will always fear [the policeman]." This fear of the law can easily develop into a paranoia which robs a criminal of sleep and peace of mind. It can drive a person to the brink of insanity so that, ironically, the only escape is surrender to the authorities. Proverbs 28:1 says: "The wicked flee when no man pursueth" (KJV). But "if you don't want to be afraid, keep the laws and you will get along well."

PRAISE :

PETITION :

Sing for joy, O heavens; shout, O earth. Break forth with song, O mountains, for the Lord has comforted his people, and will have compassion upon them in their sorrow. (Isa. 49:13)

Paying Taxes

OBEY the laws, then, for two reasons: first, to keep from being punished, and second, just because you know you should.

Pay your taxes too, for these same two reasons. For government workers need to be paid so that they can keep on doing God's work, serving you. Pay everyone whatever he ought to have: pay your taxes and import duties gladly, obey those over you, and give honor and respect to all those to whom it is due. (Romans 13:5-7)

Why should Christians be faithful in paying taxes to the government?

A man attached to his van a bumper sticker that read, "Stamp out organized crime: Abolish the IRS." When he wrote to the IRS, he addressed the envelope "Infernal Revenue Service." Although these messages were meant to be humorous, they made a point. Most people do not like to pay taxes of any sort. They view the IRS as one of Americas' greatest enemies. But although tax paying is not a delightful activity, Christians are commanded to do it "gladly." It is unlawful to cheat on income tax forms; God certainly views it as a sin. Jesus said Christians should give to Caesar (the government) what is of Caesar, and to God what is of God.

P R A I S E :

P E T I T I O N :

Those who wait for me shall never be ashamed. (Isa. 49:23)

"Quadrophenia"

PAY all your debts except the debt of love for others—never finish paying that! For if you love them, you will be obeying all of God's laws, fulfilling all his requirements. If you love your neighbor as much as you love yourself you will not want to harm or cheat him, or kill him or steal from him. And you won't sin with his wife or want what is his, or do anything else the Ten Commandments say is wrong. All ten are wrapped up in this one, to love your neighbor as you love yourself. Love does no wrong to anyone. That's why it fully satisfies all of God's requirements. It is the only law you need.

Another reason for right living is this: you know how late it is; time is running out. Wake up, for the coming of the Lord is nearer now than when we first believed. The night is far gone, the day of his return will soon be here. So quit the evil deeds of darkness and put on the armor of right living, as we who live in the daylight should! Be decent and true in everything you do so that all can approve your behavior. Don't spend your time in wild parties and getting drunk or in adultery and lust, or fighting, or jealousy. But ask the Lord Jesus Christ to help you live as you should, and don't make plans to enjoy evil. (Romans 13:8-14)

What are two reasons Christians should exercise "right living"?

A few years ago, British rock group The Who released an album called *Quadrophenia*. It was a "concept" album about an adolescent growing up in London. The lyrics tell the story of his attempts to fit into his early sixties "mod" peer group. But in spite of his dapper zoot suit, his motorscooter, and his indulgence in booze, sex, drugs, and street fighting, he doesn't find what satisfies him. High on drug-induced quadrophenia (a *four*-personality version of schizophrenia), he finally drives his motorscooter off the cliffs of Dover. In this rock opera, composer Pete Townshend has dramatically shown that a life of selfishness and debauchery leads only to death. A life of dedication to Christ, however, leads to satisfaction on earth and life in eternity.

P R A I S E :

P E T I T I O N :

In prayer we shift the center of living from self-consciousness to self-surrender. (A. Heschel)

Internal Struggles

GIVE a warm welcome to any brother who wants to join you, even though his faith is weak. Don't criticize him for having different ideas from yours about what is right and wrong. For instance, don't argue with him about whether or not to eat meat that has been offered to idols. You may believe there is no harm in this, but the faith of others is weaker; they think it is wrong, and will go without any meat at all and eat vegetables rather than eat that kind of meat. Those who think it is all right to eat such meat must not look down on those who won't. And if you are one of those who won't, don't find fault with those who do. For God has acccepted them to be his children. They are God's servants, not yours. They are responsible to him, not to you. Let him tell them whether they are right or wrong. And God is able to make them do as they should. (Romans 14:1-4)

Why should we not pass judgment on other Christians?

Brigade Leader magazine recently published a parable about two armies that set out to fight each other. At first the fighting was intense, and there were many casualties. After awhile, the combat died down, and one of the armies began to experience serious divisions within its ranks. Soon this large army was reduced to a group of smaller units. But these units did not concentrate their efforts to fight against the enemy, whose forces were still consolidated. Instead, they ignored the enemy and began to fight amongst themselves. The parable is obviously about Christianity vs. paganism and the forces of evil. Sadly, Christianity has divided itself into hundreds of small factions. These factions are often more worried about fighting each other's doctrines and standards of conduct than about defeating the enemy. Paul says the responsibility for exposing right and wrong falls into God's lap, not man's.

P R A I S E :

P E T I T I O N :

He would not have listened if I had not confessed my sins. (Ps. 66:18)

Race to Maturity

SOME think that Christians should observe the Jewish holidays as special days to worship God, but others say it is wrong and foolish to go to all that trouble, for every day alike belongs to God. On questions of this kind everyone must decide for himself. If you have special days for worshiping the Lord, you are trying to honor him; you are doing a good thing. So is the person who eats meat that has been offered to idols; he is thankful to the Lord for it; he is doing right. And the person who won't touch such meat, he, too, is anxious to please the Lord, and is thankful. We are not our own bosses to live or die as we ourselves might choose. Living or dying we follow the Lord. Either way we are his. (Romans 14:5-8)

Does this passage indicate that Paul advocates strict codes of Christian behavior? Explain.

The world champion Grand Prix racer was for a time an Argentine who could drive his car at one hundred and fifty miles per hour and who had won the great road races of Europe. On the public highway, though, he was the most careful and conscientious of drivers. Young men would drive alongside him and, recognizing him, gun their motors and honk their horns. He could have showed off by speeding ahead, leaving them as though they were standing still, but he never used his ability for his own ends. If he saw that someone wanted to pass him so as to brag about it, he would slow down so that they could pass. He sacrificed his pride for the sake of his example. Every believer stands before God in perfect liberty, but each is bound before God as to how he uses his liberty. We must not flaunt our liberty in the face of others.

PRAISE:

PETITION:

Everyone who asks, receives. Anyone who seeks, finds. If only you will knock, the door will open. (Matt. 7:8)

The Adulterous Woman

CHRIST died and rose again for this very purpose, so that he can be our Lord both while we live and when we die.

You have no right to criticize your brother or look down on him. Remember, each of us will stand personally before the Judgment Seat of God. For it is written, "As I live," says the Lord, "every knee shall bow to me and every tongue confess to God." Yes, each of us will give an account of himself to God. (Romans 14:9-12)

What does Paul have to say about criticism?

Men have no right to judge others. No story better illustrates this than Jesus' encounter with the adulterous woman (John 8:3-11) "As [Jesus] was speaking, the Jewish leaders and Pharisees brought a woman caught in adultery and placed her out in front of the staring crowd. " 'Teacher,' they said to Jesus, 'this woman was caught in the very act of adultery. Moses' law says to kill her. What about it?' "They were trying to trap him into saying something they could use against him, but Jesus stooped down and wrote in the dust with his finger. They kept demanding an answer, so he stood up and said, 'All right, hurl the stones at her until she dies. But only he who never sinned may throw the first!' "Then he stooped down again and wrote some more in the dust. And the Jewish leaders slipped away one by one, beginning with the eldest, until only Jesus was left in front of the crowd with the woman. "Then Jesus stood up again and said to her, 'Where are your accusers? Didn't even one of them condemn you?' " 'No, sir,' she said. "And Jesus said, 'Neither do I. Go and sin no more.' "

PRAISE:

PETITION:

Praying is simply a two-way conversation between you and God. (B. Graham)

Three Friends

SO don't criticize each other any more. Try instead to live in such a way that you will never make your brother stumble by letting him see you doing something he thinks is wrong.

As for myself, I am perfectly sure on the authority of the Lord Jesus that there is nothing really wrong with eating meat that has been offered to idols. But if someone believes it is wrong, then he shouldn't do it because for him it is wrong. And if your brother is bothered by what you eat, you are not acting in love if you go ahead and eat it. Don't let your eating ruin someone for whom Christ died. Don't do anything that will cause criticism against yourself even though you know that what you do is right.

For, after all, the important thing for us as Christians is not what we eat or drink but stirring up goodness and peace and joy from the Holy Spirit. (Romans 14:13-17)

If you are criticized by Christians for doing something you know is right, what should you do?

To live the Christian life as presented in the passage above is to forget about yourself and concentrate on others. Too many of us are like the one described in this ditty:

I had a little tea party,
This afternoon at three.
'Twas very small—three guests in all,
Just I, myself, and me.
Myself ate up the sandwiches,
While I drank up the tea,
'Twas also I who ate the pie
And passed the cake to me.

P R A I S E :

P E T I T I O N :

Ask, using my name, and you will receive, and your cup of joy will overflow. (John 16:24)

Stage Fright

IF you let Christ be Lord in these affairs, God will be glad; and so will others. In this way aim for harmony in the church and try to build each other up.

Don't undo the work of God for a chunk of meat. Remember, there is nothing wrong with the meat, but it is wrong to eat it if it makes another stumble. The right thing to do is to quit eating meat or drinking wine or doing anything else that offends your brother or makes him sin. You may know that there is nothing wrong with what you do, even from God's point of view, but keep it to yourself; don't flaunt your faith in front of others who might be hurt by it. In this situation, happy is the man who does not sin by doing what he knows is right. But anyone who believes that something he wants to do is wrong shouldn't do it. He sins if he does, for he thinks it is wrong, and so for him it *is* wrong. Anything that is done apart from what he feels is right is sin. (Romans 14:18-23)

Are there activities which are lawful for some yet sinful for others?

A certain nineteenth-century New York minister loved the theater. But he had to conceal his passion, for Christians of the day condemned all forms of secular entertainment. When the minister heard that the great Junius Brutus Booth was to star in a play, he wrote a letter to the actor: "I am anxious to see your play, but as Christians are opposed to theater-going, and I am a Christian minister, I have a special favor to ask. Could you admit me privately through a back door?" Booth's reply was short: "There is no door to my theater through which God cannot see."

P R A I S E :

P E T I T I O N :

You will pray to him, and he will hear you, and you will fulfill all your promises to him. (Job 22:27)

The Shaft

EVEN if we believe that it makes no difference to the Lord whether we do these things, still we cannot just go ahead and do them to please ourselves; for we must bear the "burden" of being considerate of the doubts and fears of others—of those who feel these things are wrong. Let's please the other fellow, not ourselves, and do what is for his good and thus build him up in the Lord. Christ didn't please himself. As the Psalmist said, "He came for the very purpose of suffering under the insults of those who were against the Lord." These things that were written in the Scriptures so long ago are to teach us patience and to encourage us, so that we will look forward expectantly to the time when God will conquer sin and death.

May God who gives patience, steadiness, and encouragement help you to live in complete harmony with each other—each with the attitude of Christ toward the other. And then all of us can praise the Lord together with one voice, giving glory to God, the Father of our Lord Jesus Christ. (Romans 15:1-6)

You have probably heard people say, "Well, *I* don't see anything wrong with it so *I'm* going to do it." Evaluate this attitude in light of today's Scripture reading.

In the castle of Chillon, there was once a deep, dark shaft designed for the execution of prisoners. The dungeon keeper would take the prisoners out into the dark corridor, telling them they were free to go. As they rushed ahead in their freedom, they fell into the shaft to their death. As Christians, we do have great freedom, but God has given us some guideposts to keep us from falling or causing others to fall.

PRAISE:

PETITION:

Prayer is the avenue through which God supplies man's wants. (E. M. Bounds)

Strength in Numbers

SO, warmly welcome each other into the church, just as Christ has warmly welcomed you; then God will be glorified. Remember that Jesus Christ came to show that God is true to his promises and to help the Jews. And remember that he came also that the Gentiles might be saved and give glory to God for his mercies to them. That is what the Psalmist meant when he wrote: "I will praise you among the Gentiles, and sing to your name."

And in another place, "Be glad, O you Gentiles, along with his people the Jews."

And yet again, "Praise the Lord, O you Gentiles, let everyone praise him."

And the prophet Isaiah said, "There shall be an Heir in the house of Jesse, and he will be King over the Gentiles; they will pin their hopes on him alone." (Romans 15:7-12)

Why is it important for Christians to worship together in church?

Someone once asked a man, "Can I possibly be a Christian without fellowship in a church?" The gentleman's reply was memorable. He said, "Yes it is possible, but it is something like being a student without going to school, a soldier who will not join the army, a salesman with no customers, a parent without a family, a football player without a team, a lone seaman on a ship without a crew, an author without readers, a businessman trying to operate on a deserted island, or a bee without a hive." *(Our Daily Bread)*

P R A I S E :

P E T I T I O N :

Lord, you know the hopes of humble people. Surely you will hear their cries and comfort their hearts by helping them. (Ps. 10:17)

Tools of God

SO I pray for you Gentiles that God who gives you hope will keep you happy and full of peace as you believe in him. I pray that God will help you overflow with hope in him through the Holy Spirit's power within you.

I know that you are wise and good, my brothers, and that you know these things so well that you are able to teach others all about them. But even so I have been bold enough to emphasize some of these points, knowing that all you need is this reminder from me; for I am, by God's grace, a special messenger from Jesus Christ to you Gentiles, bringing you the Gospel and offering you up as a fragrant sacrifice to God; for you have been made pure and pleasing to him by the Holy Spirit. So it is right for me to be a little proud of all Christ Jesus has done through me. I dare not judge how effectively he has used others, but I know this: he has used me to win the Gentiles to God. (Romans 15:13-18)

How has Paul been a useful tool in God's hands?

A chisel lying beside a block of stone is useless. It cannot produce a sculpture unless it is used by the hand and brain of a skillful artist. On the other hand, the artist cannot produce a sculpture—no matter how well-conceived—without a hammer and chisel. God, too, chooses to use instruments—human beings— to do his work. Christians have the tremendous privilege of being God's tools.

P R A I S E :

P E T I T I O N :

It is good to say, "Thank you" to the Lord, to sing praises to the God who is above all gods. (Ps. 92:1)

The Wrong World

I have won them by my message and by the good way I have lived before them, and by the miracles done through me as signs from God—all by the Holy Spirit's power. In this way I have preached the full Gospel of Christ all the way from Jerusalem clear over into Illyricum.

But all the while my ambition has been to go still farther, preaching where the name of Christ has never yet been heard, rather than where a church has already been started by someone else. I have been following the plan spoken of in the Scriptures where Isaiah says that those who have never heard the name of Christ before will see and understand. In fact that is the very reason I have been so long in coming to visit you. (Romans 15:19-22)

Why did Paul spend hardly any time speaking at established churches?

When David Livingstone's body was taken back to England, crowds thronged the streets to pay tribute to the noble missionary who had dotted the continent of Africa with mission stations. An elderly man among them was heard to sob aloud, and people wondered at his deep grief. It was revealed that he and Livingstone had been friends in their youth and, as an ambitious young man, he had scorned Livingstone's choice to give his life for Christ in Africa. With a life of selfish interest behind him, the man saw with regret who had made the wiser choice, and he deeply cried out, "I have put the emphasis on the wrong world."

PRAISE:

PETITION:

Our worship should not be confined to certain times and places. It should be the spirit of our life.

The Economics of Prayer

BUT now at last I am through with my work here, and I am ready to come after all these long years of waiting. For I am planning to take a trip to Spain, and when I do, I will stop off there in Rome; and after we have had a good time together for a little while, you can send me on my way again.

But before I come, I must go down to Jerusalem to take a gift to the Jewish Christians there. For you see, the Christians in Macedonia and Achaia have taken up an offering for those in Jerusalem who are going through such hard times. They were very glad to do this, for they feel that they owe a real debt to the Jerusalem Christians. Why? Because the news about Christ came to these Gentiles from the church in Jerusalem. And since they received this wonderful spiritual gift of the Gospel from there, they feel that the least they can do in return is to give some material aid. As soon as I have delivered this money and completed this good deed of theirs, I will come to see you on my way to Spain. (Romans 15:23-28)

The Jerusalem church was undergoing many difficulties. What did the churches at Macedonia and Achaia do to help?

A young widow was chatting with a wealthy businessman after church on Sunday morning. She told him that since her husband had died, things had really gotten difficult for her and her children. They were using food stamps, and the landlord had threatened her with eviction because of delinquent rent checks. The rich man looked at her with pity and said, "That's too bad. I'll pray for you." Then he walked away.   It is God's will that we pray to him on behalf of brothers and sisters. But he also expects us to use our own resources to help those in need.

PRAISE:

PETITION:

Everyone who calls upon the name of the Lord will be saved. (Joel 2:32)

Prayer Partners

AND I am sure that when I come the Lord will give me a great blessing for you.

Will you be my prayer partners? For the Lord Jesus Christ's sake, and because of your love for me—given to you by the Holy Spirit—pray much with me for my work. Pray that I will be protected in Jerusalem from those who are not Christians. Pray also that the Christians there will be willing to accept the money I am bringing them. Then I will be able to come to you with a happy heart by the will of God, and we can refresh each other.

And now may our God, who gives peace, be with you all. Amen. (Romans 15:29-33)

What are Paul's prayer requests?

We are nearing the end of March. Presumably, you have been using this devotional study book for nearly three months. Take a few moments to look back through all your prayer diary entries. On a separate sheet of paper, list the answers to prayer you have experienced so far this year. Then list your prayer requests. Thank the Lord for his faithfulness in hearing and responding to your prayers. Have you ever considered becoming a prayer partner with someone? It is valuable to have someone with whom you can share your prayer concerns. As Paul discovered, prayer partners can "refresh each other" in their sorrows and in their joys.

P R A I S E :

P E T I T I O N :

God honors no withdrawals if there have been no deposits.

Keeping Friends

PHOEBE, a dear Christian woman from the town of Cenchreae, will be coming to see you soon. She has worked hard in the church there. Receive her as your sister in the Lord, giving her a warm Christian welcome. Help her in every way you can, for she has helped many in their needs, including me. Tell Priscilla and Aquila "hello." They have been my fellow workers in the affairs of Christ Jesus. In fact, they risked their lives for me; and I am not the only one who is thankful to them: so are all the Gentile churches.

Please give my greetings to all those who meet to worship in their home. Greet my good friend Epaenetus. He was the very first person to become a Christian in Asia. Remember me to Mary, too, who has worked so hard to help us. Then there are Andronicus and Junias, my relatives who were in prison with me. They are respected by the apostles, and became Christians before I did. Please give them my greetings. Say "hello" to Ampliatus, whom I love as one of God's own children, and Urbanus, our fellow worker, and beloved Stachys.

Then there is Apelles, a good man whom the Lord approves; greet him for me. And give my best regards to those working at the house of Aristobulus. Remember me to Herodion my relative. Remember me to the Christian slaves over at Narcissus House. (Romans 16:1-11)

Who were Phoebe, Priscilla, Aquilla, Epaenetus, Apelles, and Herodion?

It is remarkable that Paul considered it important to send specific greetings to all his friends, including even the "Christian slaves over at Narcissus House." During times of transition, when we are worried about college, career moves, and leaving home, it is easy to forget about many of the people we love and appreciate. Take some time to write down the names of people whose friendships you value. Refer to your list occasionally, making sure you keep contact with these people through phone calls or letters. Remember to pray for them regularly.

PRAISE :

PETITION :

Blessings on all who reverence and trust the Lord—on all who obey him! (Ps. 128:1)

Stayin' Alive

SAY "hello" to Tryphaena and Tryphosa, the Lord's workers, and to dear Persis, who has worked so hard for the Lord. Greet Rufus for me, whom the Lord picked out to be his very own; and also his dear mother who has been such a mother to me. And please give my greetings to Asyncritus, Phlegon, Hermes, Patrobas, Hermas, and the other brothers who are with them. Give my love to Philologus, Julia, Nereus and his sister, and to Olympas, and all the Christians who are with them. Shake hands warmly with each other. All the churches here send you their greetings. (Romans 16:12-16)

What adjectives would you use to describe Paul's feelings toward these people?

When faced with adversity, it is natural for men and women to rally together in order to overcome their troubles. This fact accounts for the great enthusiasm that sports fans demonstrate when their team is on the field or court. There is strength and comfort in staying together through the "thick and thin" of life. In today's Bible reading we can certainly see this spirit of warm fellowship and oneness of cause. But we know that this "team" of Christians had more than just a cooperative spirit to hold them together. They had the Holy Spirit as well. We should attempt to be more like the Christians of the early church: dedicated to the Lord, to each other, and to the cause of evangelism.

P R A I S E :

P E T I T I O N :

Strength in prayer is better than length in prayer.

Errant Children

AND now there is one more thing to say before I end this letter. Stay away from those who cause divisions and are upsetting people's faith, teaching things about Christ that are contrary to what you have been taught. Such teachers are not working for our Lord Jesus, but only want gain for themselves. They are good speakers, and simple-minded people are often fooled by them. But everyone knows that you stand loyal and true. This makes me very happy. I want you always to remain very clear about what is right, and to stay innocent of any wrong. The God of peace will soon crush Satan under your feet. The blessings from our Lord Jesus Christ be upon you.

Timothy my fellow-worker, and Lucius and Jason and Sosipater, my relatives, send you their good wishes. (Romans 16:17-21)

What will soon happen to Satan, the father of all false teaching?

When a group called the Children of God emerged in the mid-seventies, it was commonly believed to be just another Christian youth organization. But as details about the group's leadership and practices became known, mainline evangelicals began to denounce it, labeling it a cult. The "guru" of the Children of God was an exmissionary known as Moses David. David said that while the Bible was God's Word for the people of the past, his own words of wisdom were more relevant for today. His tracts were collected by the Children, who considered them to be the inspired Word of God. The questionable practices of the Children included the use of sex to entice prospective "converts" into their cult.   Many cults have arisen since the time of Christ. Some of them contain only one or two principles that contradict Christian teaching. But Paul's advice is to stay away from those who teach "things about Christ that are contrary to what you have been taught."

P R A I S E :

P E T I T I O N :

The righteous shall move onward and forward; those with pure hearts shall become stronger and stronger. (Job 17:9)

Ghosts and Scribes

I, Tertius, the one who is writing this letter for Paul, send my greetings too, as a Christian brother. Gaius says to say "hello" to you for him. I am his guest, and the church meets here in his home. Erastus, the city treasurer, sends you his greetings and so does Quartus, a Christian brother. (Romans 16:22, 23)

Briefly identify Tertius, Gaius, Erastus, and Quartus.

A free-lance writer was contacted by a television evangelist. The evangelist said he wanted to produce a book about a certain area of Christian life. The book would be written entirely by the free-lancer, but all credit would go to the evangelist. The writer's name would appear nowhere on the book. The evangelist offered him a large sum of money for the work, and asked that the writer keep quiet about his responsibilities. The writer agreed, wrote the book, and it sold very well in bookstores across the U. S. Although this practice is generally frowned upon by publishers and the reading public, it is not uncommon. When faced with criticism, many so-called "authors" point to the fact that Tertius wrote the Epistle to the Romans on Paul's behalf. This is an incorrect analogy, however, for Tertius merely copied onto paper what Paul dictated to him. Every word in Romans originated from Paul and was inspired by God.

PRAISE:

PETITION:

Perhaps you are saying, "But I don't know what to say when I pray." God does not mind your stumbling and faltering phrases. He is not hindered by poor grammar. He is interested in your heart. (B. Graham)

Victory at Waterloo

GOODBYE. May the grace of our Lord Jesus Christ be with you all.

I commit you to God, who is able to make you strong and steady in the Lord, just as the Gospel says, and just as I have told you. This is God's plan of salvation for you Gentiles, kept secret from the beginning of time. But now as the prophets foretold and as God commands, this message is being preached everywhere, so that people all around the world will have faith in Christ and obey him. To God, who alone is wise, be the glory forever through Jesus Christ our Lord. Amen. (Romans 16:24-27)

How long has the plan of salvation existed? To whom must it be preached?

At the battle of Waterloo it was the strength and steadfastness of the British that saved the day. On the front lines, the British soldiers formed a human wall. The French poured volley after volley of shot and shell into their ranks. Men were mowed down like grain. One repeated cry was heard above the battle: "File up! File up!" As men on the front fell dead or wounded, replacements instantly took their places, stepping over the bodies of their comrades to face the enemy. Napoleon could not defeat such men. Neither can Satan overcome the strong and steadfast children of God.

PRAISE:

PETITION:

For he orders his angels to protect you wherever you go. (Ps. 91:11)

April   1 CORINTHIANS

Beautiful people are a minority—a coveted minority. Girls and guys alike dream of looking like fashion models and movie stars. And that's fine; it's natural to appreciate and desire beauty. But some people go too far in their quest for attractiveness. They concentrate on themselves to the exclusion of all else. ■ First Corinthians was written to Christians in first-century Corinth, a metropolis with a reputation for egotism, selfishness, and immoral self-gratification. In this epistle Paul teaches the Corinthians to change their focus from self to God.

Corinthian Quiz

THEN Paul left Athens and went to Corinth. There he became acquainted with a Jew named Aquila, born in Pontus, who had recently arrived from Italy with his wife, Priscilla. They had been expelled from Italy as a result of Claudius Caesar's order to deport all Jews from Rome. Paul lived and worked with them, for they were tentmakers just as he was.

Each Sabbath found Paul at the synagogue, trying to convince the Jews and Greeks alike. And after the arrival of Silas and Timothy from Macedonia, Paul spent his full time preaching and testifying to the Jews that Jesus is the Messiah. But when the Jews opposed him and blasphemed, hurling abuse at Jesus, Paul shook off the dust from his robe and said, "Your blood be upon your own heads—I am innocent—from now on I will preach to the Gentiles."

One night the Lord spoke to Paul in a vision and told him, "Don't be afraid! Speak out! Don't quit! For I am with you and no one can harm you. Many people here in this city belong to me." So Paul stayed there the next year and a half, teaching the truths of God. (Acts 18:1-6, 9-11)

When Paul became discouraged and downhearted, what did God encourage him to do?

Notice that, although we are studying 1 Corinthians, today's reading is taken from the Book of Acts. This passage provides background information to supplement Paul's epistle to the Corinthians. It is the record of the founding of the church at Corinth. Fill in the blanks in the paragraph that follows: Paul went to Corinth from _____ . He began his ministry there with a Jew named _____ , whose wife was _____ . Paul decided to stay with this couple because _____ . The apostle's ministry on the Sabbath consisted of _____ the Jews and Greeks that Jesus was the Christ. The reaction of those people was _____ .

P R A I S E :

_____

P E T I T I O N :

_____

There is no prayer so blessed as the prayer which asks for nothing. (O. J. Simon)

A Broken Christ

BUT, dear brothers, I beg you in the name of the Lord Jesus Christ to stop arguing among yourselves. Let there be real harmony so that there won't be splits in the church. I plead with you to be of one mind, united in thought and purpose. For some of those who live at Chloe's house have told me of your arguments and quarrels, dear brothers. Some of you are saying, "I am a follower of Paul"; and others say that they are for Apollos or for Peter; and some that they alone are the true followers of Christ. And so, in effect, you have broken Christ into many pieces.

But did I, Paul, die for your sins? Were any of you baptized in my name? I am so thankful now that I didn't baptize any of you except Crispus and Gaius. For now no one can think that I have been trying to start something new, beginning a "Church of Paul." Oh, yes, and I baptized the family of Stephanas. I don't remember ever baptizing anyone else. For Christ didn't send me to baptize, but to preach the Gospel; and even my preaching sounds poor, for I do not fill my sermons with profound words and high sounding ideas, for fear of diluting the mighty power there is in the simple message of the cross of Christ. (1 Corinthians 1:10-17)

When Paul discovers that some Christians are saying they are "followers of Paul," what rhetorical questions does he pose?

Since the death of Christ, the church has splintered into many major and minor denominations, each believing its theology and doctrines to be closest to the heart of God. All such divisions have come about as a result of men's differences of opinion in matters of Christian faith and conduct. What does God think of this? If Paul's pleas and admonitions are taken seriously, then we can be certain God is displeased. We have "broken Christ into many pieces." Although it appears to be quite futile to attempt to merge divergent denominations, we should not stop working toward the unity of all true Christians. Paul says we are to be "of one mind, united in thought and purpose."

P R A I S E :

P E T I T I O N :

Great and marvelous are your doings, Lord God Almighty. Just and true are your ways. (Rev. 15:3, 4)

Foolish Wisdom

SO what about these wise men, these scholars, these brilliant debaters of this world's great affairs? God has made them all look foolish, and shown their wisdom to be useless nonsense. For God in his wisdom saw to it that the world would never find God through human brilliance, and then he stepped in and saved all those who believed his message, which the world calls foolish and silly. It seems foolish to the Jews because they want a sign from heaven as proof that what is preached is true; and it is foolish to the Gentiles because they believe only what agrees with their philosophy and seems wise to them. So when we preach about Christ dying to save them, the Jews are offended and the Gentiles say it's all nonsense. But God has opened the eyes of those called to salvation, both Jews and Gentiles, to see that Christ is the mighty power of God to save them; Christ himself is the center of God's wise plan for their salvation. This so-called "foolish" plan of God is far wiser than the wisest plan of the wisest man, and God in his weakness—Christ dying on the cross—is far stronger than any man. (1 Corinthians 1:20-25)

Why does the gospel seem foolish to the Jews? To the Gentiles?

Some of the greatest minds of the past century have adamantly denied the existence of God. Others have said that there is no way to know if God exists, and that we should not waste time seeking or worshiping him. Some of the names that come to mind here are Friedrich Nietzsche, Bertrand Russell, Karl Marx, Lenin, Mao Tse-Tung, and Isaac Asimov. If these brilliant thinkers have concluded that God is either nonexistent or irrelevant, why should we question them? Why should we insist that the God of the Bible not only exists, but that he is interested in each of our lives? Isn't that a bit presumptuous?   Not if we consider the words of Paul in today's reading. He says, "For God in his wisdom saw to it that the world would never find God through human brilliance." God, the creator of the human mind, must be accepted in utter humility. He is discovered by childlike faith, not by scientific analysis.

P R A I S E :

P E T I T I O N :

I love all who love me. Those who search for me shall surely find me. (Prov. 8:17)

Simplify, Simplify

DEAR brothers, even when I first came to you I didn't use lofty words and brilliant ideas to tell you God's message. For I decided that I would speak only of Jesus Christ and his death on the cross. I came to you in weakness—timid and trembling. And my preaching was very plain, not with a lot of oratory and human wisdom, but the Holy Spirit's power was in my words, proving to those who heard them that the message was from God. I did this because I wanted your faith to stand firmly upon God, not on man's great ideas.

Yet when I am among mature Christians I do speak with words of great wisdom, but not the kind that comes from here on earth, and not the kind that appeals to the great men of this world, who are doomed to fall. Our words are wise because they are from God, telling of God's wise plan to bring us into the glories of heaven. This plan was hidden in former times, though it was made for our benefit before the world began. But the great men of the world have not understood it; if they had, they never would have crucified the Lord of Glory.

That is what is meant by the Scriptures which say that no mere man has ever seen, heard or even imagined what wonderful things God has ready for those who love the Lord. (1 Corinthians 2:1-9)

Since Paul did not preach by men's wisdom, how was the truth revealed to his hearers?

Most daily newspapers are written at a sixth-grade level, even though most of their readers are much older. Editors have discovered that with simple, direct language, they are likely to attract more readers. Even subjects as complex as foreign policy and economics are discussed in very basic language. This may help to explain why Paul didn't use lofty words and brilliant concepts to deliver God's message. He wanted to make sure everyone understood the basic fact of the gospel, so he used simple, everyday language. Paul trusted the Holy Spirit to prove to the people that the message was from God.

P R A I S E :

P E T I T I O N :

Lord, with all my heart I thank you. I will sing your praises before the armies of angels in heaven. (Ps. 138:1)

Falling Stars

DEAR brothers, I have been talking to you as though you were still just babies in the Christian life, who are not following the Lord, but your own desires; I cannot talk to you as I would to healthy Christians, who are filled with the Spirit. I have had to feed you with milk and not with solid food, because you couldn't digest anything stronger. And even now you still have to be fed on milk. (1 Corinthians 3:1, 2)

According to Paul, what characterizes "healthy Christians"?

Over the past few years several popular music personalities have become Christians. Among the new converts are Donna Summer, Van Morrison, B. J. Thomas, Bob Dylan, two members of Ireland's U2, Bruce Cockburn, Kerry Livgren (of Kansas), and Cliff Richard. We rejoice when such people come to the Lord; we know that their power to influence others is far-reaching. But often we expect too much of them. We expect them to be fully-developed, mature, witnessing Christians in the first few weeks and months of their new-found faith. Occasionally this burden of expectations takes its toll on these people, causing them to backslide or abandon the faith. Today we have read that "babies in the Christian life" need to be fed milk before they are ready for solid food. Just as a steady diet of meat can be deadly for a newborn child, a burden of heavy spirituality can overwhelm and intimidate a newborn Christian.

P R A I S E :

P E T I T I O N :

Satan trembles when he sees the weakest saint upon his knees.

Planting and Watering

WHO am I, and who is Apollos, that we should be the cause of a quarrel? Why, we're just God's servants, each of us with certain special abilities, and with our help you believed. My work was to plant the seed in your hearts, and Apollos' work was to water it, but it was God, not we, who made the garden grow in your hearts. The person who does the planting or watering isn't very important, but God is important because he is the one who makes things grow. Apollos and I are working as a team, with the same aim, though each of us will be rewarded for his own hard work. We are only God's co-workers. You are *God's* garden, not ours; you are *God's* building, not ours.

God, in his kindness, has taught me how to be an expert builder. I have laid the foundation and Apollos has built on it. But he who builds on the foundation must be very careful. And no one can ever lay any other real foundation than that one we already have—Jesus Christ. (1 Corinthians 3:5-11)

Paul and Apollos were involved in different yet related types of work. For what was each responsible?

Billy Graham's ministry is primarily evangelistic. He is involved with the winning or revival of personal commitments to Christ. He has the gift of communicating the gospel in a clear, persuasive manner. Hundreds of thousands have come to know the Lord through Graham's evangelistic crusades. For people to become mature Christians, however, they must receive training in the Word. They must fellowship with other Christians. After they've been evangelized, they need to be discipled if they are to become fruitful children of God. Local church bodies are responsible for this work of discipleship. In today's Scripture reading, Paul uses two analogies to represent evangelism and discipleship: the planting and watering of seeds, and the founding and building of structures. In both analogies, he asserts that without the guidance of God in an individual's life, there can be no spiritual growth or progress.

P R A I S E :

P E T I T I O N :

If we really know he is listening when we talk to him and make our requests, then we can be sure that he will answer us. (1 John 5:15)

Rude Christians

RELIGION has made us foolish, you say, but of course you are all such wise and sensible Christians! We are weak, but not you! You are well thought of, while we are laughed at. To this very hour we have gone hungry and thirsty, without even enough clothes to keep us warm. We have been kicked around without homes of our own. We have worked wearily with our hands to earn our living. We have blessed those who cursed us. We have been patient with those who injured us. We have replied quietly when evil things have been said about us. Yet right up to the present moment we are like dirt under foot, like garbage.

I am not writing about these things to make you ashamed, but to warn and counsel you as beloved children. For although you may have ten thousand others to teach you about Christ, remember that you have only me as your father. For I was the one who brought you to Christ when I preached the Gospel to you. So I beg you to follow my example, and do as I do. (1 Corinthians 4:10-16)

Does Paul think men admire the work of apostles? Explain.

During a summer art fair on the campus of a big university, several Christians were proclaiming the Word in an unusual fashion. They were wearing sackcloth, dragging huge wooden crosses, and shouting such phrases as, "Repent, for the end is near!" Many people dismissed them as obnoxious loudmouths. Even other Christians who saw them were embarrassed by their "rude" behavior. But although the tactics of these daring Christians were highly unorthodox, at least they drew attention to the simple gospel message. They convinced some people to read their tracts and to begin thinking about spiritual matters, while the embarrassed Christians, milling *incognito* through the crowd, had no ministry whatsoever. Paul said, "Religion has made us foolish, you say, but of course you are all such wise and sensible Christians! . . . You are well thought of, while we are laughed at."

P R A I S E :

P E T I T I O N :

Be patient. And take courage, for the coming of the Lord is near. (James 5:8)

Rust Never Sleeps

EVERYONE is talking about the terrible thing that has happened there among you, something so evil that even the heathen don't do it: you have a man in your church who is living in sin with his father's wife. And are you still so conceited, so "spiritual"? Why aren't you mourning in sorrow and shame, and seeing to it that this man is removed from your membership?

Although I am not there with you, I have been thinking a lot about this, and in the name of the Lord Jesus Christ I have already decided what to do, just as though I were there. You are to call a meeting of the church—and the power of the Lord Jesus will be with you as you meet, and I will be there in spirit—and cast out this man from the fellowship of the church and into Satan's hands, to punish him, in the hope that his soul will be saved when our Lord Jesus Christ returns.

What a terrible thing it is that you are boasting about your purity, and yet you let this sort of thing go on. Don't you realize that if even one person is allowed to go on sinning, soon all will be affected? Remove this evil cancer—this wicked person—from among you, so that you can stay pure. Christ, God's Lamb, has been slain for us. (1 Corinthians 5:1-7)

What is "this terrible thing that has happened" among the Corinthians? What does Paul suggest as a solution?

When a dam breaks and the water comes pounding through, it appears as though the destruction were the work of a few seconds. The tremendous pressure of the water seems to effortlessly pulverize the man-made barrier. Behind those few moments of calamity, though, lie weeks, even years, of general weakening and deterioration. So with the downfall of a man. The slow process of carnal corruption eats at the thought centers, slowly corrupting character—then comes the crash.

P R A I S E :

P E T I T I O N :

Sometimes God's answers to prayer are *direct.*
Sometimes God's answers to prayer are *delayed.*
Sometimes God's answers to prayer are *denied.*

The Pretenders

WHEN I wrote to you before I said not to mix with evil people. But when I said that I wasn't talking about unbelievers who live in sexual sin, or are greedy cheats and thieves and idol worshipers. For you can't live in this world without being with people like that. What I meant was that you are not to keep company with anyone who claims to be a brother Christian but indulges in sexual sins, or is greedy, or is a swindler, or worships idols, or is a drunkard, or abusive. Don't even eat lunch with such a person.

It isn't our job to judge outsiders. But it certainly is our job to judge and deal strongly with those who are members of the church, and who are sinning in these ways. God alone is the Judge of those on the outside. But you yourselves must deal with this man and put him out of your church. (1 Corinthians 5:9-13)

Are we to judge others' relationships to God and the church? Explain.

When Paul speaks of "evil people," he is not referring to the non-Christians of the day. Rather, he reserves this term for hypocrites who claim to be Christians while secretly indulging in all forms of deviance and sin. It appears as though Paul is saying that God finds sinning unbelievers more palatable than sinning hypocrites. For besides committing the same sins as unbelievers commit, hypocrites seek to deceive God and men into thinking they are blameless. God has no patience with such cunning deceivers. Paul asks believers to throw these people out of the church. "Don't even eat lunch with such a person," he says.

P R A I S E :

P E T I T I O N :

He keeps his eye upon you as you come and go, and always guards you. (Ps. 121:8)

God's Law

HOW is it that when you have something against another Christian, you "go to law" and ask a heathen court to decide the matter instead of taking it to other Christians to decide which of you is right? Don't you know that some day we Christians are going to judge and govern the world? So why can't you decide even these little things among yourselves? Don't you realize that we Christians will judge and reward the very angels in heaven? So you should be able to decide your problems down here on earth easily enough. Why then go to outside judges who are not even Christians? I am trying to make you ashamed. Isn't there anyone in all the church who is wise enough to decide these arguments? But, instead, one Christian sues another and accuses his Christian brother in front of unbelievers.

To have such lawsuits at all is a real defeat for you as Christians. Why not just accept mistreatment and leave it at that? It would be far more honoring to the Lord to let yourselves be cheated. But, instead, you yourselves are the ones who do wrong, cheating others, even your own brothers. (1 Corinthians 6:1-8)

What are Paul's reasons for settling our disputes with other believers outside of a court of law?

When you feel that another Christian has severely wronged you, what action do you take? Do you "turn the other cheek"? Do you sue him? Or do you try to seek some form of settlement outside of court? An increasing number of Christians in such situations are turning to Christian reconciliation services. These services bring together the parties in question with an objective, Christian mediator. The parties present their cases, then, based upon biblical principles of fairness and justice, the mediator seeks to negotiate a settlement between them. These reconciliation services appear to be an excellent alternative to taking fellow believers to court. (For more information on such services, write to the Christian Legal Society, P. O. Box 2069, Oak Park, IL 60303.)

P R A I S E :

P E T I T I O N :

He is a mighty Savior. He will give you victory. He will rejoice over you in great gladness. (Zeph. 3:17, 18)

The End of Sex

BUT sexual sin is never right: our bodies were not made for that, but for the Lord, and the Lord wants to fill our bodies with himself. And God is going to raise our bodies from the dead by his power just as he raised up the Lord Jesus Christ. Don't you realize that your bodies are actually parts and members of Christ? So should I take part of Christ and join him to a prostitute? Never! And don't you know that if a man joins himself to a prostitute she becomes a part of him and he becomes a part of her? For God tells us in the Scripture that in his sight the two become one person. But if you give yourself to the Lord, you and Christ are joined together as one person.

That is why I say to run from sex sin. No other sin affects the body as this one does. When you sin this sin it is against your own body. Haven't you yet learned that your body is the home of the Holy Spirit God gave you, and that he lives within you? Your own body does not belong to you. For God has bought you with a great price. So use every part of your body to give glory back to God, because he owns it. (1 Corinthians 6:13-20)

What reasons does Paul give for believers to abstain from sex sin?

In *The End of Sex* (Houghton Mifflin, 1983), George Leonard writes that the sexual revolution in the United States is coming to an abrupt halt. He says that the fever of promiscuity that characterized the sixties and seventies is becoming passé. People are learning that sex is meaningless and dissatisfying if not coupled with love. Among the other factors for the "death of sex" are fear of venereal diseases (especially recent strains such as herpes and AIDS), boredom, and a reluctance to lower vulnerabilities. Leonard is certainly premature in tolling the death of sex. There is still an abundance of extramarital affairs, fornication, homosexuality, and pornography. But he is right in that the unrestrained debauchery of a few years ago has cooled off. But apart from a strict adherence to God's Word, we will never be completely free of sexual sin.

P R A I S E :

P E T I T I O N :

If there were more private prayer, there would be shorter prayers in public.

Stranger with a Destination

NOW about those questions you asked in your last letter: my answer is that if you do not marry, it is good. But usually it is best to be married, each man having his own wife, and each woman having her own husband, because otherwise you might fall back into sin.

The man should give his wife all that is her right as a married woman, and the wife should do the same for her husband: for a girl who marries no longer has full right to her own body, for her husband then has his rights to it, too; and in the same way the husband no longer has full right to his own body, for it belongs also to his wife. So do not refuse these rights to each other. The only exception to this rule would be the agreement of both husband and wife to refrain from the rights of marriage for a limited time, so that they can give themselves more completely to prayer. Afterwards, they should come together again so that Satan won't be able to tempt them because of their lack of self-control.

I'm not saying you *must* marry; but you certainly *may* if you wish. I wish everyone could get along without marrying, just as I do. But we are not all the same. God gives some the gift of a husband or wife, and others he gives the gift of being able to stay happily unmarried. (1 Corinthians 7:1-7)

According to Paul, why is it "best to be married"?

Philip Henry, father of Bible commentator Matthew Henry, wanted to marry a bright young girl from Wales. He was a Presbyterian minister; she was an only daughter and heiress of a considerable fortune. When she told her father they wanted to be married, her father objected. He said, "You see, he may be a perfect gentleman, a brilliant scholar, and an excellent preacher, but he is a stranger and we do not even know where he comes from."   "**T**rue," replied the girl, with all the insight that her son later displayed, "But we know where he is going, and I'd like to go with him!"

P R A I S E :

P E T I T I O N :

Let him have all your worries and cares, for he is always thinking about you and watching everything that concerns you. (1 Pet. 5:7)

The Throw-Away Marriage

HERE I want to add some suggestions of my own. These are not direct commands from the Lord, but they seem right to me: If a Christian has a wife who is not a Christian, but she wants to stay with him anyway, he must not leave her or divorce her. And if a Christian woman has a husband who isn't a Christian, and he wants her to stay with him, she must not leave him. For perhaps the husband who isn't a Christian may become a Christian with the help of his Christian wife. And the wife who isn't a Christian may become a Christian with the help of her Christian husband. Otherwise, if the family separates, the children might never come to know the Lord.

But if the husband or wife who isn't a Christian is eager to leave, it is permitted. In such cases the Christian husband or wife should not insist that the other stay, for God wants his children to live in peace and harmony. For, after all, there is no assurance to you wives that your husbands will be converted if they stay; and the same may be said to you husbands concerning your wives. (1 Corinthians 7:12-16)

If a woman becomes a believer but her husband does not, should she leave him?

We live in a society of disposability, where very little is designed to last. Many eating and cooking utensils, household appliances and accessories, and articles of clothing are designed to be used just once, or a very few times. They are then thrown away and replaced. Rental centers that stock everything from screwdrivers to semi-trucks are doing a booming business. Even the housing industry is now building modular homes, and many autos have built-in life expectancies of just six or seven years. The "disposable" mentality now affects even human relationships. If a marriage partner is unhappy with a spouse, for example, he or she can be easily divorced and replaced with a "new model." This, of course, is against the plan of God. Marriage was intended to be for life. In this age of transience, we must remember that marriage is one of the few permanent institutions.

P R A I S E :

P E T I T I O N :

Rest in the Lord; wait patiently for him to act. (Ps. 37:7)

The Sense of Common Sense

IN all you do, I want you to be free from worry. An unmarried man can spend his time doing the Lord's work and thinking how to please him. But a married man can't do that so well; he has to think about his earthly responsibilities and how to please his wife. His interests are divided. It is the same with a girl who marries. She faces the same problem. A girl who is not married is anxious to please the Lord in all she is and does. But a married woman must consider other things such as housekeeping and the likes and dislikes of her husband.

I am saying this to help you, not to try to keep you from marrying. I want you to do whatever will help you serve the Lord best, with as few other things as possible to distract your attention from him.

But if anyone feels he ought to marry because he has trouble controlling his passions, it is all right, it is not a sin; let him marry.

The wife is part of her husband as long as he lives; if her husband dies, then she may marry again, but only if she marries a Christian. (1 Corinthians 7:32-36, 39)

Does this passage permit Christian widows and/or widowers to remarry? Explain.

Some people believe the Bible dictates how believers should behave. They think every detail is laid out in clear, black-and-white terms. But it is not so. The Bible often asks us to use our common sense in making an ethical decision. Today's Scripture passage exemplifies this. Paul says that our highest desire should be to serve the Lord. For some, he says, this will mean avoiding the "distractions" of marriage. But others might need to be married, in order to keep away from the distractions of unfulfilled passions. Each is to decide for himself/herself which way of life—married or single—will allow the greatest freedom to serve the Lord. Entrusted with such a decision, we should be greatly motivated to praise and worship the Lord who grants us so much freedom.

P R A I S E :

P E T I T I O N :

In all your prayers, let your heart be without words, lest your words be without heart.

Stumbling Blocks

SHOULD we eat meat that has been sacrificed to idols? Well, we all know that an idol is not really a god, and that there is only one God, and no other. According to some people, there are a great many gods, both in heaven and on earth. But we know that there is only one God, the Father, who created all things and made us to be his own; and one Lord Jesus Christ, who made everything and gives us life.

However, some Christians don't realize this. All their lives they have been used to thinking of idols as alive, and have believed that food offered to the idols is really being offered to actual gods. So when they eat such food it bothers them and hurts their tender consciences. Just remember that God doesn't care whether we eat it or not. We are no worse off if we don't eat it, and no better off if we do. But be careful not to use your freedom to eat it, lest you cause some Christian brother to sin whose conscience is weaker than yours. (1 Corinthians 8:4-9)

Why is it sometimes wrong for us to do things we personally don't see anything wrong with?

"I don't see anything wrong with what I'm doing. It's nobody's business but my own!" Have you ever heard anyone say that? Perhaps you've said it yourself. You may have indulged in some habit which you felt was harmless in itself, forgetting what effect it might have on others. A man was entertaining some children by lighting a match and extinguishing it by placing the burning end in his mouth. The father of the children saw the man and said, "I wish you would stop; that's dangerous." The man replied, "But I'm not hurting myself." Then the father pointed at his little son who had a dressing on his upper lip. He said, "Yesterday Johnny saw you do this trick. He thought it was OK for him to try it. He not only burned his lip, but set fire to the tablecloth. We barely kept the flames from spreading. You may not hurt yourself with your little trick, but you have caused someone else to get hurt by your example."

P R A I S E :

P E T I T I O N :

You can get anything—*anything* you ask for in prayer—if you believe. (Matt. 21:22)

Go, Pray, Pay

WE have planted good spiritual seed in your souls. Is it too much to ask, in return, for mere food and clothing? You give them to others who preach to you, and you should. But shouldn't we have an even greater right to them? Yet we have *never* used this right, but supply our own needs without your help. We have never demanded payment of any kind for fear that, if we did, you might be less interested in our message to you from Christ.

Don't you realize that God told those working in his temple to take for their own needs some of the food brought there as gifts to him? And those who work at the altar of God get a share of the food that is brought by those offering it to the Lord. In the same way the Lord has given orders that those who preach the Gospel should be supported by those who accept it. (1 Corinthians 9:11-14)

What grievance does Paul express toward the Christians in Corinth?

Every three years an important missions conference is held on the campus of the University of Illinois at Champaign-Urbana. Thousands of high school and college students attend it. Known simply as *Urbana,* the conference seeks to inform interested young people about missions work around the world. Over a period of five days, world-famous evangelists and missions authorities speak about the importance of becoming "world Christians." Dozens of related seminars and workshops are offered. All conference guests are urged to become active supporters of world missions through direct participation (going to a field), prayer, and/or financial help. If we are to take seriously Christ's command to preach the gospel to all nations, we must be actively involved in the missions movement. Let us not be among the apathetic group Paul calls irresponsible and negligent.

P R A I S E :

P E T I T I O N :

If our consciences are clear, we can come to the Lord with perfect assurance and trust, and get whatever we ask for because we are obeying him and doing the things that please him. (1 John 3:21, 22)

Rader of the Lost Souls

WHEN I am with the Jews I seem as one of them so that they will listen to the Gospel and I can win them to Christ. When I am with Gentiles who follow Jewish customs and ceremonies I don't argue, even though I don't agree, because I want to help them. When with the heathen I agree with them as much as I can, except of course that I must always do what is right as a Christian. And so, by agreeing, I can win their confidence* and help them too.

When I am with those whose consciences bother them easily, I don't act as though I know it all and don't say they are foolish; the result is that they are willing to let me help them. Yes, whatever a person is like, I try to find common ground with him so that he will let me tell him about Christ and let Christ save him. I do this to get the Gospel to them and also for the blessing I myself receive when I see them come to Christ. (1 Corinthians 9:20-23)

What is Paul's strategy for approaching someone with the gospel?

Evangelist Paul Rader had often spoken to a certain banker in New York concerning his soul, but to no avail. One day God seemed to speak to Rader, urging him to go immediately and once again seek out this individual. Obediently he caught a train and went to the banker's house. As he approached the house, he saw the banker standing in the doorway. "Oh, Rader," the banker said, "I'm so glad to see you. I wrote a letter begging you to come, but I tore it up." "That may be so," replied the evangelist, "but your message came by way of heaven." Under deep conviction of sin, the man was impressed by Rader's special effort to reach him with the gospel. Consequently, that very hour he accepted the Lord. In his new-found joy he exclaimed, "Rader, did you ever see the sky so blue or the grass so green?" Suddenly the banker leaned heavily against Rader, then with a gasp fell into his arms—dead! He had been saved on the very brink of eternity. What if Paul Rader had delayed to come, taking the promptings of the Lord with less urgency? Let us always be keenly sensitive to the Lord's leadings.

P R A I S E :

P E T I T I O N :

Prayer forms the godliest men and makes the godliest world.

Gay Sin

ANOTHER lesson for us is what happened when some of them sinned with other men's wives, and 23,000 fell dead in one day. And don't try the Lord's patience—they did, and died from snake bites. And don't murmur against God and his dealings with you, as some of them did, for that is why God sent his Angel to destroy them.

All these things happened to them as examples—as object lessons to us—to warn us against doing the same things; they were written down so that we could read about them and learn from them in these last days as the world nears its end.

So be careful. If you are thinking, "Oh, I would never behave like that"—let this be a warning to you. For you too may fall into sin. But remember this—the wrong desires that come into your life aren't anything new and different. Many others have faced exactly the same problems before you. And no temptation is irresistible. You can trust God to keep the temptation from becoming so strong that you can't stand up against it, for he has promised this and will do what he says. He will show you how to escape temptation's power so that you can bear up patiently against it. (1 Corinthians 10:8-13)

Who is susceptible to temptation?

Most of us cannot understand what drives men and women to homosexuality. Psychologists believe it may be caused by heredity, environment, family situations, or even hormonal imbalance. But regardless of how these feelings begin, there is no doubt that active homosexuality is a sin against God and nature. It is repeatedly condemned in the Bible. But what about people who feel homosexual attractions but refuse to give in to them? Are they sinful merely because they have such temptations? I believe not. Temptation in itself is not sin; it merely points the way to sin. In God's eyes, indulgence in any form of licentiousness—heterosexual or homosexual—is wrong. Remember that God has promised to keep temptation from becoming so strong that we find it irresistible.

P R A I S E :

P E T I T I O N :

O my people, trust him all the time. Pour out your longings before him, for he can help! (Ps. 62:8)

Space Idol

SO, dear friends, carefully avoid idol-worship of every kind.

You are intelligent people. Look now and see for yourselves whether what I am about to say is true. When we ask the Lord's blessing upon our drinking from the cup of wine at the Lord's Table, this means, doesn't it, that all who drink it are sharing together the blessing of Christ's blood? And when we break off pieces of the bread from the loaf to eat there together, this shows that we are sharing together in the benefits of his body. No matter how many of us there are, we all eat from the same loaf, showing that we are all parts of the one body of Christ. And the Jewish people, all who eat the sacrifices, are united by that act.

What am I trying to say? Am I saying that the idols to whom the heathen bring sacrifices are really alive and are real gods, and that these sacrifices are of some value? No, not at all. What I am saying is that those who offer food to these idols are united together in sacrificing to demons, certainly not to God. (1 Corinthians 10:14-20)

Should meat offered to idols be eaten along with the Lord's Supper? Why/why not?

A few years ago a major television network released a series called *Battlestar Galactica*. Starring Lorne Green, the series was set in the distant future and chronicled the adventures of a crew of space warriors. The series attracted a large following; many teens were enthralled with it. But the ratings were not high enough, and soon it was cancelled. After the last episode was broadcast, one young viewer went to his room and wrote a short note which read, "Life without *Battlestar Galactica* is not worth living." Then he committed suicide. An idol can be anything that takes the place of God in our hearts. For some it may be a TV show, a movie star, or an automobile. For others it may be money or fame. Paul says, "Avoid idol-worship of every kind." List the ten things (people, objects, etc.) you value most. Have any of these taken the place of God in your heart?

P R A I S E :

P E T I T I O N :

God sometimes uses sorrow in our lives to help us turn away from sin and seek eternal life. (2 Cor. 7:10)

Hypocrisy and Love

YOU are certainly free to eat food offered to idols if you want to; it's not against God's laws to eat such meat, but that doesn't mean that you should go ahead and do it. It may be perfectly legal, but it may not be best and helpful. Don't think only of yourself. Try to think of the other fellow, too, and what is best for him.

If someone who isn't a Christian asks you out to dinner, go ahead; accept the invitation if you want to. Eat whatever is on the table and don't ask any questions about it. Then you won't know whether or not it has been used as a sacrifice to idols, and you won't risk having a bad conscience over eating it. But if someone warns you that this meat has been offered to idols, then don't eat it for the sake of the man who told you, and of his conscience. In this case *his* feeling about it is the important thing, not yours.

I try to please everyone in everything I do, not doing what I like or what is best for me, but what is best for them, so that they may be saved. (1 Corinthians 10:23-24, 27-29, 33)

What was Paul's ultimate goal as expressed in this passage?

A few days ago we read about that most vile of sins—hypocrisy. Paul commanded the Corinthians to not even eat lunch with people who pretended to be virtuous believers while living in sinful indulgence. Here, though, he says that we should always act in a way that will not offend or bewilder other believers. But if we refrain from our normal behavior in order to not scandalize someone, are we not also guilty of hypocrisy? There is a difference between hypocrisy (pretending to have virtues or qualities one does not have) and being sensitive to the beliefs of other Christians. In one case we are deliberately deceiving; in the other, we are putting others' feelings before our own. While hypocrisy leads to destruction and hurt feelings, sensitivity to the beliefs and behavior of other Christians leads to peace and good will.

P R A I S E :

P E T I T I O N :

Every time you pray, if your prayer is sincere, there will be new feeling and new meaning in it which will give you fresh courage, and you will understand that prayer is an education. (F. Dostoevski)

Modest Hair

I am so glad, dear brothers, that you have been remembering and doing everything I taught you. But there is one matter I want to remind you about: that a wife is responsible to her husband, her husband is responsible to Christ, and Christ is responsible to God. That is why, if a man refuses to remove his hat while praying or preaching, he dishonors Christ. And that is why a woman who publicly prays or prophesies without a covering on her head dishonors her husband [for her covering is a sign of her subjection to him]. Yes, if she refuses to wear a head covering, then she should cut off all her hair.

What do you yourselves really think about this? Is it right for a woman to pray in public without covering her head? Doesn't even instinct itself teach us that women's heads should be covered? For women are proud of their long hair, while a man with long hair tends to be ashamed. (1 Corinthians 11:2-6, 13-15)

What does Paul teach women regarding the use of head coverings? Should we follow these instructions today? Explain.

Why is Paul making such a big deal about women covering their heads in public? And if it *is* important, why don't women cover their heads today? These questions come to mind immediately as we read this passage. In this portion of Scripture, as in many others, we must remember the cultural context. Paul was writing to the Christians in Corinth, an immoral city. Its temple "priestesses" were nothing more than common prostitutes. In that city the mark of a sinful woman was short hair and the lack of a head covering. When we look at Paul's words under this light, we see that he is merely telling the women to avoid the appearance of immorality. In our culture, this means women (as well as men) should be modest in their clothing, mannerisms, language and associations.

P R A I S E :

P E T I T I O N :

Watch with me and pray lest the Tempter overpower you. For though the spirit is willing enough, the body is weak. (Mark 14:38)

Pledging Returns

FOR this is what the Lord himself has said about his Table, and I have passed it on to you before: That on the night when Judas betrayed him, the Lord Jesus took bread, and when he had given thanks to God for it, he broke it and gave it to his disciples and said, "Take this and eat it. This is my body, which is given for you. Do this to remember me." In the same way, he took the cup of wine after supper, saying, "This cup is the new agreement between God and you that has been established and set in motion by my blood. Do this in remembrance of me whenever you drink it." For every time you eat this bread and drink this cup you are re-telling the message of the Lord's death, that he has died for you. Do this until he comes again.

So if anyone eats this bread and drinks from this cup of the Lord in an unworthy manner, he is guilty of sin against the body and the blood of the Lord. That is why a man should examine himself careful- ly before eating the bread and drinking from the cup. For if he eats the bread and drinks from the cup unworthily, not thinking about the body of Christ and what it means, he is eating and drinking God's judgment upon himself; for he is trifling with the death of Christ. (1 Corinthians 11:20, 21, 23-29)

What might happen to one who participates in the Lord's Supper in an unworthy manner?

The Jacobites of Scotland never met one another on the mountain paths, never sat down to a table of council or conference, without first lifting a cup to pledge the return of their king and prince, Charles. At last Charles came back, only to bring Scotland defeat, disaster, humiliation, and suffering. When we partake of the Lord's Supper, we also pledge the return of a Prince. But when he comes back to earth, it will be in triumph and glory.

PRAISE:

PETITION:

O God, my heart is quiet and confident. No wonder I can sing your praises! (Ps. 57:7)

The Gift of Fame

TO one person the Spirit gives the ability to give wise advice; someone else may be especially good at studying and teaching, and this is his gift from the same Spirit. He gives special faith to another, and to someone else the power to heal the sick. He gives power for doing miracles to some, and to others power to prophesy and preach. He gives someone else the power to know whether evil spirits are speaking through those who claim to be giving God's messages—or whether it is really the Spirit of God who is speaking. Still another person is able to speak in languages he never learned; and others, who do not know the language either, are given power to understand what he is saying. It is the same and only Holy Spirit who gives all these gifts and powers, deciding which each one of us should have. (1 Corinthians 12:8-11)

Who decides which spiritual gift(s) you should receive?

To many people, fame is nearly as desirable as wealth. This is because acceptance is one of our basic needs, and there's nothing like seeing your name in bright lights to make you feel accepted and admired. Some come to fame because of exceptional talent or brilliance. Others just happen upon it, being at the right place at the right time. Artist Andy Warhol once predicted that, due to expanding TV technology, we'll all experience fame at some point in our lives, even if for just ten or fifteen minutes. Fame is fleeting, as they say; but elusiveness only adds to its enticement. Christians should avoid the allure of fame. It can seduce us away from our foremost desire to serve God. Paul tells us that the Holy Spirit gives us gifts. We are to discover our gifts and be diligent with them, using them for God's glory. Because of the nature of certain gifts, some of their beneficiaries may incidentally become famous. But the real purpose of spiritual gifts is to lead the church to a more meaningful relationship with the Lord.

PRAISE:

PETITION:

Prayer is the unfolding of one's will to God that he may fulfill it. (T. Aquinas)

Hurricane in a Teacup

OUR bodies have many parts, but the many parts make up only one body when they are all put together. So it is with the "body" of Christ. Each of us is a part of the one body of Christ. Some of us are Jews, some are Gentiles, some are slaves and some are free. But the Holy Spirit has fitted us all together into one body. We have been baptized into Christ's body by the one Spirit, and have all been given that same Holy Spirit.

Yes, the body has many parts, not just one part. If the foot says, "I am not a part of the body because I am not a hand," that does not make it any less a part of the body. And what would you think if you heard an ear say, "I am not part of the body because I am only an ear, and not an eye"? Would that make it any less a part of the body? Suppose the whole body were an eye—then how would you hear? Or if your whole body were just one big ear, how could you smell anything?

But that isn't the way God has made us. He has made many parts for our bodies and has put each part just where he wants it. What a strange thing a body would be if it had only one part! So he has made many parts, but still there is only one body. (1 Corinthians 12:12-20)

Are any parts of the "body" more important than others?

George Whitefield was an eighteenth-century itinerant evangelist. He divided his time between Europe and America. Once he was confronted by a Pennsylvania Quaker. They soon came to some hot words over matters of appearance and behavior. When it seemed they had come to a stalemate, the Quaker said, "George, we are brothers. We both long to see men come to Christ. But while we are fighting, no souls are being saved. If you will forget to quarrel about the broad brim on my hat, I'll promise not to quarrel about your black clerical gown." With that, they shook hands, smiling sheepishly at their foolishness. We are often tempted to overemphasize our trivial differences. Let us remember that God "has made many parts, but still there is only one body."

P R A I S E :

P E T I T I O N :

Pray all the time. (Eph. 6:18)

On Tempers and Temperance

IF I had the gift of being able to speak in other languages without learning them, and could speak in every language there is in all of heaven and earth, but didn't love others, I would only be making noise. If I had the gift of prophecy and knew all about what is going to happen in the future, knew everything about *everything*, but didn't love others, what good would it do? Even if I had the gift of faith so that I could speak to a mountain and make it move, I would still be worth nothing at all without love. If I gave everything I have to poor people, and if I were burned alive for preaching the Gospel but didn't love others, it would be of no value whatever.

Love is very patient and kind, never jealous or envious, never boastful or proud, never haughty or selfish or rude. Love does not demand its own way. It is not irritable or touchy. It does not hold grudges and will hardly even notice when others do it wrong. It is never glad about injustice, but rejoices whenever truth wins out.

There are three things that remain—faith, hope, and love—and the greatest of these is love. (1 Corinthians 13:1-6, 13)

After reading this passage, write out a one-sentence definition of love.

In the biography of D. L. Moody, we learn that a man once grossly and deliberately insulted the great preacher. Mr. Moody momentarily flared up in anger at the unjust attack. Coming to the pulpit a moment later, however, he made this humble admission: "Friends, before beginning tonight, I want to confess that out in the hall just now I yielded to my temper. I have done wrong. I want to confess my error before you all, and if that man is present here whom I thrust from me in anger, I want to ask his forgiveness and God's. Let us pray." Moody's sincere apology reflected not a hint of excuse or self-vindication for the insult he had suffered. The meeting which followed was a scene of unusual blessing due to his straightforward, Christian confession. This is a great example of Christian love in action.

PRAISE:

PETITION:

May the Lord bless and protect you; may the Lord's face radiate with joy because of you; may he be gracious to you, show you his favor, and give you his peace. (Num. 6:24-26)

Speaking in Tongues

LET love be your greatest aim; nevertheless, ask also for the special abilities the Holy Spirit gives, and especially the gift of prophecy, being able to preach the messages of God.

But if your gift is that of being able to "speak in tongues," that is, to speak in languages you haven't learned, you will be talking to God but not to others, since they won't be able to understand you. You will be speaking by the power of the Spirit but it will all be a secret. But one who prophesies, preaching the messages of God, is helping others grow in the Lord, encouraging and comforting them. So a person "speaking in tongues" helps himself grow spiritually, but one who prophesies, preaching messages from God, helps the entire church grow in holiness and happiness. (1 Corinthians 14:1-4)

How does Paul define the gift of prophesy?

A young missionary heard reports of an unevangelized tribe deep in the heart of an African nation. He prepared his gear, then entered the uncharted jungle alone. After several hours of hacking his way through the bush, he was suddenly surrounded by hostile natives. The chief raised his spear to kill the stranger. The missionary opened his mouth to protest; instead, he began to babble and gesticulate strangely. *Am I going crazy?* he thought. Then he noticed that the leader had lowered his spear and his features had softened. Soon the other warriors were smiling and came over to greet him. Only then did the missionary realize that the Holy Spirit had given him the ability to speak to them. He was befriended and taken to the natives' settlement. Upon arriving, he found himself once again unable to communicate. But the ice had been broken, and in the ensuing months he "relearned" the language, then evangelized the village. **S**peaking in tongues is one of the most misunderstood of all the spiritual gifts. It has been the source of much controversy. The young missionary learned that, mysterious as it is, the gift of tongues had saved his life.

P R A I S E :

P E T I T I O N :

What is the use of praying if at the very moment of prayer we have so little confidence in God that we are busy planning our own kind of answer to our prayer? (T. Merton)

Defining the Gospel

NOW let me remind you, brothers, of what the Gospel really is, for it has not changed—it is the same Good News I preached to you before. You welcomed it then and still do now, for your faith is squarely built upon this wonderful message; and it is this Good News that saves you if you still firmly believe it, unless of course you never really believed it in the first place.

I passed on to you right from the first what had been told to me, that Christ died for our sins just as the Scriptures said he would, and that he was buried and that three days afterwards he arose from the grave just as the prophets foretold. (1 Corinthians 15:1-4)

According to this passage, what is the gospel?

Duncan McNeil, the Scottish evangelist, once said that in school he had a seminary professor who insisted on opening his theology classes with a question. No one could ever anticipate what the question would be. One day he said to his students, "Gentlemen, can someone give me a definition of the gospel?" A student rose and read John 3:16: "For God loved the world so much that he gave his only Son so that anyone who believes in him shall not perish but have eternal life." The professor said, "That is a good gospel text, but it is not a *definition* of the gospel." Another student read 1 Timothy 1:15: "How true it is, and how I long that everyone should know it, that Christ Jesus came into the world to save sinners—and I was the greatest of them all." Again the professor declined to accept it; he waited for what he wanted. Finally, a student stood and read 1 Corinthians 15:3, 4 (italicized in the passage above), much to the professor's delight. It was evident that he had the reply he desired; he said, "Gentlemen, that is the gospel. Believe it, live it, preach it, and die for it if necessary!"

P R A I S E :

P E T I T I O N :

Answer me, O Lord my God; give me light in my darkness lest I die. (Ps. 13:3)

Through the Fire

OUR earthly bodies which die and decay are different from the bodies we shall have when we come back to life again, for they will never die. The bodies we have now embarrass us for they become sick and die; but they will be full of glory when we come back to life again. Yes, they are weak, dying bodies now, but when we live again they will be full of strength. They are just human bodies at death, but when they come back to life they will be superhuman bodies. For just as there are natural, human bodies, there are also supernatural, spiritual bodies.

The Scriptures tell us that the first man, Adam, was given a natural, human body but Christ is more than that, for he was life-giving Spirit.

First, then, we have these human bodies and later on God gives us spiritual, heavenly bodies. Adam was made from the dust of the earth, but Christ came from heaven above. Every human being has a body just like Adam's, made of dust, but all who become Christ's will have the same kind of body as his—a body from heaven. Just as each of us now has a body like Adam's, so we shall some day have a body like Christ's. (1 Corinthians 15:42-49)

What will happen to our physical bodies when we are resurrected?

The certainty of the resurrection takes away the fear that would otherwise surround the destruction of the body. A child who sees precious metal being thrown into a furnace might be saddened. He thinks the metal is being destroyed. But one who understands the refining process knows that only the impurities will be lost. The pure metal will emerge safe. As Christians, we need not fear death. The grave is the room where we shall be fashioned according to the glorious body of the Lord Jesus.

P R A I S E :

P E T I T I O N :

The Lord is my strength, my song, and my salvation. He is my God, and I will praise him. (Exod. 15:2)

The Death of Death

BUT I am telling you this strange and wonderful secret: we shall not all die, but we shall all be given new bodies! It will all happen in a moment, in the twinkling of an eye, when the last trumpet is blown. For there will be a trumpet blast from the sky and all the Christians who have died will suddenly become alive, with new bodies that will never, never die; and then we who are still alive shall suddenly have new bodies too. For our earthly bodies, the ones we have now that can die, must be transformed into heavenly bodies that cannot perish but will live forever.

When this happens, then at last this Scripture will come true—"Death is swallowed up in victory." O death, where then your victory? Where then your sting? For sin—the sting that causes death—will all be gone; and the law, which reveals our sins, will no longer be our judge. How we thank God for all of this! It is he who makes us victorious through Jesus Christ our Lord!

So, my dear brothers, since future victory is sure, be strong and steady, always abounding in the Lord's work, for you know that nothing you do for the Lord is ever wasted as it would be if there were no resurrection. (1 Corinthians 15:51-58)

What is Paul's secret?

Death is Satan's greatest weapon. He uses it to bring confusion and fear into the hearts of those facing it. Thousands have turned away from the Lord because of death. They haven't been able to understand how a good God could permit such evil to have free reign. We must remember that death is not of God. It is part of the satanic curse that has the universe in its grasp. As Christians, we know death is not final. It is only a necessary phase of life. When a Christian dies, Satan feels no victory, for the believer moves on immediately to eternal life. At the end of the age, when Christ returns in glory, the curse of death will be abolished forever.

P R A I S E :

P E T I T I O N :

In prayer, as in nothing else, we can find refuge from the degradation of self-love. (W. L. Sullivan)

Special Season

NOW here are the directions about the money you are collecting to send to the Christians in Jerusalem; (and, by the way, these are the same directions I gave to the churches in Galatia). On every Lord's Day each of you should put aside something from what you have earned during the week, and use it for this offering. The amount depends on how much the Lord has helped you earn. Don't wait until I get there and then try to collect it all at once. When I come I will send your loving gift with a letter to Jerusalem, to be taken there by trustworthy messengers you yourselves will choose. And if it seems wise for me to go along too, then we can travel together.

I am coming to visit you after I have been to Macedonia first, but I will be staying there only for a little while. It could be that I will stay longer with you, perhaps all winter, and then you can send me on to my next destination. This time I don't want to make just a passing visit and then go right on; I want to come and stay awhile, if the Lord will let me. I will be staying here at Ephesus until the holiday of Pentecost, for there is a wide open door for me to preach and teach here. So much is happening, but there are many enemies. (1 Corinthians 16:1-9)

How long does Paul intend to stay when he goes to visit the Corinthians?

In our culture, churches often invite special speakers to come and minister to their congregations. But these invitations seldom extend for more than just a few days at a time. In most cases it is considered inconvenient for both the church and the speaker to have him or her remain for longer than a week.   In Paul's time, though, things were different. When he went to visit a church, it wasn't just for a Sunday morning worship service. He often stayed for two or three months! Maybe that is not such a bad idea. A visiting minister cannot truly sense the needs of the congregation until he or she has been among them for a while. Even though it seems highly "impractical" today, it is something churches should consider. What do you think?

P R A I S E :

P E T I T I O N :

The Lord [says], "I will arise and defend the oppressed, the poor, the needy. I will rescue them as they have longed for me to do." (Ps. 12:5)

May 2 CORINTHIANS

High school is a time when emotions run high. The combination of sports, close friends, dating, and self-discovery creates an environment of excitement and intense feelings. It is said that high school friends are friends forever, and that the experiences of high school are important in one's self-concept. ■ This epistle is marked by the deep emotions of a man of God. In 2 Corinthians Paul runs the gamut of human emotions: disappointment, despair, joy, relief. Through his heartfelt writing we see Paul's relationship to the church and to God. This passionate letter allows us to peer into Paul's soul.

Silent Comfort

WHAT a wonderful God we have—he is the Father of our Lord Jesus Christ, the source of every mercy, and the one who so wonderfully comforts and strengthens us in our hardships and trials. And why does he do this? So that when others are troubled, needing our sympathy and encouragement, we can pass on to them this same help and comfort God has given us. You can be sure that the more we undergo sufferings for Christ, the more he will shower us with his comfort and encouragement. We are in deep trouble for bringing you God's comfort and salvation. But in our trouble God had comforted us—and this, too, to help you: to show you from our personal experience how God will tenderly comfort you when you undergo these same sufferings. He will give you the strength to endure. (2 Corinthians 1:3-7)

Why does God strengthen us in our hardships and trials?

A person who has just experienced a devastating loss needs desperately to be comforted. He needs to know that life has not come to an end, that his friends and family love him, and that the semblance of normalcy will return. What do you say to such a person? Often it is best to say nothing, offering no so-called "words of encouragement" or homespun advice. During periods of intense grief, most words sound hopelessly contrived and meaningless. At such times, the purest comfort comes through the help, love, and presence of friends, the knowledge of God's infinite love, and the hope that life—now almost intolerable—will shortly reduce its demands. Paul says that those who have experienced God's comfort in times of tribulation are responsible for comforting others. We can all help each other to draw from Christ's limitless well of comfort and encouragement.

P R A I S E :

P E T I T I O N :

By running an errand to God for others, you'll never fail to get something for yourself.

The Branded Ones

IT was because I was so sure of your understanding and trust that I planned to stop and see you on my way to Macedonia, as well as afterwards when I returned, so that I could be a double blessing to you and so that you could send me on my way to Judea.

Then why, you may be asking, did I change my plan? Hadn't I really made up my mind yet? Or am I like a man of the world who says "yes" when he really means "no"? Never! As surely as God is true, I am not that sort of person. My "yes" means "yes."

Timothy and Silvanus and I have been telling you about Jesus Christ the Son of God. He isn't one to say "yes" when he means "no." He always does exactly what he says. He carries out and fulfills all of God's promises, no matter how many of them there are; and we have told everyone how faithful he is, giving glory to his name. It is this God who has made you and me into faithful Christians and commissioned us apostles to preach the Good News. He has put his brand upon us—his mark of ownership—and given us his Holy Spirit in our hearts as guarantee that we belong to him, and as the first installment of all that he is going to give us.

I call upon this God to witness against me if I am not telling the absolute truth: the reason I haven't come to visit you yet is that I don't want to sadden you with a severe rebuke. (2 Corinthians 1:15-23)

Give one reason for Paul's decision to postpone his trip to Corinth.

Many tribes in Africa have rituals which involve placing permanent marks upon the bodies of adolescents. Such marks—usually cuts made on the face and chest—are meant to identify people as members of a certain tribe. Because these natives are fiercely loyal to their tribes, they are proud to be branded with these distinguishing marks. Paul says that when we become Christians, God brands our souls with the mark of his ownership. What an honor! We should love our distinguishing marks and bear them proudly.

P R A I S E :

P E T I T I O N :

Your heavenly Father will forgive you if you forgive those who sin against you. (Matt. 6:14, 15)

The Sugarcoated Lie

REMEMBER that the man I wrote about, who caused all the trouble, has not caused sorrow to me as much as to all the rest of you—though I certainly have my share in it too. I don't want to be harder on him than I should. He has been punished enough by your united disapproval. Now it is time to forgive him and comfort him. Otherwise he may become so bitter and discouraged that he won't be able to recover. Please show him now that you still do love him very much.

I wrote to you as I did so that I could find out how far you would go in obeying me. When you forgive anyone, I do too. And whatever I have forgiven (to the extent that this affected me too) has been by Christ's authority, and for your good. A further reason for forgiveness is to keep from being outsmarted by Satan; for we know what he is trying to do. (2 Corinthians 2:5-11)

Why should the Corinthians forgive the sinful man?

People who believe in the reality of Satan and evil spirits are often considered unenlightened, bigoted, and fanatical. They are scoffed at by non-Christians; even some liberal Christians laugh at the idea. But the very fact that they deny his existence means that Satan is powerful. He is clever enough to delude even the brightest minds, making people believe that evil comes from man and nature, not from a real, live devil. Satan often disguises himself as an "angel of light," posing as truth, culture, education, or religious reform. Dressed in the garb of supposed spiritual advancement, he seeks to lead men astray. Underneath the pleasing exterior and the thin sugarcoating of truth lies the bitter pill of deception and the fatal dose of error.

P R A I S E :

P E T I T I O N :

I will rescue you and free you from the grip of your enemies. (Mic. 4:10)

The Price of Patience

WELL, when I got as far as the city of Troas, the Lord gave me tremendous opportunities to preach the Gospel. But Titus, my dear brother, wasn't there to meet me and I couldn't rest, wondering where he was and what had happened to him. So I said good-bye and went right on to Macedonia to try to find him.

But thanks be to God! For through what Christ has done, he has triumphed over us so that now wherever we go he uses us to tell others about the Lord and to spread the Gospel like a sweet perfume. As far as God is concerned there is a sweet, wholesome fragrance in our lives. It is the fragrance of Christ within us, an aroma to both the saved and the unsaved all around us. To those who are not being saved, we seem a fearful smell of death and doom, while to those who know Christ we are a life-giving perfume. But who is adequate for such a task as this? Only those who, like ourselves, are men of integrity, sent by God, speaking with Christ's power, with God's eye upon us. We are not like those hucksters—and there are many of them—whose idea in getting out the Gospel is to make a good living out of it. (2 Corinthians 2:12-17)

To what does Paul compare the spreading of the gospel?

A young man went to see an old saint and asked for prayer. He said, "I find myself continually giving way to impatience. Will you please pray for me that I may be more patient?" The old man agreed. They knelt together and the man of God began to pray: "Lord, send this young man tribulation in the morning, tribulation in the afternoon, . . ." The young man nudged him and whispered, "No, no, not tribulation. Patience!" **"B**ut," replied the old man, "it is tribulation that works patience! If you would know patience, you must have tribulation." If you would know victory, you must have conflict. It is ridiculous for anybody to talk about having a victory when they have never been in a battle. You must be prepared to enter into the arena with Jesus Christ himself, and he will give you lessons daily.

P R A I S E :

P E T I T I O N :

Prayer is our need crying out for help. Prayer is the voice of faith to the Father. (E. W. Kenyon)

Epitaphs of Glory

ARE we beginning to be like those false teachers of yours who must tell you all about themselves and bring long letters of recommendation with them? I think you hardly need someone's letter to tell you about us, do you? And we don't need a recommendation from you, either! The only letter I need is you yourselves! By looking at the good change in your hearts, everyone can see that we have done a good work among you. They can see that you are a letter from Christ, written by us. It is not a letter written with pen and ink, but by the Spirit of the living God; not one carved on stone, but in human hearts.

We dare to say these good things about ourselves only because of our great trust in God through Christ, that he will help us to be true to what we say, and not because we think we can do anything of lasting value by ourselves. Our only power and success comes from God. He is the one who has helped us tell others about his new agreement to save them. We do not tell them that they must obey every law of God or die; but we tell them there is life for them from the Holy Spirit. (2 Corinthians 3:1-6)

What does Paul point to as proof for his ministry?

Most of us would like to leave a lasting impression on humanity, so that we would be remembered with fondness and admiration long after our deaths. Here's what Henry Van Dyke had to say about this: "We long to leave something behind us which shall last, some influence of good which shall be transmitted through our children, some impress of character or action which shall endure and perpetuate itself. There is only one way in which we can do this, only one way in which our lives can receive any lasting beauty and dignity; and that is by being taken up into the great plan of God. Then the fragments of broken glass glow with an immortal meaning in the design of his grand mosaic. Our work is then established, because it becomes a part of his work." (From *The Friendly Year,* 1907)

P R A I S E :

P E T I T I O N :

Accept our praise, O Lord, for all your glorious power. We will write songs to celebrate your mighty acts! (Ps. 21:13)

The Ugly Queen

SINCE we know that this new glory will never go away, we can preach with great boldness, and not as Moses did, who put a veil over his face so that the Israelis could not see the glory fade away.

Not only Moses' face was veiled, but his people's minds and understanding were veiled and blinded too. Even now when the Scripture is read it seems as though Jewish hearts and minds are covered by a thick veil, because they cannot see and understand the real meaning of the Scriptures. For this veil of misunderstanding can be removed only by believing in Christ. Yes, even today when they read Moses' writings their hearts are blind and they think that obeying the Ten Commandments is the way to be saved.

But whenever anyone turns to the Lord from his sins, then the veil is taken away. The Lord is the Spirit who gives them life, and where he is there is freedom [from trying to be saved by keeping the laws of God]. But we Christians have no veil over our faces; we can be mirrors that brightly reflect the glory of the Lord. And as the Spirit of the Lord works within us, we become more and more like him. (2 Corinthians 3:12-18)

How can the "veil of misunderstanding" be removed?

An African queen had never seen her own reflection and was made to believe she was a very beautiful woman. One day a trader came to the community to barter with the natives, and some of the articles of trade were mirrors. The queen, eager to see herself for the first time, was given one of the best and clearest. When she looked at her image, she was shocked to see that she was not beautiful at all, as she had imagined. Enraged, she dashed the mirror to the ground and expelled the trader from the community. How foolish, we say. But it is not more foolish than what thousands of educated, refined people do today: The Bible reveals their ugliness and sin, so they seek to destroy the validity of the Bible.

P R A I S E :

P E T I T I O N :

Remember, your Father knows exactly what you need even before you ask him! (Matt. 6:8)

Thorny Roses

IT is God himself, in his mercy, who has given us this wonderful work [of telling his Good News to others], and so we never give up. We do not try to trick people into believing—we are not interested in fooling anyone. We never try to get anyone to believe that the Bible teaches what it doesn't. All such shameful methods we forego. We stand in the presence of God as we speak and so we tell the truth, as all who know us will agree.

If the Good News we preach is hidden to anyone, it is hidden from the one who is on the road to eternal death. Satan, who is the god of this evil world, has made him blind, unable to see the glorious light of the Gospel that is shining upon him, or to understand the amazing message we preach about the glory of Christ, who is God. We don't go around preaching about ourselves, but about Christ Jesus as Lord. All we say of ourselves is that we are your slaves because of what Jesus has done for us. For God, who said, "Let there be light in the darkness," has made us understand that it is the brightness of his glory that is seen in the face of Jesus Christ. (2 Corinthians 4:1-6)

Who is blind to the light of the gospel?

A few so-called Christian evangelists today would have their audiences believe that all their earthly problems will depart when they accept Jesus as Savior. They say that God has indeed promised a rose garden, and that all sorrow, anxiety, suffering, and pain will cease if they choose to follow his path. Through such dubious teaching, many are enticed into the kingdom, only to soon discover that there are quite a few thistles in the garden of roses. God never promised deliverance from all earthly concerns, though he did promise us divine strength and comfort during tribulation. Paul denounces those who would bring people to Christ through deception and trickery. He is not interested in fooling anyone. He says we should never try to get anyone to believe that the Bible teaches what it doesn't.

PRAISE:

PETITION:

Prayer is always affected by the character and conduct of him who prays. Water cannot rise above its own level, and the spotless prayer cannot flow from the spotted heart. Straight praying is never born of crooked conduct.

Cheap Containers

BUT this precious treasure—this light and power that now shine within us—is held in a perishable container, that is, in our weak bodies. Everyone can see that the glorious power within must be from God and is not our own.

We are pressed on every side by troubles, but not crushed and broken. We are perplexed because we don't know why things happen as they do, but we don't give up and quit. We are hunted down, but God never abandons us. We get knocked down, but we get up again and keep going. These bodies of ours are constantly facing death just as Jesus did; so it is clear to all that it is only the living Christ within [who keeps us safe].

Yes, we live under constant danger to our lives because we serve the Lord, but this gives us constant opportunities to show forth the power of Jesus Christ within our dying bodies. Because of our preaching we face death, but it has resulted in eternal life for you. (2 Corinthians 4:7-12)

How can people tell that the "glorious power" within Christians is not their own?

One of the world's most expensive perfumes is Opium, by Yves Saint-Laurent. Its fragrance is exquisite, contemporary yet timeless, and subtle as the scent of a single rosebud. Yet this singular essence, costing over $160 per ounce, is sold in simple glass vials, worth just a few cents. These fragile bottles can crack if exposed to low temperatures, and will shatter if dropped onto a hard surface.   In today's reading we see that we are like these glass bottles. We too are perishable containers holding a precious treasure; the weak, fragile bodies of Christians contain the priceless glory of God. And just as the perfume adds beauty and value to a bottle, the divine presence within transforms a mere human into a child of God.

P R A I S E :

P E T I T I O N :

God will hear and answer and receive [you] with joy. (Job 33:26)

Blind Visions

THAT is why we never give up. Though our bodies are dying, our inner strength in the Lord is growing every day. These troubles and sufferings of ours are, after all, quite small and won't last very long. Yet this short time of distress will result in God's richest blessing upon us forever and ever! So we do not look at what we can see right now, the troubles all around us, but we look forward to the joys in heaven which we have not yet seen. The troubles will soon be over, but the joys to come will last forever. (2 Corinthians 4:16-18)

During our times of trouble, what should we look forward to?

Fanny Crosby was one of the greatest hymn writers ever. As an infant, she was blinded as a result of negligence on the part of a doctor. To compensate for the loss of her sight, she keenly developed her other senses. One of her most beautiful hymns, "I Shall See Him Face to Face," could never have been written were it not for the fact that she had never looked upon the green fields, the evening sunset, or the twinkle in her mother's eye. It was the loss of her vision that helped her to gain her remarkable spiritual discernment.   As we read in today's passage, "This short time of distress will result in God's richest blessing upon us forever and ever!"

P R A I S E :

P E T I T I O N :

I will sing to the Lord because he has blessed me so richly. (Ps. 13:6)

The Dilapidated House

FOR we know that when this tent we live in now is taken down—when we die and leave these bodies—we will have wonderful new bodies in heaven, homes that will be ours forevermore, made for us by God himself, and not by human hands. How weary we grow of our present bodies. That is why we look forward eagerly to the day when we shall have heavenly bodies which we shall put on like new clothes. For we shall not be merely spirits without bodies. These earthly bodies make us groan and sigh, but we wouldn't like to think of dying and having no bodies at all. We want to slip into our new bodies so that these dying bodies will, as it were, be swallowed up by everlasting life. This is what God has prepared for us and, as a guarantee, he has given us his Holy Spirit.

Now we look forward with confidence to our heavenly bodies, realizing that every moment we spend in these earthly bodies is time spent away from our eternal home in heaven with Jesus. (2 Corinthians 5:1-6)

What will happen to us when we leave the bodies we now possess?

When former President John Quincy Adams was eighty years old, he was met by an old friend who shook his trembling hand and said, "Good morning. How is John Quincy Adams today?" The retired chief executive looked at him for a moment and then said, "John Quincy Adams himself is quite well, sir, quite well. But the house in which he lives at present is becoming dilapidated. It is tottering upon its foundations. Time and the seasons have almost destroyed it. Its roof is pretty worn out. Its walls are much shattered, and it crumbles with every wind. The old tenement is becoming almost uninhabitable, and I think that John Quincy Adams will have to move out of it soon. But he himself is well, sir, quite well!" It was not long afterward that he had his second and fatal stroke and John Quincy Adams moved from his "shaky tabernacle," as he called it, to his "house not made with hands."

PRAISE:

PETITION:

It is God himself who prays through us, when we pray to him. . . . We cannot bridge the gap between God and ourselves even through the most intensive and frequent prayers; the gap between God and ourselves can only be bridged by God. (P. Tillich)

Grading People

SINCE we believe that Christ died for all of us, we should also believe that we have died to the old life we used to live. He died for all so that all who live—having received eternal life from him—might live no longer for themselves, to please themselves, but to spend their lives pleasing Christ who died and rose again for them. So stop evaluating Christians by what the world thinks about them or by what they seem to be like on the outside. Once I mistakenly thought of Christ that way, merely as a human being like myself. How differently I feel now! When someone becomes a Christian he becomes a brand new person inside. He is not the same any more. A new life has begun! (2 Corinthians 5:14-17)

How did Paul formerly think of Christ? What changed his mind?

Paul urges us to stop evaluating Christians by what the world thinks of them or by what they seem to be. This is difficult for us, because it is tempting to attach labels to people we often hear about. After each of the names below, write in your impressions of that person based upon what you've seen and heard of them.

Jerry Falwell _____

Billy Graham _____

Charles Colson _____

Debby Boone _____

Oral Roberts _____

Look at your remarks. How many of them are evaluative? Let us guard against the temptation to pigeonhole fellow Christians. We should let God be the Judge.

P R A I S E : _____

P E T I T I O N : _____

Yes, ask *anything* using my name, and I will do it! (John 14:14)

Bride of the Falls

ALL these new things are from God who brought us back to himself through what Christ Jesus did. And God has given us the privilege of urging everyone to come into his favor and be reconciled to him. For God was in Christ, restoring the world to himself, no longer counting men's sins against them but blotting them out. This is the wonderful message he has given us to tell others. We are Christ's ambassadors. God is using us to speak to you: we beg you, as though Christ himself were here pleading with you, receive the love he offers you—be reconciled to God. For God took the sinless Christ and poured into him our sins. Then, in exchange, he poured God's goodness into us! (2 Corinthians 5:18-21)

As Christ's ambassador, what was Paul's official message?

It was the annual custom of a tribe of North American Indians living near Niagara Falls to offer a young virgin to the Spirit of the Mighty River. One year the lot fell upon the beautiful daughter of the old chieftain. When he received the sad news, he said nothing, and went on smoking his pipe. On the appointed day, the young girl entered the frail canoe and was pushed out into the mighty current of the river. To the amazement of the crowd, a second canoe was seen to dart out from the river's bank further downstream. It was the old chieftain. His canoe met his daughter's, and with a last look of love, they plunged over the cataract and perished side by side. In their death they were not divided. The father was in it with his child. Our heavenly Father was also with his Son on the day of Christ's death. The motivating force behind that sacrifice was God's immeasurable love for his lost world.

P R A I S E :

P E T I T I O N :

All of us, whether Jews or Gentiles, may come to God the Father with the Holy Spirit's help because of what Jesus Christ has done for us. (Eph. 2:18)

Bad Shepherds

AS God's partners we beg you not to toss aside this marvelous message of God's great kindness. For God says, "Your cry came to me at a favorable time, when the doors of welcome were wide open. I helped you on a day when salvation was being offered." Right now God is ready to welcome you. Today he is ready to save you.

We try to live in such a way that no one will ever be offended or kept back from finding the Lord by the way we act, so that no one can find fault with us and blame it on the Lord. In fact, in everything we do we try to show that we are true ministers of God.

We patiently endure suffering and hardship and trouble of every kind. We have been beaten, put in jail, faced angry mobs, worked to exhaustion, stayed awake through sleepless nights of watching, and gone without food. We have proved ourselves to be what we claim by our wholesome lives and by our understanding of the Gospel and by our patience. We have been kind and truly loving and filled with the Holy Spirit. (2 Corinthians 6:1-6)

What is Paul's suggestion for how Christian ministers should live?

Mr. and Mrs. Deloe were members of a church in Los Angeles. Both young Christians, Mr. Deloe was the director of the youth group, while Mrs. Deloe sang in the choir. One day Mr. Deloe found out that his company would soon transfer him to New Orleans. A few weeks before their move, the Deloes were astounded to receive the news that their pastor had left his wife for another woman. The Deloes were deeply hurt. How could a man of God suddenly turn from the Lord to such sin? They were so disillusioned that when they moved to New Orleans they didn't even bother to look for a new church. Over the course of a few years, they completely left the faith. To some degree, the errant pastor in Los Angeles was responsible for the Deloes' drift away from the church. This emphasizes the need for church leaders to lead exemplary lives. Paul says, "We try to live in such a way that no one will ever be . . . kept back from finding the Lord by the way we act."

P R A I S E :

P E T I T I O N :

Prayer is the channel through which all good flows from God to man, and all good from men to men. (E. M. Bounds)

Incompatible Teams

OH, my dear Corinthian friends! I have told you all my feelings; I love you with all my heart. Any coldness still between us is not because of any lack of love on my part, but because your love is too small and does not reach out to me and draw me in. I am talking to you now as if you truly were my very own children. Open your hearts to us! Return our love!

Don't be teamed with those who do not love the Lord, for what do the people of God have in common with the people of sin? How can light live with darkness? And what harmony can there be between Christ and the devil? How can a Christian be a partner with one who doesn't believe? And what union can there be between God's temple and idols? For you are God's temple, the home of the living God, and God has said of you, "I will live in them and walk among them, and I will be their God and they shall be my people." That is why the Lord has said, "Leave them; separate yourselves from them; don't touch their filthy things, and I will welcome you, and be a Father to you, and you will be my sons and daughters." (2 Corinthians 6:11-18)

What advice does Paul offer Christians here?

Advice is often the last thing young people want to hear. They feel that the "wise words" of adults are not valid, because older people usually are out of touch with the problems of the young. That may be somewhat true; nevertheless, there are certain biblical principles that are universal. We see one such principle in today's reading: "Don't be teamed up with those who do not love the Lord." This passage has been quoted many times to Christian young people who are contemplating marriage to an unbeliever. Those who take this advice often avert disaster. Those who do not take it invite a multitude of problems into their relationships. As Christians, we are forced to make many difficult decisions. Our decisions reveal our priorities. Let us strive to always be faithful and obedient to God and his Word.

P R A I S E :

P E T I T I O N :

Sing to the Lord, O kingdoms of the earth—sing praises to the Lord. (Ps. 68:32)

Head in the Stars

HAVING such great promises as these, dear friends, let us turn away from everything wrong, whether of body or spirit, and purify ourselves, living in the wholesome fear of God, giving ourselves to him alone. Please open your hearts to us again, for not one of you has suffered any wrong from us. Not one of you was led astray. We have cheated no one nor taken advantage of anyone. I'm not saying this to scold or blame you, for, as I have said before, you are in my heart forever and I live and die with you. I have the highest confidence in you, and my pride in you is great. You have greatly encouraged me; you have made me so happy in spite of all my suffering. (2 Corinthians 7:1-4)

What do you think Paul means by the "fear of God"?

A well-known television actress was traveling in the first-class section of a commercial airliner. Two body guards sat across the aisle from her. Soon a stewardess came by to see if the actress was comfortable. **"M**ay I get you anything?" she asked politely. The TV star didn't even acknowledge her presence, and continued reading her magazine. The stewardess, thinking the actress might not have heard her, repeated the question. Still there was no response. The stewardess shrugged and returned to her service area, one of the bodyguards on her heels. **"I** saw you talking to Miss _____," he said, adjusting his tie. "There's one thing you should know. She *never* speaks to help." **P**aul, a "celebrity" among early Christians, could have taken an equally disdainful attitude toward the common people. But there is never a hint of this anywhere in the epistles. He told the people of Corinth: "You are in my heart forever and I live and die with you."

P R A I S E :

P E T I T I O N :

When the Holy Spirit, who is truth, comes, he shall guide you into all truth. (John 16:13)

When Feeling Good Is Bad

I am no longer sorry that I sent that letter to you, though I was very sorry for a time, realizing how painful it would be to you. But it hurt you only for a little while. Now I am glad I sent it, not because it hurt you, but because the pain turned you to God. It was a good kind of sorrow you felt, the kind of sorrow God wants his people to have, so that I need not come to you with harshness. For God sometimes uses sorrow in our lives to help us turn away from sin and seek eternal life. We should never regret his sending it. But the sorrow of the man who is not a Christian is not the sorrow of true repentance and does not prevent eternal death.

Just see how much good this grief from the Lord did for you! You no longer shrugged your shoulders, but became earnest and sincere, and very anxious to get rid of the sin that I wrote you about. You became frightened about what had happened, and longed for me to come and help. You went right to work on the problem and cleared it up [punishing the man who sinned]. You have done everything you could to make it right. (2 Corinthians 7:8-11)

Why was Paul initially sorry for sending the first letter to the Corinthians?

Analgesia is a medical condition meaning the absence of pain. Certain diseases and injuries can cause this condition, which interrupts normal communication between nerves and the brain. Although analgesia seems to be desirable (after all, who wants to go through pain?), it is a wolf in sheep's clothing. People with analgesia can be seriously ill and not know it, due to the absence of painful symptoms. Or they can badly injure themselves without realizing it. No one likes to suffer, but pain is part of being human. It is a necessary part of the early-warning mechanism that helps us to detect physical problems. Spiritual "pain" is also a blessing in disguise. Though it produces suffering, it can ultimately lead to God.

P R A I S E :

P E T I T I O N :

Anchor yourself to the throne of God, then shorten the rope.

The Burning Bush

NOW I want to tell you what God in his grace has done for the churches in Macedonia.

Though they have been going through much trouble and hard times, they have mixed their wonderful joy with their deep poverty, and the result has been an overflow of giving to others. They gave not only what they could afford, but far more; and I can testify that they did it because they wanted to, and not because of nagging on my part. They begged us to take the money so they could share in the joy of helping the Christians in Jerusalem. Best of all, they went beyond our highest hopes, for their first action was to dedicate themselves to the Lord and to us, for whatever directions God might give to them through us. They were so enthusiastic about it that we have urged Titus, who encouraged your giving in the first place, to visit you and encourage you to complete your share in this ministry of giving. (2 Corinthians 8:1-6)

How much money does Paul say the Macedonians gave to the Jerusalem church?

Hugh Macmillan tells this story: "One September, on an afternoon walk, I saw an aspen tree that reminded me of Moses' burning bush. Its foliage was a blaze of the most vivid scarlet. The leaves were not dead like most autumn leaves; they were quite fresh and full of life. I soon discovered that the tree grew on a little mound from which the waters of a stream that existed only in rainy weather had been washing away the soil, leaving most of the roots bare and exposed. The conditions of life were thus unfavorable; but instead of being made less beautiful, the plant became more beautiful. **"D**eep in my soul I reflected that so it is with human life, from which the stream of circumstances washes away all worldly concerns, leaving the roots bare. God's breath kindles in it a new beauty, which no worldly condition could have developed. And the poverty of its state, which men pity, only makes it glow with the light of heaven, and its cross becomes its crown."

P R A I S E :

P E T I T I O N :

The Lord hates the gifts of the wicked, but delights in the prayers of his people. (Prov. 15:8)

Church of Charity

I want to suggest that you finish what you started to do a year ago, for you were not only the first to propose this idea, but the first to begin doing something about it. Having started the ball rolling so enthusiastically, you should carry this project through to completion just as gladly, giving whatever you can out of whatever you have. Let your enthusiastic idea at the start be equalled by your realistic action now. If you are really eager to give, then it isn't important how much you have to give. God wants you to give what you have, not what you haven't.

Of course, I don't mean that those who receive your gifts should have an easy time of it at your expense, but you should divide with them. Right now you have plenty and can help them; then at some other time they can share with you when you need it. In this way each will have as much as he needs. Do you remember what the Scriptures say about this? "He that gathered much had nothing left over, and he that gathered little had enough." So you also should share with those in need. (2 Corinthians 8:10-15)

What had the Corinthians enthusiastically proposed, then failed to follow through with?

In a society as affluent as America, it is difficult to realize that thousands of desperately poor people roam our city streets daily. Most of us have little or no contact with extreme poverty, so we tend to assume that the problem has been taken care of. We believe that it is the government's job to aid the poor through welfare and financial assistance programs. But this is not always the case. For various reasons, many poor people are ineligible for such assistance. Obviously, their ineligibility does not reduce their needs for the basics of survival and well-being. The church in America must become more attentive to the needs of the poor. It must use its resources to help ease their suffering. I believe the function of the church extends to more than meeting spiritual needs. The church should be a nucleus of charity and good will.

P R A I S E :

P E T I T I O N :

Blessed be God who didn't turn away when I was praying and didn't refuse me his kindness and love. (Ps. 66:20)

Christian Money

I am thankful to God that he has given Titus the same real concern for you that I have. He is glad to follow my suggestion that he visit you again—but I think he would have come anyway, for he is very eager to see you! I am sending another well-known brother with him, who is highly praised as a preacher of the Good News in all the churches. In fact, this man was elected by the churches to travel with me to take the gift to Jerusalem. This will glorify the Lord and show our eagerness to help each other. By traveling together we will guard against any suspicion, for we are anxious that no one should find fault with the way we are handling this large gift. God knows we are honest, but I want everyone else to know it too. That is why we have made this arrangement.

And I am sending you still another brother, whom we know from experience to be an earnest Christian. He is especially interested, as he looks forward to this trip, because I have told him all about your eagerness to help. (2 Corinthians 8:16-22)

Why did the churches elect a man to travel with Paul?

When it comes to collecting and managing money, some Christian organizations have better reputations than others. Unfortunately, several such organizations have been accused and convicted of gross misappropriations of donations. As a result, even the most blameless Christian groups have undergone public scrutiny and criticism. To counteract this trend, a Christian council for financial accountability was formed. Council members—mostly nonprofit Christian organizations—keep open records, available for examination at any time. Although these council members know in their hearts that they are honest, by joining this council they can effectively demonstrate their honesty to the public at large. In an imperfect world, where cheating and dishonesty abound, it is necessary for Christian organizations to be doubly careful about monetary concerns. As Paul says, "God knows we are honest, but I want everyone else to know it too."

PRAISE:

PETITION:

If God is not first in our thoughts in the morning, he will be last in our thoughts all day.

Gifts of Life

I realize that I really don't even need to mention this to you, about helping God's people. For I know how eager you are to do it, and I have boasted to the friends in Macedonia that you were ready to send an offering a year ago. In fact, it was this enthusiasm of yours that stirred up many of them to begin helping. But I am sending these men just to be sure that you really are ready, as I told them you would be, with your money all collected; I don't want it to turn out that this time I was wrong in my boasting about you. I would be very much ashamed—and so would you—if some of these Macedonian people come with me, only to find that you still aren't ready after all I have told them!

So I have asked these other brothers to arrive ahead of me to see that the gift you promised is on hand and waiting. I want it to be a real gift and not look as if it were being given under pressure. (2 Corinthians 9:1-5)

What motivated the Macedonians to donate money for church growth?

Too often we forget that it is a blessing to be able to give. If we were as eager to do things for others as we are to receive favors, we would better understand the words of Jesus, "It is more blessed to give than to receive." A spring of water continually gives, while a pool continually receives. That is why the spring is always fresh, while the pool becomes stagnant and filled with refuse. If we knew the blessing of giving, there would be no need for drives, schemes, rummage sales, car washes, entertainments, and circuses to support church work. The poor preacher would not need to plead and urge and beg to keep things going. A giving church cannot die, but when a people stop giving, the church dies—spiritually as well as materially.   After a minister had earnestly pled for the cause of missions, a stingy old deacon complained, "All this giving will kill the church." The pastor replied, "Take me to one church which died from giving and I will leap upon its grave and shout to high heaven, 'Blessed are the dead which die in the Lord!' " (Rev. 14:13).

PRAISE:

PETITION:

In his love and pity he redeemed them and carried them through all the years. (Isa. 63:9)

Glass and Silver

GOD is able to make it up to you by giving you everything you need and more, so that there will not only be enough for your own needs, but plenty left over to give joyfully to others. It is as the Scriptures say: "The godly man gives generously to the poor. His good deeds will be an honor to him forever."

For God, who gives seed to the farmer to plant, and later on, good crops to harvest and eat, will give you more and more seed to plant and will make it grow so that you can give away more and more fruit from your harvest.

Yes, God will give you much so that you can give away much, and when we take your gifts to those who need them they will break out into thanksgiving and praise to God for your help. So, two good things happen as a result of your gifts—those in need are helped, and they overflow with thanks to God. Those you help will be glad not only because of your generous gifts to themselves and to others, but they will praise God for this proof that your deeds are as good as your doctrine. And they will pray for you with deep fervor and feeling because of the wonderful grace of God shown through you.

Thank God for his Son—his Gift too wonderful for words. (2 Corinthians 9:8-15)

What two good things can happen as a result of our gifts to the Lord?

A recent *Moody Monthly* article told the story of a rich old man of miserable disposition who went to visit a rabbi. The rabbi led the rich man to the window, and asked, "Look out there and tell me what you see." The old man peered out and said he saw nothing but men, women, and children. Again the rabbi took him by the hand, this time leading him to a mirror.   "Now what do you see?" asked the rabbi.   "Only myself," the rich man replied. At that, the rabbi wisely remarked, "Look, in the window there is glass and in the mirror there is glass. But the glass of the mirror is covered with reflecting silver. No sooner is the silver added than you cease to see others and see only yourself."

P R A I S E :

P E T I T I O N :

When you pray, go away by yourself, all alone, and shut the door behind you and pray to your Father secretly, and your Father, who knows your secrets, will reward you. (Matt. 6:6)

Prayer Attack

I hope I won't need to show you when I come how harsh and rough I can be. I don't want to carry out my present plans against some of you who seem to think my deeds and words are merely those of an ordinary man. It is true that I am an ordinary, weak human being, but I don't use human plans and methods to win my battles. I use God's mighty weapons, not those made by men, to knock down the devil's strongholds. These weapons can break down every proud argument against God and every wall that can be built to keep men from finding him. With these weapons I can capture rebels and bring them back to God, and change them into men whose hearts' desire is obedience to Christ. I will use these weapons against every rebel who remains after I have first used them on you yourselves, and you surrender to Christ. (2 Corinthians 10:2-6)

How does Paul attack the devil's strongholds?

During World War I, the French decided to take one of the enemy's strategic strongholds. But the enemy's lines were so defended by trenches, parapets, and barbed wire that it was virtually impossible for the infantry to get through. But the attacking general had amassed a large amount of powerful artillery. He began to fire round after round of the most explosive shells at them. With this excessive strength, a continuous fire was kept up for over five hours, until all the trenches were covered, palisades thrown down, and wire entanglements blown to pieces. The infantry was then able to enter and capture the base with ease.   This incident is analogous to spiritual warfare. There are positions of the adversary that cannot be stormed or starved. There are defenses which seem impregnable. But with a barrage of constant prayer, the defenses can be lowered, and souls will be ready to surrender to the Lord. Let us be productive soldiers in the battle against sin and Satan.

P R A I S E :

P E T I T I O N :

When I pray, you answer me, and encourage me by giving me the strength I need. (Ps. 138:3)

Empty Boastings

BUT we will not boast of authority we do not have. Our goal is to measure up to God's plan for us, and this plan includes our working there with you. We are not going too far when we claim authority over you, for we were the first to come to you with the Good News concerning Christ. It is not as though we were trying to claim credit for the work someone else has done among you. Instead, we hope that your faith will grow and that, still within the limits set for us, our work among you will be greatly enlarged.

After that, we will be able to preach the Good News to other cities that are far beyond you, where no one else is working; then there will be no question about being in someone else's field. As the Scriptures say, "If anyone is going to boast, let him boast about what the Lord has done and not about himself." When someone boasts about himself and how well he has done, it doesn't count for much. But when the Lord commends him, that's different! (2 Corinthians 10:13-18)

On what basis can Paul claim authority over the Corinthians?

Pravda, the most well-known Soviet newspaper, is tightly controlled by the Communist Party of that country. The newspaper "neglects" to report anything which might reflect negatively on the USSR. It boasts that the Soviet Union is the world's most civilized country with the best possible political regime. If you were to read only *Pravda,* you would be left with the impression that the USSR is a progressive, humanitarian country that grants total freedom to its citizens. As most people know, however, *Pravda's* claims and boasts are not borne out by facts. The rest of the world knows the truth—communism in the USSR has resulted in the mass oppression of the masses and the prevalence of totalitarian injustice. We must be careful to not brag about ourselves. For if our boasting is false, we appear foolish. If we are humble, serving the Lord with gladness and diligence, someday *he* will commend us.

PRAISE:

PETITION:

We can prove the reality of prayer only by praying. (S. Eddy)

Spiritual Malpractice

I hope you will be patient with me as I keep on talking like a fool. Do bear with me and let me say what is on my heart. I am anxious for you with the deep concern of God himself—anxious that your love should be for Christ alone, just as a pure maiden saves her love for one man only, for the one who will be her husband. But I am frightened, fearing that in some way you will be led away from your pure and simple devotion to our Lord, just as Eve was deceived by Satan in the Garden of Eden. You seem so gullible: you believe whatever anyone tells you even if he is preaching about another Jesus than the one we preach, or a different spirit than the Holy Spirit you received, or shows you a different way to be saved. You swallow it all.

Yet I don't feel that these marvelous "messengers from God," as they call themselves, are any better than I am. If I am a poor speaker, at least I know what I am talking about, as I think you realize by now, for we have proved it again and again. (2 Corinthians 11:1-6)

What is Paul's concern for the Corinthian church?

The Faith Assembly Church, based near Warsaw, Indiana, has been the site of much controversy. The leader of the church has convinced his congregation that medicine and medical care are of the devil. He teaches that medicine is just another satanic substitute for faith. True Christians should not need the "crutch" of medicine, he says. As a result of this teaching, dozens of church members have died from their untreated diseases or injuries. One young mother hemorrhaged to death while another church member—an ex-nurse—passively looked on, offering no assistance and waiting for "God's will to be done." Medicine and medical treatment are gifts from God. To deny them is to reject common sense and godly wisdom. Any minister who urges a congregation to refuse medical attention is either seriously mistaken or deliberately deceptive. We must be careful of men and women who claim to be ministers but who are actually sent by Satan to create confusion.

P R A I S E :

P E T I T I O N :

Here on earth you will have many trials and sorrows; but cheer up, for I have overcome the world. (John 16:33)

The Humility of Bragging

THEY say they serve Christ? But I have served him far more! (Have I gone mad to boast like this?) I have worked harder, been put in jail oftener, been whipped times without number, and faced death again and again and again. Five different times the Jews gave me their terrible thirty-nine lashes. Three times I was beaten with rods. Once I was stoned. Three times I was shipwrecked. Once I was in the open sea all night and the whole next day.

Then, besides all this, I have the constant worry of how the churches are getting along: Who makes a mistake and I do not feel his sadness? Who falls without my longing to help him? Who is spiritually hurt without my fury rising against the one who hurt him?

But if I must brag, I would rather brag about the things that show how weak I am. God, the Father of our Lord Jesus Christ, who is to be praised forever and ever, knows I tell the truth. For instance, in Damascus the governor under King Aretas kept guards at the city gates to catch me; but I was let down by rope and basket from a hole in the city wall, and so I got away! [What popularity!] (2 Corinthians 11:23-25, 28-33)

What does Paul say he would prefer to brag about?

Paul was a humble man, and he did not like to talk about himself. He had been put in a corner by the Corinthians, however, and had to come to his own defense. He was frightened to think about what might happen to the people if they challenged his authority and began to accept heretical teachings. Paul put forth his unwilling defense in an effort to convince the people of his God-given authority. He did this with great hesitation. But when he believed it was essential for him to maintain credibility, he demonstrated no false modesty— he boldly listed all his accomplishments. He was humble enough to run the risk of appearing like a braggart. But he spoke anyway, for the sake of the kingdom.

PRAISE:

PETITION:

God gives strength to the humble. (James 4:6)

More Than Enough

I am going to boast only about how weak I am and how great God is to use such weakness for his glory. I have plenty to boast about and would be no fool in doing it, but I don't want anyone to think more highly of me than he should from what he can actually see in my life and my message.

I will say this: because these experiences I had were so tremendous, God was afraid I might be puffed up by them; so I was given a physical condition which has been a thorn in my flesh, a messenger from Satan to hurt and bother me, and prick my pride. Three different times I begged God to make me well again.

Each time he said, "No. But I am with you; that is all you need. My power shows up best in weak people." Now I am glad to boast about how weak I am; I am glad to be a living demonstration of Christ's power, instead of showing off my own power and abilities. Since I know it is all for Christ's good, I am quite happy about "the thorn," and about insults and hardships, persecutions and difficulties; for when I am weak, then I am strong—the less I have, the more I depend on him. (2 Corinthians 12:5-10)

How does Paul feel about his hardships and persecutions?

As famed British preacher Charles Spurgeon once reflected on the meaning of the verse "I am with you; that is all you need" (KJV: "My grace is sufficient for thee"), he suddenly burst out laughing. The verse seemed absurd to him. For God to say this would be like the River Thames to say to a thirsty fish, "Drink, for my waters are sufficient for you." Or for the earth to say to a panting man, "Breathe, for my oxygen is sufficient for you."   But Spurgeon later realized that, even when faced with the limitless grace of God, man can remain ignorantly unmoved. Spurgeon ended his reflection with these words: "Oh, brethren, be great believers! Little faith will bring your souls to heaven, but great faith will bring heaven to your souls."

P R A I S E :

P E T I T I O N :

Consider it a blessing when God delays the answer to your prayer in order to enlarge your capacity to receive.

Miracles of Faith

YOU have made me act like a fool—boasting like this—for you people ought to be writing about me and not making me write about myself. There isn't a single thing these other marvelous fellows have that I don't have too, even though I am really worth nothing at all. When I was there I certainly gave you every proof that I was truly an apostle, sent to you by God himself: for I patiently did many wonders and signs and mighty works among you. The only thing I didn't do for you, that I do everywhere else in all other churches, was to become a burden to you—I didn't ask you to give me food to eat and a place to stay. Please forgive me for this wrong! (2 Corinthians 12:11-13)

What was the only thing Paul did *not* do for the Corinthians?

Paul apologizes for defending himself, but again tells the Corinthians that they have forced him to do so. Then he offers a final proof of his apostleship—he says he "patiently did many wonders and signs and mighty works among [them]." This is surprising, for we don't often think of Paul as a miracle-worker. In the space below, record the most memorable miracle you have ever seen or experienced. How do you know it was truly a miracle? How has this affected your relationship with the Lord?

PRAISE:

PETITION:

Search me, O God, and know my heart; test my thoughts. (Ps. 139:23)

Unrequited Love

NOW I am coming to you again, the third time; and it is still not going to cost you anything, for I don't want your money. I want *you!* And anyway, you are my children, and little children don't pay for their father's and mother's food—it's the other way around; parents supply food for their children. I am glad to give you myself and all I have for your spiritual good, even though it seems that the more I love you, the less you love me.

Some of you are saying, "It's true that his visits didn't seem to cost us anything, but he is a sneaky fellow, that Paul, and he fooled us. As sure as anything he must have made money from us some way."

But how? Did any of the men I sent to you take advantage of you? When I urged Titus to visit you, and sent our other brother with him, did they make any profit? No, of course not. For we have the same Holy Spirit, and walk in each other's steps, doing things the same way. (2 Corinthians 12:14-18)

Does Paul believe the Corinthians love him?

Just as a father would not bill a child for living expenses, so Paul does not require any payment from the Corinthians, his spiritual children. He says he is glad to give them himself and all he has for their spiritual good. Paul is understandably hurt when he hears that some people are saying that he is trying to trick them into giving him some money. Again he defends himself. It is amazing that Paul didn't lose his patience with these fickle people. He had done everything to ensure their salvation and growth as Christians, and they repaid him with backbiting and slander. But Paul did not give up on them. Because of his humility and patience, he remained loyal to them.

P R A I S E :

P E T I T I O N :

I am with you and no one can harm you. (Acts 18:10)

Quarreling Christians

I suppose you think I am saying all this to get back into your good graces. That isn't it at all. I tell you, with God listening as I say it, that I have said this to help *you*, dear friends—to build you up spiritually and not to help myself. For I am afraid that when I come to visit you I won't like what I find, and then you won't like the way I will have to act. I am afraid that I will find you quarreling, and envying each other, and being angry with each other, and acting big, and saying wicked things about each other and whispering behind each other's backs, filled with conceit and disunity. Yes, I am afraid that when I come God will humble me before you and I will be sad and mourn because many of you who have sinned became sinners and don't even care about the wicked, impure things you have done: your lust and immorality, and the taking of other men's wives. (2 Corinthians 12:19-21)

What does Paul think he will encounter when he finally goes to Corinth?

Several missionary families lived in close quarters in a certain Latin American mission station. They held many things in common, including a large dining room where all the missionaries took their meals. Because of their constant contact with each other, frictions began to develop. Before long, major fights took place, and several people refused to come to the dining room during the regular hours. Their hard feelings toward each other affected their ministry, and soon all of the local people knew of the bickering. It didn't take long for the nationals to become disillusioned with this strange brand of bitter Christianity. Paul feared that when he finally went to Corinth he would find an unpleasant situation. He was afraid that he would encounter an atmosphere of contention and hostility. There is no reason for Christians to quarrel. This causes rifts within the church, and, worse yet, it turns people off to Christianity. As ambassadors of Christ on earth, we need to show love, not divisiveness.

PRAISE:

PETITION:

Give thanks part of the time and *live* thanks the rest of the time.

Cozy Commitment

CHECK up on yourselves. Are you really Christians? Do you pass the test? Do you feel Christ's presence and power more and more within you? Or are you just pretending to be Christians when actually you aren't at all? I hope you can agree that I have stood that test and truly belong to the Lord.

I pray that you will live good lives, not because that will be a feather in our caps, proving that what we teach is right; no, for we want you to do right even if we ourselves are despised. Our responsibility is to encourage the right at all times, not to hope for evil. We are glad to be weak and despised if you are really strong. Our greatest wish and prayer is that you will become mature Christians.

I am writing this to you now in the hope that I won't need to scold and punish when I come; for I want to use the Lord's authority which he has given me, not to punish you but to make you strong. (2 Corinthians 13:5-10)

What is Paul's greatest wish and prayer?

How can you know if you are a Christian? Contrary to what some Christians think, the certainty of salvation is not just a warm, cozy feeling inside. It is dangerous to rely on feelings. Emotions are as intangible as a summer breeze. They come and go without warning. We can be certain of our salvation through an objective review of our commitment to Christ:

- Have you accepted the basic doctrine of the gospel?
- Have you repented of your sins, asking Jesus to become the Lord of your life?
- Are you striving to live a pure life based on biblical teaching?

If you can answer yes to these questions, then you are a Christian, regardless of how you may feel at times. Remember to always remain faithful to Christ.

PRAISE:

PETITION:

Pray to the one in charge of the harvesting. (Matt. 9:38)

Seeing through Ingratitude

I close my letter with these last words:
Be happy.
Grow in Christ.
Pay attention to what I have said.
Live in harmony and peace.
And may the God of love and peace be with you.

Greet each other warmly in the Lord. All the Christians here send you their best regards. May the grace of our Lord Jesus Christ be with you all. May God's love and the Holy Spirit's friendship be yours. (2 Corinthians 13:11-14)

What is the attribute of Christ mentioned here? Of God? Of the Holy Spirit?

During the course of his ministry, Paul discovered a truth that was often evident: Those for whom we do the most, and love "most abundantly," are the ones who seem to appreciate it least and show their love least. Nevertheless, Christians should continue to love and help them. We should not depend on their gratitude to motivate us to greater love and action. Our love is solely dependent on the love of Christ being shed abroad in our hearts. This is the message of Christian maturity that Paul sought to bring to the Corinthians.

PRAISE:

PETITION:

Jehovah himself is caring for you! He is your defender. He protects you day and night. (Ps. 121:5, 6)

June EPHESIANS

To be successful, a team must be unified. It must have singleness of purpose, action, and strategy. All members must work together in harmony. ■ Ephesians was written at a time when many new churches had come into being. These churches were experiencing growing pains; there were hard feelings between Jewish and Gentile Christians. This epistle emphasizes the oneness and universality of the church. Paul wants the Christians of Ephesus to realize that, like a team, they should be unified in every way.

Future Goals

PAUL stayed in the city several days after that and then said good-bye to the Christians and sailed for the coast of Syria, taking Priscilla and Aquila with him. At Cenchreae, Paul had his head shaved according to Jewish custom, for he had taken a vow. Arriving at the port of Ephesus, he left us aboard ship while he went over to the synagogue for a discussion with the Jews. They asked him to stay for a few days, but he felt that he had no time to lose.

"I must by all means be at Jerusalem for the holiday," he said. But he promised to return to Ephesus later if God permitted; and so we set sail again. (Acts 18:18-21)

In order to learn about the founding of the church at Ephesus, we will spend four days in Acts before proceeding to Ephesians. In today's reading, what reason does Paul give for not remaining in Ephesus? What promise did he give the Ephesians?

June is the first month of summer vacation for most students. It is a month of anticipation and excitement. Many graduations occur during this month, and thousands of young couples choose to have June weddings. From where you now stand, at the onset of summer, what goals do you have for the future? Now is a good time to start thinking about them. Fill in the chart below with your personal goals. What obstacles do you need to overcome in order to accomplish them? Remember to seek God's will as you set goals.

When	Where I want to be:	What I want to be doing:
This fall		
One year		
Two years		
Five years		

PRAISE:

PETITION:

Prayer is not monologue, but dialogue; God's voice in response to mine is its most essential part. Listening to God's voice is the secret of the assurance that he will listen to mine.

On Beating a Dead Horse

THEN Paul went to the synagogue and preached boldly each Sabbath day for three months, telling what he believed and why, and persuading many to believe in Jesus. But some rejected his message and publicly spoke against Christ, so he left, refusing to preach to them again. Pulling out the believers, he began a separate meeting at the lecture hall of Tyrannus and preached there daily. This went on for the next two years, so that everyone in the Turkish province of Ausia—both Jews and Greeks—heard the Lord's message. (Acts 19:8-10)

Why did Paul stop teaching in the synagogue at Ephesus?

Paul was a persuasive evangelist; thousands came to Christ through his ministry. But although Paul had a heavy burden for the unsaved, he would go only so far in trying to convince them to repent of their sins and follow Christ. If he sensed that people had no intention of mending their ways, he wouldn't waste a lot of time with them. We see in today's passage that when an influential few rejected the message Paul preached in the synagogue, Paul realized it was pointless to continue. He left the synagogue and went somewhere else to preach.   If you have spoken to someone about Christ, but they seem to be totally uninterested, you must make a decision: Should you continue to spend time evangelizing him or her? Or should you "move on"? Remember that, regardless of your decision, you should never cease to pray for the salvation of unbelievers.

PRAISE:

PETITION:

No matter what happens, always be thankful, for this is God's will for you who belong to Christ Jesus. (1 Thess. 5:18)

Unholy Spirits

AND God gave Paul the power to do unusual miracles, so that even when his handkerchiefs or parts of his clothing were placed upon sick people, they were healed, and any demons within them came out.

A team of itinerant Jews who were traveling from town to town casting out demons planned to experiment by using the name of the Lord Jesus. The incantation they decided on was this: "I adjure you by Jesus, whom Paul preaches, to come out!" Seven sons of Sceva, a Jewish priest, were doing this. But when they tried it on a man possessed by a demon, the demon replied, "I know Jesus and I know Paul, but who are you?" And he leaped on two of them and beat them up, so that they fled out of his house naked and badly injured. (Acts 19:11-16)

In whose name were the non-Christian Jews casting out demons?

Books and other materials on the occult are growing in popularity. There are now stores that deal in nothing but occult paraphernalia. Many young people are becoming interested in astrology, witchcraft, Satan-worship, and other forms of spiritualism. Part of the new fascination with the occult is due to popular culture. Fantasy role-playing games such as Dungeons & Dragons can easily lead into unhealthy quests into the worlds of black magic and satanism. Several rock groups and singers openly promote occultism; among these are Ozzy Osbourne, Blue Oyster Cult, Judas Priest, Black Sabbath, and Kiss. The Bible categorically condemns spiritualism and the practicing of black magic. In popular culture, this would include listening to Black Sabbath and "playing" with a Ouija board. As Christians, we have the Holy Spirit in our hearts. Why should we need any other spirits?

PRAISE :

PETITION :

How great you are, Lord God! We have never heard of any other god like you. And there is no other god. (2 Sam. 7:22)

The Cult of Diana

BUT about that time, a big blowup developed in Ephesus concerning the Christians. It began with Demetrius, a silversmith who employed many craftsmen to manufacture silver shrines of the Greek goddess Diana. He called a meeting of his men, together with others employed in related trades, and addressed them as follows:

"Gentlemen, this business is our income. As you know so well from what you've seen and heard, this man Paul has persuaded many, many people that handmade gods aren't gods at all. As a result, our sales volume is going down! And this trend is evident not only here in Ephesus, but throughout the entire province! Of course, I am not only talking about the business aspects of this situation and our loss of income, but also of the possibility that the temple of the great goddess Diana will lose its influence, and that Diana—this magnificent goddess worshiped not only throughout this part of Turkey but all around the world—will be forgotten!"

At this their anger boiled and they began shouting, "Great is Diana of the Ephesians!"

A crowd began to gather and soon the city was filled with confusion. Everyone rushed to the amphitheater, dragging along Gaius and Aristarchus, Paul's traveling companions, for trial. Paul wanted to go in, but the disciples wouldn't let him. Some of the Roman officers of the province, friends of Paul, also sent a message to him, begging him not to risk his life by entering.

Inside, the people were all shouting, some one thing and some another—everything was in confusion. In fact, most of them didn't even know why they were there. (Acts 19:23-32)

Why did Demetrius hate Paul? What two things did he fear would result from Paul's ministry?

P R A I S E : _____

P E T I T I O N : _____

He will never let me stumble, slip or fall. For he is always watching, never sleeping. (Ps. 121:3)

Losing Count

DEAR Christian friends at Ephesus, ever loyal to the Lord: This is Paul writing to you, chosen by God to be Jesus Christ's messenger. May his blessings and peace be yours, sent to you from God our Father and Jesus Christ our Lord.

How we praise God, the Father of our Lord Jesus Christ, who has blessed us with every blessing in heaven because we belong to Christ.

Long ago, even before he made the world, God chose us to be his very own, through what Christ would do for us; he decided then to make us holy in his eyes, without a single fault—we who stand before him covered with his love. His unchanging plan has always been to adopt us into his own family by sending Jesus Christ to die for us. And he did this because he wanted to! (Ephesians 1:1-5)

What credentials does Paul present to his readers at the beginning of his letter?

A family was sitting together on the front porch of their home. They were enjoying the evening darkness after their supper. The youngest child, a girl of eight, looked up into the night sky and said, "I'm going to count the stars." And she started counting, beginning with the stars on her left. After a few minutes she reached three hundred, and she was still looking left. **"I** give up," she sighed. "I had no idea there were so many up there!" **We** often take our spiritual blessings for granted. But whenever we begin to count them, we, like this child, are amazed at their number.

PRAISE:

PETITION:

Prayer is not a lazy substitute for work. Sometimes God delays the answer to our prayer in final form until we have time to build up the strength, accumulate the knowledge, or fashion the character that would make it possible for him to say "yes" to what we ask.

The Crooked Path

NOW all praise to God for his wonderful kindness to us and his favor that he has poured out upon us, because we belong to his dearly loved Son. So overflowing is his kindness toward us that he took away all our sins through the blood of his Son, by whom we are saved. (Ephesians 1:6, 7)

Through what did God take away our sins?

A man walked across the desolate Valley of Dead Men in New Zealand's South Island. Looking back over his way, he saw his tracks in the sand and how crooked his path had been, though he had intended to walk straight. He thought, "This is my life. Every footprint crooked." Then the man fell asleep. When he awakened hours later, he could see no marks on the sand. Every footprint was gone—not one to be seen. The wind had leveled them; there was no record of his crooked path. He said to himself, "This is a fresh reminder of what God has done for me."

PRAISE :

PETITION :

The Lord is faithful to his promises. Blessed are those who wait for him to help them. (Isa. 30:18)

Programmed to Worship

AND he has showered down upon us the richness of his grace—for how well he understands us and knows what is best for us at all times.

God has told us his secret reason for sending Christ, a plan he decided on in mercy long ago; and this was his purpose: that when the time is ripe he will gather us all together from wherever we are—in heaven or on earth—to be with him in Christ, forever. Moreover, because of what Christ has done we have become gifts to God that he delights in, for as part of God's sovereign plan we were chosen from the beginning to be his, and all things happen just as he decided long ago. God's purpose in this was that we should praise God and give glory to him for doing these mighty things for us, who were the first to trust in Christ. (Ephesians 1:8-12)

What was God's "secret reason" for sending Christ to earth?

God could have chosen to create a race of mindless droids which would inhabit the earth, praising him twenty-four hours a day. Instead, he created man. He gave to man the priceless gift of free will. Men do not have to praise God if they choose not to. But when they do praise him, God's joy is abundant, for he knows that such worship springs from sincere, convicted, loving hearts. To God, no voice of praise is insignificant; to him, men's praises sound sweeter than the singing of the angels.

PRAISE:

PETITION:

Through Christ, all the kindness of God has been poured out upon us undeserving sinners. (Rom. 1:5)

Marking Logs

AND because of what Christ did, all you others too, who heard the Good News about how to be saved, and trusted Christ, were marked as belonging to Christ by the Holy Spirit, who long ago had been promised to all of us Christians. His presence within us is God's guarantee that he really will give us all that he promised; and the Spirit's seal upon us means that God has already purchased us and that he guarantees to bring us to himself. This is just one more reason for us to praise our glorious God. (Ephesians 1:13, 14)

What confirms the truth of God's promises?

Corinth and Ephesus were great centers of the lumber industry. Large rafts of logs would be brought in from the Black Sea, and different lumber firms would be notified that the lumber was in the harbor. The men from each firm would pay earnest money on the logs of their choice and cut their special identifying wedge onto each log. This was the seal of ownership. The logs might stay in the water for several weeks, but eventually they were redeemed by the owners. So Christ has put his seal on us; one day he will redeem his chosen people!

P R A I S E :

P E T I T I O N :

Answer quickly when I cry to you; bend low and hear my whispered plea. (Ps. 31:2)

A Multitude of Crowds

THAT is why, ever since I heard of your strong faith in the Lord Jesus and of the love you have for Christians everywhere, I have never stopped thanking God for you. I pray for you constantly, asking God, the glorious Father of our Lord Jesus Christ, to give you wisdom to see clearly and really understand who Christ is and all that he has done for you. I pray that your hearts will be flooded with light so that you can see something of the future he has called you to share. I want you to realize that God has been made rich because we who are Christ's have been given to him! I pray that you will begin to understand how incredibly great his power is to help those who believe him. It is that same mighty power that raised Christ from the dead and seated him in the place of honor at God's right hand in heaven, far, far above any other king or ruler or dictator or leader. Yes, his honor is far more glorious than that of anyone else either in this world or in the world to come. And God has put all things under his feet and made him the supreme Head of the Church—which is his body, filled with himself, the Author and Giver of everything everywhere. (Ephesians 1:15-23)

What was Paul's first request to God on behalf of the Ephesians?

Think of the people who receive the greatest honor and adulation these days. There is the pope, who draws throngs of people wherever he goes. There are the rock supergroups—such as the Police, the Rolling Stones, the Beach Boys, and Journey—which attract many thousands to their concerts. There are political leaders who live under the eyes of the worldwide media attention. There are sports heroes, loved and venerated by thousands, even millions, of fans.   But all the honor ever bestowed upon humans will be as nothing when compared to the praise and worship God will ultimately receive. As Paul says here, "His honor is far more glorious than that of anyone else either in this world or in the world to come."

P R A I S E :

P E T I T I O N :

Hem your blessings with praise, lest they unravel.

The Free Lunch

ONCE you were under God's curse, doomed forever for your sins. You went along with the crowd and were just like all the others, full of sin, obeying Satan, the mighty prince of the power of the air, who is at work right now in the hearts of those who are against the Lord. All of us used to be just as they are, our lives expressing the evil within us, doing every wicked thing that our passions or our evil thoughts might lead us into. We started out bad, being born with evil natures, and were under God's anger just like everyone else.

But God is so rich in mercy; he loved us so much that even though we were spiritually dead and doomed by our sins, he gave us back our lives again when he raised Christ from the dead—only by his undeserved favor have we ever been saved—and lifted us up from the grave into glory along with Christ, where we sit with him in the heavenly realms—all because of what Christ Jesus did. And now God can always point to us as examples of how very, very rich his kindness is, as shown in all he has done for us through Jesus Christ. (Ephesians 2:1-7)

Fill in the blank: God can point to us as examples of his _____ .

An often-used phrase these days is: "There's no such thing as a free lunch." This refers to the fact that nothing on earth can be obtained for free, no strings attached. Recipients of favors, for example, feel they must "repay" their benefactors with similar favors or simply with a grateful attitude. Free merchandise is given away in order to encourage people to become paying customers. The list goes on. . . . But for Christians, there *is* indeed a "free lunch." It is salvation through Christ. There is nothing we can do to merit it. Salvation is not only something for nothing; it is *everything* for nothing.

P R A I S E :

P E T I T I O N :

The Lord will guide continually, and satisfy you with all good things, and keep you healthy too. (Isa. 58:11)

The Rejected Best

BECAUSE of his kindness you have been saved through trusting Christ. And even trusting is not of yourselves; it too is a gift from God. Salvation is not a reward for the good we have done, so none of us can take any credit for it. It is God himself who has made us what we are and given us new lives from Christ Jesus; and long ages ago he planned that we should spend these lives in helping others. (Ephesians 2:8-10)

Is salvation a reward for our good works? Explain.

A certain evangelist was sitting in a barber's chair waiting for a shave. While the barber was sharpening his razor, the evangelist asked, "Sir, are you saved?" **"I** am doing the best I can, and that's enough, isn't it?" was the barber's stock answer. The evangelist was silent until after he was shaven and the next customer was in the chair. Then the evangelist grabbed the razor and said, "Let me shave this customer." **"O**h, no," protested the barber, "not you." **"B**ut," said the evangelist, "I would do my very best." **"Y**our best would not be good enough for this customer." The evangelist laid down the razor and said, "Neither is your best good enough for God."

PRAISE:

PETITION:

God is my strong fortress; he has made me safe. (2 Sam. 22:33)

Love and Death

FOR Christ himself is our way of peace. He has made peace between us Jews and you Gentiles by making us all one family, breaking down the wall of contempt that used to separate us. By his death he ended the angry resentment between us, caused by the Jewish laws which favored the Jews and excluded the Gentiles, for he died to annul that whole system of Jewish laws. Then he took the two groups that had been opposed to each other and made them parts of himself; thus he fused us together to become one new person, and at last there was peace. As parts of the same body, our anger against each other has disappeared, for both of us have been reconciled to God. And so the feud ended at last at the cross. And he has brought this Good News of peace to you Gentiles who were very far away from him, and to us Jews who were near. Now all of us, whether Jews or Gentiles, may come to God the Father with the Holy Spirit's help because of what Christ has done for us. (Ephesians 2:14-18)

How did Christ make peace between the Jews and the Gentiles?

Shakespeare's great tragedy *Romeo and Juliet* is a play about the strength of love over hatred. As the storyline goes, the young lovers come from families that bitterly hate each other. They must keep their love secret or suffer the terrible consequences of their families' wrath. They go to such lengths to hide their romance that a great tragedy occurs; both Romeo and Juliet meet their deaths. Only through this calamity do the opposing families see the folly of their feuding, and are reconciled to each other.   In a greater story, the Son of God offered his life so that we humans might be reconciled to him and to each other in love. "The feud ended at last at the cross."

P R A I S E :

P E T I T I O N :

I have lived to thank God that all of my prayers have not been answered. (J. Ingelow)

Gone with the Mice

NOW you are no longer strangers to God and foreigners to heaven, but you are members of God's very own family, citizens of God's country, and you belong in God's household with every other Christian.

What a foundation you stand on now: the apostles and the prophets; and the cornerstone of the building is Jesus Christ himself! We who believe are carefully joined together with Christ as parts of a beautiful, constantly growing temple for God. And you also are joined with him and with each other by the Spirit, and are part of this dwelling place of God. (Ephesians 2:19-22)

What is the "cornerstone" of the church?

An elderly woman thought she was a Christian because she had a church membership certificate. She believed her salvation rested on that old piece of paper. One day as she was cleaning she discovered that mice had gotten into her cabinet and had eaten the certificate. She lamented, "Oh, no! I'm no longer a Christian!" Though Paul emphasized the importance of the church, he never gave any reason to believe that salvation is connected to church membership.

PRAISE:

PETITION:

He will listen to the prayers of the destitute, for he is never too busy to heed their requests. (Ps. 102:17)

The Beauty of Truth

I Paul, the servant of Christ, am here in jail because of you—for preaching that you Gentiles are a part of God's house. No doubt you already know that God has given me this special work of showing God's favor to you Gentiles, as I briefly mentioned before in one of my letters. God himself showed me this secret plan of his, that the Gentiles, too, are included in his kindness. I say this to explain to you how I know about these things. In olden times God did not share this plan with his people, but now he has revealed it by the Holy Spirit to his apostles and prophets.

And this is the secret: that the Gentiles will have their full share with the Jews in all the riches inherited by God's sons; both are invited to belong to his Church, and all of God's promises of mighty blessings through Christ apply to them both when they accept the Good News about Christ and what he has done for them. (Ephesians 3:1-6)

Paul was a prisoner in Rome when he wrote the Ephesians. What was the reason for his imprisonment?

Presbyterian minister Clarence E. Macartney once wrote these words: "When young Timothy was pastor at Ephesus, he often passed on his pastoral rounds the great temple of Diana. The sight of that great building with the sun reflecting from its structure reminded him that he was the minister of a grander temple, the temple of Christian truth, for the church of the living God is the pillar and ground of truth." The beauty of God's church is in its truth, not necessarily in its physical structure.

P R A I S E :

P E T I T I O N :

When you pray, don't be like the hypocrites who pretend piety by praying publicly on street corners and in the synagogues where everyone can see them. Truly, that is all the reward they will ever get. (Matt. 6:5)

Homicidal Judge

GOD has given me the wonderful privilege of telling everyone about this plan of his; and he has given me his power and special ability to do it well.

Just think! Though I did nothing to deserve it, and though I am the most useless Christian there is, yet I was the one chosen for this special joy of telling the Gentiles the Glad News of the endless treasures available to them in Christ; and to explain to everyone that God is the Savior of the Gentiles too, just as he who made all things had secretly planned from the very beginning.

And his reason? To show to all the rulers in heaven how perfectly wise he is when all of his family—Jews and Gentiles alike—are seen to be joined together in his Church, in just the way he had always planned it through Jesus Christ our Lord.

Now we can come fearlessly right into God's presence, assured of his glad welcome when we come with Christ and trust in him. (Ephesians 3:7-12)

What responsibility has God given to Paul?

King Lubengula was a much-feared chief of an African tribe. Besides being the ruler, he was also the supreme judge. He held his court upon the top of a steep hill. Once a prisoner was being brought before him. As the guards led him up the slope, the king lifted his rifle and shot the prisoner dead—not even waiting to hear the charges. Men would come to this savage king crawling fearfully along, their faces pale with terror.   Judgments by men are sometimes unfair, but we may have boldness to come before God through the blood of Jesus Christ.

P R A I S E :

P E T I T I O N :

We pray as we live; we live as we pray.

More Is Less

SO please don't lose heart at what they are doing to me here. It is for you I am suffering and you should feel honored and encouraged.

When I think of the wisdom and scope of his plan I fall down on my knees and pray to the Father of all the great family of God—some of them already in heaven and some down here on earth—that out of his glorious, unlimited resources he will give you the mighty inner strengthening of his Holy Spirit. And I pray that Christ will be more and more at home in your hearts, living within you as you trust in him. May your roots go down deep into the soil of God's marvelous love; and may you be able to feel and understand, as all God's children should, how long, how wide, how deep, and how high his love really is; and to experience this love for yourselves, though it is so great that you will never see the end of it or fully know or understand it. And so at last you will be filled up with God himself.

Now glory be to God who by his mighty power at work within us is able to do far more than we would ever dare to ask or even dream of—infinitely beyond our highest prayers, desires, thoughts, or hopes. May he be given glory forever and ever through endless ages because of his master plan of salvation for the Church through Jesus Christ. (Ephesians 3:13-21)

What will Christians ultimately be filled with?

A wise old scholar once told a reporter that the more he discovers, the more ignorant he feels. This statement might appear illogical at first; but the man meant merely that the more he finds out about our world and the universe, the more he realizes that there are vast areas of knowledge beyond his scope or comprehension. Even the most brilliant of minds cannot contain more than an infinitesimal amount of the sum total of all knowledge. **P**aul presents a paradox in this passage when he says we are to know the love of Christ which is beyond comprehension. But although we can never attain perfect understanding of Christ's love, we are to seek to know it as deeply as possible.

P R A I S E :

P E T I T I O N :

All those who listen to my instructions and follow them are wise, like a man who builds his house on solid rock. (Matt. 7:24)

Daily Walk

I beg of you—I, a prisoner here in jail for serving the Lord—to live and act in a way worthy of those who have been chosen for such wonderful blessings as these. Be humble and gentle. Be patient with each other, making allowance for each other's faults because of your love. Try always to be led along together by the Holy Spirit, and so be at peace with one another.

We are all parts of one body, we have the same Spirit, and we have all been called to the same glorious future. For us there is only one Lord, one faith, one baptism, and we all have the same God and Father who is over us all and in us all, and living through every part of us. (Ephesians 4:1-6)

List the requests and suggestions that Paul makes to the Ephesians.

The first three chapters of Ephesians deal with Christian doctrine. Starting with chapter four, though, the emphasis shifts to another area. In chapters four through six, Paul offers advice and direction to people who want to live godly lives. As you read these chapters, evaluate your own life. In your daily walk, how close are you to Christ's footsteps?

P R A I S E :

P E T I T I O N :

Hold me safe above the heads of all my enemies; then I can continue to obey all your laws. (Ps. 119:117)

Alexander's Gift

HOWEVER, Christ has given each of us special abilities—whatever he wants us to have out of his rich storehouse of gifts.

The Psalmist tells about this, for he says that when Christ returned triumphantly to heaven after his resurrection and victory over Satan, he gave generous gifts to men. Notice that it says he returned to heaven. This means that he had first come down from the heights of heaven, far down to the lowest parts of the earth. The same one who came down is the one who went back up, that he might fill all things everywhere with himself, from the very lowest to the very highest.

Some of us have been given special ability as apostles; to others he has given the gift of being able to preach well; some have special ability in winning people to Christ, helping them to trust him as their Savior; still others have a gift for caring for God's people as a shepherd does his sheep, leading and teaching them in the ways of God.

Why is it that he gives us these special abilities to do certain things best? It is that God's people will be equipped to do better work for him, building up the Church, the body of Christ, to a position of strength and maturity; until finally we all believe alike about our salvation and about our Savior, God's Son, and all become full-grown in the Lord—yes, to the point of being filled full with Christ. (Ephesians 4:7-13)

Do all Christians have the same gifts? Explain.

Alexander the Great once wanted to honor one of his faithful servants. He called together his entire household, and asked the servant to come up beside him. Alexander said a few words of appreciation, then presented the man with an expensive gold cup.   "But Emperor," protested the servant, "this is too much for me to take." The emperor replied, "That may be so, but it isn't too much for me to give."   The gifts of the Spirit are second only to the gift of the Spirit himself, the greatest gift ever given to the believer. Thank God for his gift!

P R A I S E :

P E T I T I O N :

Failure to pray is failure along the whole line of life. It is failure of duty, service, and spiritual progress.

Doctrine of Love

THEN we will no longer be like children, forever changing our minds about what we believe because someone has told us something different, or has cleverly lied to us and made the lie sound like the truth. Instead, we will lovingly follow the truth at all times—speaking truly, dealing truly, living truly—and so become more and more in every way like Christ who is the Head of his body, the Church. Under his direction the whole body is fitted together perfectly, and each part in its own special way helps the other parts, so that the whole body is healthy and growing and full of love. (Ephesians 4:14-16)

To what does Paul compare Christ and the church?

"Paul here emphasizes the importance of doctrine. Believers who are doctrinally ignorant can be led astray easily. Every Christian should be acquainted with the great doctrines of the faith. Some people say: doctrine divides; love unites or brings peace. Peace without right doctrinal agreement will destroy the foundations of the faith; right doctrine without love can be mere formalism. Right doctrine and love should go hand in hand." (From *Lindsell Study Bible*, Tyndale)

P R A I S E :

P E T I T I O N :

I will cleanse away your sins. (Ezek. 36:29)

New Men

LET me say this, then, speaking for the Lord: Live no longer as the unsaved do, for they are blinded and confused. Their closed hearts are full of darkness; they are far away from the life of God because they have shut their minds against him, and they cannot understand his ways. They don't care anymore about right and wrong and have given themselves over to impure ways. They stop at nothing, being driven by their evil minds and reckless lusts.

But that isn't the way Christ taught you! If you have really heard his voice and learned from him the truths concerning himself, then throw off your old evil nature—the old you that was a partner in your evil ways—rotten through and through, full of lust and sham.

Now your attitudes and thoughts must all be constantly changing for the better. Yes, you must be a new and different person, holy and good. Clothe yourself with this new nature. (Ephesians 4:17-24)

Why are the unsaved far away from the life of God?

When we become Christians, we are called to more than just a few new steps in life. We are expected to accumulate more than some new habits, ways, motives, or prospects. We are called to an entirely new life. This "new life" is not merely the old life retouched. It is not a broken column repaired, a soiled picture cleaned, a defaced inscription restored. The Christian is a new creation, born again. He is a new man.

I am the Vine; you are the branches. Whoever lives in me and I in him shall produce a large crop of fruit. (John 15:5)

The Pain of Hate

STOP lying to each other; tell the truth, for we are parts of each other and when we lie to each other we are hurting ourselves. If you are angry, don't sin by nursing your grudge. Don't let the sun go down with you still angry—get over it quickly; for when you are angry you give a mighty foothold to the devil.

If anyone is stealing he must stop it and begin using those hands of his for honest work so he can give to others in need. Don't use bad language. Say only what is good and helpful to those you are talking to, and what will give them a blessing.

Don't cause the Holy Spirit sorrow by the way you live. Remember, he is the one who marks you to be present on that day when salvation from sin will be complete.

Stop being mean, bad-tempered and angry. Quarreling, harsh words, and dislike of others should have no place in your lives. Instead, be kind to each other, tenderhearted, forgiving one another, just as God has forgiven you because you belong to Christ. (Ephesians 4:25-32)

According to this passage, why has God forgiven us?

An interview with the brother of a murdered policeman recently appeared in the *Chicago Tribune.* Although the murder had occurred four years prior to the interview, the brother demonstrated no trace of forgiveness toward the killers. "I smile whenever I think of their sweaty, smelly bodies rotting away in jail," he said. "That's the only thought that gives me any comfort." The man had obviously suffered because of his feelings of revenge and hatred. A man full of hate cannot have peace. As Paul says in today's reading, "When you are angry you give a mighty foothold to the devil." As difficult as it may sometimes be, we should strive to forgive others as our Father in heaven has forgiven us.

P R A I S E :

P E T I T I O N :

Put your thanksgiving into the present tense. It's a sure cure for grumbling.

Holy High

FOLLOW God's example in everything you do just as a much loved child imitates his father. Be full of love for others, following the example of Christ who loved you and gave himself to God as a sacrifice to take away your sins. And God was pleased, for Christ's love for you was like sweet perfume to him.

Let there be no sex sin, impurity or greed among you. Let no one be able to accuse you of any such things. Dirty stories, foul talk and coarse jokes—these are not for you. Instead, remind each other of God's goodness and be thankful.

You can be sure of this: The Kingdom of Christ and of God will never belong to anyone who is impure or greedy, for a greedy person is really an idol worshiper—he loves and worships the good things of this life more than God. Don't be fooled by those who try to excuse these sins, for the terrible wrath of God is upon all those who do them. Don't even associate with such people. (Ephesians 5:1-7)

To what does Paul compare Christ's love?

Evangelist Lehman Strauss relates that one summer at a Bible conference where he was speaking, he had exhorted the people about the fact that Christians don't often talk about the things of the Lord when they are together casually. He told them how the early Christians used to greet one another by saying, "Maranatha" ("the Lord cometh"). The next day as Dr. Strauss was walking to the meeting, he noticed two old ladies along the side of the path leading to the tabernacle. One whispered to the other, "There goes the preacher who scolded us for the way we talk. Let's go the other way." The other lady replied, "No, I'm going to greet him." She walked up to Dr. Strauss, and raising her hand, said, "Marijuana!"

P R A I S E :

P E T I T I O N :

O Lord, I have longed for your salvation, and your law is my delight. (Ps. 119:174)

A Significant Nothing

FOR though once your heart was full of darkness, now it is full of light from the Lord, and your behavior should show it! Because of this light within you, you should do only what is good and right and true.

Learn as you go along what pleases the Lord. Take no part in the worthless pleasures of evil and darkness, but instead, rebuke and expose them. It would be shameful even to mention here those pleasures of darkness which the ungodly do. But when you expose them, the light shines in upon their sin and shows it up, and when they see how wrong they really are, some of them may even become children of light! That is why God says in the Scriptures, "Awake, O sleeper, and rise up from the dead; and Christ shall give you light." (Ephesians 5:8-14)

As Christians, what should be evident from our behavior?

The storming of the Bastille, the government prison in Paris, on July 14, 1789, was the first significant act of the populace in the French Revolution. In this revolution, the monarchy was overthrown and the king, Louis XVI, lost his life. Yet Louis was so blind to the signs of the times that he wrote in his diary at the close of July 14, 1789, the one French word, "Rien," meaning that nothing had happened that day. By all means, let us who are awake and who are children of light be aware of the urgency of this hour!

PRAISE:

PETITION:

If you want to know what God wants you to do, ask him, and he will gladly tell you. (James 1:5)

Christian Alcoholism

SO be careful how you act; these are difficult days. Don't be fools; be wise: make the most of every opportunity you have for doing good. Don't act thoughtlessly, but try to find out and do whatever the Lord wants you to. Don't drink too much wine, for many evils lie along that path; be filled instead with the Holy Spirit, and controlled by him.

Talk with each other much about the Lord, quoting psalms and hymns and singing sacred songs, making music in your hearts to the Lord. Always give thanks for everything to our God and Father in the name of our Lord Jesus Christ. (Ephesians 5:15-20)

What does Paul say about drinking "too much wine"?

Drunkenness is one of the greatest social evils of our time. Every year thousands of people die in accidents caused by drunks. And there are millions of people who have let drinking destroy their relationships and careers. Casualties of alcohol lie all around us. Young people under the legal drinking age are consuming more alcohol than ever. *Christianity Today* has reported that an increasing number of Christians are suffering from alcoholism. Excessive alcohol deprives us of our minds; it robs us of our very selves. Paul says it is immoral to be drunk; we should seek instead to be filled with the Holy Spirit.

PRAISE :

PETITION :

God's promises are like giant corpses without life, only to decay and turn to dust, unless men claim these promises by sincere prayer.

The Submission Question

HONOR Christ by submitting to each other. You wives must submit to your husbands' leadership in the same way you submit to the Lord. For a husband is in charge of his wife in the same way Christ is in charge of his body the Church. (He gave his very life to take care of it and be its Savior!) So you wives must willingly obey your husbands in everything, just as the Church obeys Christ. (Ephesians 5:21-24)

To what is the husband's leadership over the wife compared?

Much of Paul's specific commands in the epistles must be considered in light of cultural context. For example, today we don't have to worry about wearing appropriate head coverings or eating the meat offered to idols. But what about today's passage? Should it be taken literally? Most evangelical leaders would say yes, it should. They say that these verses contain a universal principle, not a cultural one. The husband should be the head of the home, and the wife should be submissive to him. This is hard for many modern women to swallow, for this command appears to undermine the equality of women. Nevertheless, Paul's words are clear. There seems to be no ambiguity about them. What do you think? What is the role of women in the home, and in the church?

P R A I S E :

P E T I T I O N :

We cannot imagine the power of the Almighty, and yet he is so just and merciful that he does not destroy us. (Job 37:23)

Love in Action

AND you husbands, show the same kind of love to your wives as Christ showed to the Church when he died for her, to make her holy and clean, washed by baptism and God's Word; so that he could give her to himself as a glorious Church without a single spot or wrinkle or any other blemish, being holy and without a single fault. That is how husbands should treat their wives, loving them as parts of themselves. For since a man and his wife are now one, a man is really doing himself a favor and loving himself when he loves his wife! No one hates his own body but lovingly cares for it, just as Christ cares for his body the Church, of which we are parts.

(That the husband and wife are one body is proved by the Scripture which says, "A man must leave his father and mother when he marries, so that he can be perfectly joined to his wife, and the two shall be one.") I know this is hard to understand, but it is an illustration of the way we are parts of the body of Christ.

So again I say, a man must love his wife as a part of himself; and the wife must see to it that she deeply respects her husband—obeying, praising and honoring him. (Ephesians 5:25-33)

How should husbands love their wives?

Yesterday's Bible reading is one that creates a lot of controversy. Today's, though it is a continuation of Paul's words to wives and husbands, hardly raises any eyebrows at all. Everyone agrees that husbands should love their wives. Although you are probably unmarried, now is a good time to start thinking about love in marriage. Think of the married couples you know. Which ones seem to demonstrate a lot of love? How do you recognize this love? As in many aspects of life, in love, actions speak louder than words. Helping a wife with the dishes is equivalent to one hundred whispered "I love you's." Although emotions are important in marriage, the strongest evidence of love is action. When a man commits himself to his wife and to the institution of marriage, he is truly loving his wife as part of himself.

P R A I S E :

P E T I T I O N :

The Lord watches over all the plans and paths of godly men, but the paths of the godless lead to doom. (Ps. 1:6)

Parent Honor

CHILDREN, obey your parents; this is the right thing to do because God has placed them in authority over you. Honor your father and mother. This is the first of God's Ten Commandments that ends with a promise. And this is the promise: that if you honor your father and mother, yours will be a long life, full of blessing.

And now a word to you parents. Don't keep on scolding and nagging your children, making them angry and resentful. Rather, bring them up with the loving discipline the Lord himself approves, with suggestions and godly advice. (Ephesians 6:1-4)

What does God promise to children who honor their parents?

A gang of young boys was bent on doing mischief. They wanted to break into an abandoned home, go to the second floor, and throw the old bathtub down the stairs. One of the boys was unwilling to go along. The others chided him by saying, "You're just afraid that if your father finds out, he'll hurt you. Sissy!" The boy, who had been raised in a Christian home, replied, "No, I'm only afraid that if he found out, *I* would hurt *him*."

P R A I S E :

P E T I T I O N :

A grateful thought toward heaven is a complete prayer.

Modern Slavery

SLAVES, obey your masters; be eager to give them your very best. Serve them as you would Christ. Don't work hard only when your master is watching and then shirk when he isn't looking; work hard and with gladness all the time, as though working for Christ, doing the will of God with all your hearts. Remember, the Lord will pay you for each good thing you do, whether you are slave or free.

And you slave owners must treat your slaves right, just as I have told them to treat you. Don't keep threatening them; remember, you yourselves are slaves to Christ; you have the same Master they do, and he has no favorites. (Ephesians 6:5-9)

According to this passage, how should we serve our "masters"?

In the late seventies a country singer with the unlikely name of Johnny Paycheck released a hit song called, "Take This Job and Shove It." At about the same time, the movie *9 to 5* was released; it was about three female office workers who get back at their nasty boss. It was a blockbuster. Such entertainment was produced as harmless satire on the modern work world. But it accurately reflects a current trend in our society—the trend toward self-fulfillment and away from all those who would impose "limitations" upon us. This includes parents, teachers, employers, and the clergy. **"S**laves, obey your masters" might today be paraphrased, "Employees, obey your employers." It is honorable to treat our bosses with respect and obedience. As Paul has said elsewhere, all authority comes from God himself.

P R A I S E :

P E T I T I O N :

For the Lord is watching his children, listening to their prayers. (1 Pet. 3:12)

Invisible Armor

LAST of all I want to remind you that your strength must come from the Lord's mighty power within you. Put on all of God's armor so that you will be able to stand safe against all strategies and tricks of Satan. For we are not fighting against people made of flesh and blood, but against persons without bodies—the evil rulers of the unseen world, those mighty satanic beings and great evil princes of darkness who rule this world; and against huge numbers of wicked spirits in the spirit world.

So use every piece of God's armor to resist the enemy whenever he attacks, and when it is all over, you will still be standing up.

But to do this, you will need the strong belt of truth and the breastplate of God's approval. Wear shoes that are able to speed you on as you preach the Good News of peace with God. In every battle you will need faith as your shield to stop the fiery arrows aimed at you by Satan. And you will need the helmet of salvation and the sword of the Spirit—which is the Word of God. (Ephesians 6:10-17)

List the six pieces of equipment that constitute a Christian's armor.

J. R. R. Tolkien's trilogy, *The Lord of the Rings,* is a popular fantasy series. A central element in the books is a coveted ring which, when slipped onto a finger, renders the wearer invisible. Many forces struggle to possess the ring. They want it not for the value of its gold, but for its magic. They know that, with the power of invisibility, they can get or do whatever they desire. It is frightening to think that we, as Christians, are continually doing battle with the evil rulers of the unseen world. If it were not for the protection of God's impenetrable armor, we would all be lost.

P R A I S E :

P E T I T I O N :

Let all the joys of the godly well up in praise to the Lord, for it is right to praise him. (Ps. 33:1)

The Pieces of Prayer

PRAY all the time. Ask God for anything in line with the Holy Spirit's wishes. Plead with him, reminding him of your needs, and keep praying earnestly for all Christians everywhere. Pray for me, too, and ask God to give me the right words as I boldly tell others about the Lord, and as I explain to them that his salvation is for the Gentiles too. I am in chains now for preaching this message from God. But pray that I will keep on speaking out boldly for him even here in prison, as I should.

Tychicus, who is a much loved brother and faithful helper in the Lord's work, will tell you all about how I am getting along. I am sending him to you for just this purpose, to let you know how we are and be encouraged by his report.

May God give peace to you, my Christian brothers, and love, with faith from God the Father and the Lord Jesus Christ. May God's grace and blessing be upon all who sincerely love our Lord Jesus Christ. (Ephesians 6:18-24)

How does Paul want the Ephesians to pray for him?

How to pray is a question each Christian must decide for himself. There is no secret formula or prescribed method. A careful study of the Bible shows us that there are certain elements which should be incorporated into our prayers, regardless of our method of praying. These are the following: worship of God, gratitude and thanksgiving, confession of sins, petition (on behalf of self), and intercession (on behalf of others). On certain days, thanksgiving may outweigh the other elements; on others, petition and intercession may be most prominent. But in our walk with Christ, and in our communication with him, all the elements of prayer should be exercised regularly.

P R A I S E :

P E T I T I O N :

Those who always pray are necessary to those who never pray. (V. Hugo)

EXOTICAR, BENSENVILLE, IL

July PHILIPPIANS

The treasures of this world are tempting. It is easy to fantasize about owning an expensive sports car, or state-of-the-art stereo equipment, or a luxurious yacht, or diamond jewelry. . . . These things can entrance and mesmerize those who crave the material treasures of life. ▪ Philippians is a letter about treasures. It is rich with descriptions of the good life. But Paul's idea of the good life is the "God life." From a lonely prison cell, Paul writes of his intention to accumulate wealth. His treasures, however, will be stored in heaven, not on earth.

The Lonely Million

FROM: Paul and Timothy, slaves of Jesus Christ.

To: The pastors and deacons and all the Christians in the city of Philippi.

May God bless you all. Yes, I pray that God our Father and the Lord Jesus Christ will give each of you his fullest blessings, and his peace in your hearts and your lives. (Philippians 1:1, 2)

To whom does Paul write this epistle?

Suppose that someone with a cashier's check for one million dollars were to say, "I will give this check to the first person who will accept it on my terms. The person who takes it may keep all the money and buy with it anything he or she desires. You are not restricted to any commodity or to any condition—except one. Promptly after spending all his money, you must go to live in a place where you will never again see or talk to another human being." **H**ow many would come to take the money? Perhaps a few antisocial cynics would jump at the chance. But all things being equal, most people would not sacrifice the fellowship of the human race even for a million dollars. **P**aul has not seen the people to whom he writes for over ten years. Yet the letter he writes to them is an example of the greatest fellowship of all—the fellowship within the body of Christ.

PRAISE:

PETITION:

There is nothing that makes us love a man so much as praying for him. (W. Law)

Desire for Growth

ALL my prayers for you are full of praise to God! When I pray for you, my heart is full of joy, because of all your wonderful help in making known the Good News about Christ from the time you first heard it until now. And I am sure that God who began the good work within you will keep right on helping you grow in his grace until his task within you is finally finished on that day when Jesus Christ returns.

How natural it is that I should feel as I do about you, for you have a very special place in my heart. We have shared together the blessings of God, both when I was in prison and when I was out, defending the truth and telling others about Christ. (Philippians 1:3-7)

How would you describe Paul's attitude in this passage?

The fact that you are reading this devotional book means that you are interested in developing and maintaining a close relationship with the Lord. You are probably seeking new depth in your spiritual life. God honors such dedication and diligence, and he truly desires to help his children to "grow in his grace." Although it is critically important for us to receive Christ's salvation, growth in wisdom and spirituality is essential as well. We are responsible not only for our own salvation, but also for the spiritual development necessary for leading others to Christ.

P R A I S E :

P E T I T I O N :

O Lord God of Israel, sitting on your throne high above the angels, you alone are the God of all the kingdoms of the earth. (2 Kings 19:15)

Mixing Sex and Love

ONLY God knows how deep is my love and longing for you—with the tenderness of Jesus Christ. My prayer for you is that you will over-flow more and more with love for others, and at the same time keep on growing in spiritual knowledge and insight, for I want you always to see clearly the difference between right and wrong, and to be inwardly clean, no one being able to criticize you from now until our Lord returns. May you always be doing those good, kind things which show that you are a child of God, for this will bring much praise and glory to the Lord. (Philippians 1:8-11)

What is Paul's prayer for the Philippians?

In popular culture the term "love" has become a synonym for *sex*. People refer to having sex as "making love." Partners in illicit sex are called "lovers." And popular songs with sexual overtones bear such titles as "Love to Love You, Baby," "Love the One You're With," and "Love Me Tender." The true meaning of love has been blurred by abuse and misuse. We now feel compelled to define the term every time we use it.   When Paul prays that the Philippians "will overflow more and more with love for others," he is talking about pure love, the kind of love that includes self-denial, compassion, and charity. Paul demon-strated his love for the churches by giving them his time, energy, and lifeblood. We should strive to commit our love to the cause of Christ.

P R A I S E :

P E T I T I O N :

The earnest prayer of a righteous man has great power and wonderful results. (James 5:16)

Joy in Chains

AND I want you to know this, dear brothers: Everything that has happened to me here has been a great boost in getting out the Good News concerning Christ. For everyone around here, including all the soldiers over at the barracks, knows that I am in chains simply because I am a Christian. And because of my imprisonment many of the Christians here seem to have lost their fear of chains! Somehow my patience has encouraged them and they have become more and more bold in telling others about Christ. (Philippians 1:12-14)

What good has come about through Paul's imprisonment?

Paul has a remarkable attitude throughout this epistle. He is suffering in prison, yet his ecstasy at being a Christian shines through as if he were in heaven itself. He could have started this episode with a sob story about the lousy prison conditions with its inadequate food supply, brutal guards, and infestation of rats. He could have made the Philippians feel sorry for him. But the pure joy of knowing Christ is much greater than all these hardships. He rejoices that his enthusiasm and patience have encouraged other Christians in prison.   What an example for us! A reading of Philippians should be enough to lift the spirits of any downhearted Christian.

P R A I S E :

P E T I T I O N :

I will be glad, yes, filled with joy because of you. I will sing your praises, O Lord God above all gods. (Ps. 9:2)

God's Hat Trick

SOME, of course, are preaching the Good News because they are jealous of the way God has used me. They want reputations as fearless preachers! But others have purer motives, preaching because they love me, for they know that the Lord has brought me here to use me to defend the Truth. And some preach to make me jealous, thinking that their success will add to my sorrows here in jail! But whatever their motive for doing it, the fact remains that the Good News about Christ is being preached and I am glad. (Philippians 1:15-18)

What two motivations were behind the preaching of the gospel?

Richard Storrs and Gordon Hall were students at the same theological seminary. One Saturday near the end of the semester, Hall was preparing to go to Braintree, Mass., to preach, hoping that he might receive an invitation to become their pastor. That afternoon as he was splitting some wood, his hat fell beneath the axe and was destroyed. He didn't have the money to replace it and the weather was bitter cold, so he asked his friend to take the assignment. Storrs preached and was offered the job. He accepted it, and he remained the minister of that parish until his dying day—a period of over half a century! Hall, although disappointed, sought other outlets for his talents. He went to India and became the first American missionary to Bombay. He was quite influential in the Indian missions movement. No one who believes in divine providence will for a moment doubt that God stationed Storrs at Braintree and Hall in India. By means of that ruined hat, the courses of two lives were changed. Nevertheless, in God's divine will, the Good News was proclaimed.

PRAISE:

PETITION:

Prayer is the spiritual gymnasium in which we exercise and practice godliness. (V. L. Crawford)

The Edge of Life

I am going to keep on being glad, for I know that as you pray for me, and as the Holy Spirit helps me, this is all going to turn out for my good. For I live in eager expectation and hope that I will never do anything that will cause me to be ashamed of myself but that I will always be ready to speak out boldly for Christ while I am going through all these trials here, just as I have in the past; and that I will always be an honor to Christ, whether I live or whether I must die. For to me, living means opportunities for Christ, and dying—well, that's better yet! But if living will give me more opportunities to win people to Christ, then I really don't know which is better, to live or die! (Philippians 1:19-22)

Did Paul prefer to live or die?

An eleven-year-old Chicago girl went to the dentist's office for a routine checkup. The dentist found a cavity and made the preparations to fill it. He gave her a shot of novocaine and placed cotton pads around the tooth. Then he stepped out of the room for a few minutes. When he returned, he was stunned to find the girl slumped over in the chair, dead! Later the paramedics told him she had choked on one of the cotton pads he had placed in her mouth. Most of us never realize how close we are to death. We are so afraid of dying that we cloak ourselves in illusions of immortality. Paul, though, viewed death as a gateway to heaven. He looked with hope to the day when he could finally die and go to meet Jesus.

PRAISE:

PETITION:

Don't worry about anything; instead, pray about everything; tell God your needs and don't forget to thank him for his answers. (Phil. 4:6)

The Peacefulness of Death

SOMETIMES I want to live and at other times I don't, for I long to go and be with Christ. How much happier for *me* than being here! But the fact is that I can be of more help to *you* by staying!

Yes, I am still needed down here and so I feel certain I will be staying on earth a little longer, to help you grow and become happy in your faith; my staying will make you glad and give you reason to glorify Christ Jesus for keeping me safe, when I return to visit you again. (Philippians 1:23-26)

Why does Paul decide that, at this point in his life, living is better than dying?

It is not hard to praise the Lord as you sit in your comfortable home in a free country. But suppose you were kneeling on a hill in far away China with an executioner's sword raised above your head? Would you praise him then? The Rev. and Mrs. R. W. Porteous faced this situation in the spring of 1931. They were taken prisoners by communist bandits in China. Led to a lonely spot on top of a hill, the leader said, "This is the place." The executioner took the long knife from its holder and raised it above the necks of the courageous couple. Certain death seemed imminent. However, instead of cringing and begging for mercy, the Porteouses began to sing. The executioner's knife did not fall; the bandits stared open-mouthed as the missionary couple sang:

Face to face with Christ, my Savior,
Face to face—what will it be?
When with rapture I behold him,
Jesus Christ who died for me.

These two saintly souls were ready for death, but to their surprise, no order was given. The executioner returned the knife to its place, and the couple was released. Subsequently, they told the story of the perfect peace which the Lord Jesus gives to his children in the face of certain death.

P R A I S E :

P E T I T I O N :

Now glory be to God who by his mighty power at work within us is able to do far more than we would ever dare to ask or even dream of—infinitely beyond our highest prayers, desires, thoughts, or hopes. (Eph. 3:20)

Heavenly School

BUT whatever happens to me, remember always to live as Christians should, so that, whether I ever see you again or not, I will keep on hearing good reports that you are standing side by side with one strong purpose—to tell the Good News fearlessly, no matter what your enemies may do. They will see this as a sign of their downfall, but for you it will be a clear sign from God that he is with you, and that he has given you eternal life with him. (Philippians 1:27, 28)

What should be the "one strong purpose" of the Philippian Christians?

Theodore L. Cuyler once compared spiritual life to academic life: "God keeps a costly school. Many of its lessons are spelled out through tears. This school of our heavenly Father will soon close for us. The term time is shortening every day. Let us not shrink from a hard lesson or wince under any rod of chastisement. The richer will be the crown, and the sweeter will be heaven, if we endure cheerfully to the end and graduate in glory."

PRAISE: _____

PETITION: _____

Prayer fills man's emptiness with God's fullness; fills man's poverty with God's riches; puts away man's weakness with God's strength.

Scars of Beauty

FOR to you has been given the privilege not only of trusting him but also of suffering for him. We are in this fight together. You have seen me suffer for him in the past; and I am still in the midst of a great and terrible struggle now, as you know so well. (Philippians 1:29, 30)

Paul mentions two privileges that Christians have in serving God. What are they?

The world's finest china is put through the fire at least three times. The expert craftsmen have learned that one firing in the kiln is not enough to produce china of world-class quality. Why must it go through such intense fire more than once? So that the applied gold and crimson elements will be brought out more beautifully, bonded permanently. Mature Christians are fashioned after the same principle. Our trials are burned into us once, twice, many times. By God's grace, the beautiful characteristics that emerge are immutable; they are there to stay forever.

P R A I S E :

P E T I T I O N :

My eyes are ever looking to the Lord for help, for he alone can rescue me. (Ps. 25:15)

Christian Chameleons

IS there any such thing as Christians cheering each other up? Do you love me enough to want to help me? Does it mean anything to you that we are brothers in the Lord, sharing the same Spirit? Are your hearts tender and sympathetic at all? Then make me truly happy by loving each other and agreeing wholeheartedly with each other, working together with one heart and mind and purpose.

Don't be selfish; don't live to make a good impression on others. Be humble, thinking of others as better than yourself. Don't just think about your own affairs, but be interested in others, too, and in what they are doing. (Philippians 2:1-4)

How can the Philippians make Paul happy?

In the film *Zelig,* Woody Allen plays the role of a man obsessed with imitating whoever he happens to be with. Minutes after joining a group of doctors, for example, Zelig has learned their gestures and lingo, and for all appearances, *becomes* a doctor. Later he sits down to chat with an Indian friend. He soon assumes all of the poses, comments, and looks of a Navajo. And on he goes, "becoming" every imaginable sort of human being. He is called a chameleon, and gains worldwide fame for his uncanny ability to change personalities as easily as one changes a shirt. He ultimately discovers, of course, that making impressions on others is not satisfying to one's own soul.   Paul has said that Christians ought to live in imitation of Christ. But here he says that we should not be concerned about making good impressions on people. We should be faithful to the Word and to our consciences, being honest and open with others.

P R A I S E :

P E T I T I O N :

Sing to the Lord, for he has done wonderful things. Make known his praise around the world. (Isa. 12:5)

God of Humility

YOUR attitude should be the kind that was shown us by Jesus Christ, who, though he was God, did not demand and cling to his rights as God, but laid aside his mighty power and glory, taking the disguise of a slave and becoming like men. And he humbled himself even further, going so far as actually to die a criminal's death on a cross. (Philippians 2:5-8)

How was Christ's humility demonstrated at the end of his earthly life?

We have no greater example of humility than Christ himself. He humbled himself in many ways. He came to earth as a human; he lived in poverty; he withstood the verbal and physical abuses of a haughty, self-righteous people; and he died the horrible death of a common criminal. I cannot think of greater humiliation than for God the Creator to become one of his created beings. That is exactly what Christ did for us.   To be a Christian means to be Christlike. Let us strive for the brand of humility that characterized the life of our Savior.

P R A I S E :

P E T I T I O N :

Pray . . . for kings and all others who are in authority over us, or are in places of high responsibility, so that we can live in peace and quietness, spending our time in godly living and thinking much about the Lord. (1 Tim. 2:2)

Rags to Riches

YET it was because of this that God raised him up to the heights of heaven and gave him a name which is above every other name, that at the name of Jesus every knee shall bow in heaven and on earth and under the earth, and every tongue shall confess that Jesus Christ is Lord, to the glory of God the Father. (Philippians 2:9-11)

Christ will be exalted in three places. What are they?

Christ spent his time on earth in utter humility. But his time of glory is yet to come. During the end-times events, everyone living and dead will recognize Christ as the Lord of the universe. All shall bow to him in adoration, and all shall speak glories to his name. Jesus humbled himself to prove his love for man; but now he lives in the glory he so richly deserves. As Christ himself said, "Many that are first shall be last; and the last shall be first" (Matt. 19:30, KJV).

PRAISE:

PETITION:

The most important thing in any prayer is not what we say to God, but what God says to us. We are apt to pray and then hurry away without giving God a chance to answer.

Musicians' Instruments

DEAREST friends, when I was there with you, you were always so careful to follow my instructions. And now that I am away you must be even more careful to do the good things that result from being saved, obeying God with deep reverence, shrinking back from all that might displease him. For God is at work within you, helping you want to obey him, and then helping you do what he wants.

In everything you do, stay away from complaining and arguing, so that no one can speak a word of blame against you. You are to live clean, innocent lives as children of God in a dark world full of people who are crooked and stubborn. Shine out among them like beacon lights, holding out to them the Word of Life.

Then when Christ returns how glad I will be that my work among you was so worthwhile. (Philippians 2:12-16)

Why does Paul look forward to Christ's return?

The great German composer Mendelssohn once went to see one of the world's greatest musical instruments, the Freiburg organ. The old custodian, not recognizing the composer, at first refused to grant him permission to play the organ. At length, however, he reluctantly agreed to let him play just a few notes. Mendelssohn took his seat, and soon the most beautiful music was breaking forth from the organ. The custodian was spellbound. He came up beside the great musician and asked his name. Learning it, he stood humiliated, self-condemned, saying, "And I refused you permission to play upon my organ."   Often God comes to us, wanting to take our lives and use them for his glory. But we withhold ourselves from him, because of our distrust and insecurity. If we would yield ourselves to him, he would bring heavenly music from our souls.

P R A I S E :

P E T I T I O N :

Each believer should confess his sins to God when he is aware of them, while there is time to be forgiven. (Ps. 32:6)

Shoe-Shine Service

AND if my lifeblood is, so to speak, to be poured out over your faith which I am offering up to God as a sacrifice—that is, if I am to die for you—even then I will be glad, and will share my joy with each of you. For you should be happy about this, too, and rejoice with me for having this privilege of dying for you. (Philippians 2:17, 18)

What does Paul say he will gladly do for the Philippians?

Samuel Brengle was a brilliant university student. He was the leading orator of his senior class. Upon graduation, a very influential church called him to join their pastoral staff; they wanted to groom him for the pulpit. But Brengle's heart was not satisfied. He resigned his position at the church, sailed for London, and offered his services to General William Booth, head of the Salvation Army. He was accepted for service, but was put in the training garrison with cadets. His first assignment was to clean the shoes of the cadets. As he knelt, polish and brush in hand, he prayed, "Lord, if you could take soap and towels and wash the disciples' dirty feet, surely I can take a brush and clean the cadets' dirty boots." Brengle, as Paul, considered service, even unto death, a privilege.

P R A I S E :

P E T I T I O N :

They shall be my people and I will be their God. (Jer. 32:38)

The Apprentice

IF the Lord is willing, I will send Timothy to see you soon. Then when he comes back he can cheer me up by telling me all about you and how you are getting along. There is no one like Timothy for having a real interest in you; everyone else seems to be worrying about his own plans and not those of Jesus Christ. But you know Timothy. He has been just like a son to me in helping me preach the Good News. I hope to send him to you just as soon as I find out what is going to happen to me here. And I am trusting the Lord that soon I myself may come to see you. (Philippians 2:19-24)

How does Paul describe his relationship with Timothy?

Many years ago, before there were any technical schools, young men learned professional trades by becoming apprentices. They agreed to work with skilled craftsmen for several months or years without pay. In exchange, the craftsmen would teach the young men everything they knew about their trade. Apprenticeships were an excellent way of learning a trade; in some countries this method is still used today.   Although Timothy wasn't actually an apprentice of Paul, the two worked closely together for a long period. Timothy was inspired by Paul's commitment to Christ. He went on to be an influential leader himself.

P R A I S E :

P E T I T I O N :

Spread out your petition before God, and then say, "Thy will, not mine, be done." The sweetest lesson I have learned in God's school is to let the Lord choose for me. (D. L. Moody)

The Best Violins

MEANWHILE, I thought I ought to send Epaphroditus back to you. You sent him to help me in my need; well, he and I have been real brothers, working and battling side by side. Now I am sending him home again, for he has been homesick for all of you and upset because you heard that he was ill. And he surely was; in fact, he almost died. But God had mercy on him, and on me too, not allowing me to have this sorrow on top of everything else.

So I am all the more anxious to get him back to you again, for I know how thankful you will be to see him, and that will make me happy and lighten all my cares. Welcome him in the Lord with great joy, and show your appreciation, for he risked his life for the work of Christ and was at the point of death while trying to do for me the things you couldn't do because you were far away. (Philippians 2:25-30)

How does Paul instruct the Philippians to treat Epaphroditus?

An old violin maker was much envied by fellow artisans because of the superior quality of the instruments he produced. He finally disclosed the secret of his success. He said that while the others went into the protected valleys to cut wood to make their violins, he climbed the rugged crags of a nearby mountain in order to secure trees which had become severely twisted and gnarled by storms. From these weatherbeaten monarchs of the forest he then fabricated his violins—famous for their tone and beauty. He knew that the fierce trial of the mountain gales caused such trees to strengthen and toughen their fibers. It was this—their storm-tortured heart and grain—that produced the deep, colorful sound when the instrument was played. Likewise, the Lord allows sore difficulties to come into our lives that we may more fully bring forth the music of his grace when our soul-trying experiences have done their sanctifying work.

P R A I S E :

P E T I T I O N :

We are praying . . . that you will be filled with his mighty, glorious strength so that you can keep going no matter what happens— always full of the joy of the Lord. (Col. 1:11)

Church Dogs

WHATEVER happens, dear friends, be glad in the Lord. I never get tired of telling you this and it is good for you to hear it again and again.

Watch out for those wicked men—dangerous dogs, I call them—who say you must be circumcised to be saved. For it isn't the *cutting of our bodies* that makes us children of God; it is *worshiping him with our spirits.* That is the only true "circumcision." We Christians glory in what Christ Jesus has done for us and realize that we are helpless to save ourselves. (Philippians 3:1-3)

What should be the attitude of the Philippians, regardless of the circumstances?

The "dangerous dogs" Paul refers to are people who would have us believe that God's grace is not enough to save us. They teach that other things—such as baptism, confession to man, and speaking in tongues—are necessary for us to enter God's kingdom. Here's what theologian F. B. Meyer says about such people: "They are fanatical, unbalanced, and unable to distinguish between a part and the whole, magnifying some tiny point in Christianity until it blinds the eye to the symmetry, proportion, and beauty of heaven's glorious scheme. These people are the 'cranks' of our churches. They introduce fads and hobbies. They exaggerate the importance of trifles. They catch up every new theory and vagary, and follow it to the detriment of truth and love. It is impossible to exaggerate the harm that these people can do."

P R A I S E :

P E T I T I O N :

Come, Lord, and rescue me. Ransom me from all my enemies. (Ps. 69:18)

The Essentials

YET if anyone ever had reason to hope that he could save himself, it would be I. If others could be saved by what they are, certainly I could! For I went through the Jewish initiation ceremony when I was eight days old, having been born into a pure-blooded Jewish home that was a branch of the old original Benjamin family. So I was a real Jew if there ever was one! What's more, I was a member of the Pharisees who demand the strictest obedience to every Jewish law and custom. And sincere? Yes, so much so that I greatly persecuted the Church; and I tried to obey every Jewish rule and regulation right down to the very last point. (Philippians 3:4-6)

Before Paul's conversion to Christ, was he obedient to Jewish law?

Listed below are twelve Christian practices. Although all of them should be a part of every Christian's life, only three of them are necessary to one's salvation. Which are they? (Ask your pastor or Sunday school teacher to check your answers.)

_____ 1. Dedication/baptism of children
_____ 2. Confession of sins to Christ
_____ 3. Baptism
_____ 4. Daily devotions
_____ 5. Repentance of one's sins
_____ 6. Tithing one's income
_____ 7. Communion (the Lord's Supper)
_____ 8. Daily prayers
_____ 9. Acceptance of Christ as Savior
_____ 10. Regular church attendance
_____ 11. Helping the poor
_____ 12. Regular Bible study

P R A I S E :

P E T I T I O N :

The praise-life wears out the self-life.

Super Churches

BUT all these things that I once thought very worthwhile—now I've thrown them all away so that I can put my trust and hope in Christ alone. Yes, everything else is worthless when compared with the priceless gain of knowing Christ Jesus my Lord. I have put aside all else, counting it worth less than nothing, in order that I can have Christ, and become one with him, no longer counting on being saved by being good enough or by obeying God's laws, but by trusting Christ to save me; for God's way of making us right with himself depends on faith—counting on Christ alone. (Philippians 3:7-9)

What is God's way of making us right with him?

Sometimes churches embark upon ambitious building programs of doubtful necessity. They invest hundreds of thousands of dollars building mammoth churches equipped with expensive furnishings and the latest technological devices. I dare say that the motivations of such churches are not always sound. The temptation to impress people can sometimes overwhelm the desire to simply serve God. Let us make a practice of examining our hearts, asking God to root out unhealthy priorities. As Paul says in today's reading, "Everything else is worthless when compared with the priceless gain of knowing Christ Jesus."

P R A I S E :

P E T I T I O N :

If you stay in me and obey my commands, you may ask any request you like, and it will be granted! (John 15:7)

Endless Journey

NOW I have given up everything else—I have found it to be the only way to really know Christ and to experience the mighty power that brought him back to life again, and to find out what it means to suffer and to die with him. So, whatever it takes, I will be one who lives in the fresh newness of life of those who are alive from the dead.

I don't mean to say I am perfect. I haven't learned all I should even yet, but I keep working toward that day when I will finally be all that Christ saved me for and wants me to be.

No, dear brothers, I am still not all I should be but I am bringing all my energies to bear on this one thing: Forgetting the past and looking forward to what lies ahead, I strain to reach the end of the race and receive the prize for which God is calling us up to heaven because of what Christ Jesus did for us. (Philippians 3:10-14)

What is Paul's ultimate goal in life?

It is impossible for humans to attain perfection in any area of life. The perfect song has not been composed. The perfect athlete is still only a dream. The perfect sermon has not yet been preached. And the perfect automobile has not yet been designed. Nothing that man is or can create will ever be perfect in this world. For only God holds the key to perfection. But even though perfection is unattainable in this life, we should still try to get as close to it as possible. Everything we do should be done as unto the Lord; that is, we ought to always make perfection our goal. Paul says, "I keep working toward that day when I will finally be all that Christ saved me for and wants me to be."

PRAISE:

PETITION:

I would no more reject my people than I would change my laws of night and day, of earth and sky. (Jer. 33:25, 26)

Running the Race

I hope all of you who are mature Christians will see eye-to-eye with me on these things, and if you disagree on some point, I believe that God will make it plain to you—if you fully obey the truth you have. (Philippians 3:15, 16)

Does Paul insist that the "mature Christians" agree with him on every point he has made? Explain your answer.

Paul wants to make one thing clear: He considers himself a growing, changing, developing person. No matter what the record of his past achievements or how great his standing in their sight, he wants the Philippians to know that he has not reached the pinnacle of Christian growth. Therefore, he says that he is not concentrating on past defeats or past victories. Instead, he is concentrating all his effort and energy on running the race to which God has called him.   John Newton once wrote, "I am not what I ought to be, I am far from what I wish to be, but by God's grace I am not what I once was." This is what Paul is saying in the passage beginning yesterday and ending today.

P R A I S E :

P E T I T I O N :

The first purpose of prayer is to move the pray-er. (R. L. Smith)

One-Eyed King

DEAR brothers, pattern your lives after mine and notice who else lives up to my example. (Philippians 3:17)

After whose life should the Philippians pattern theirs?

"In the land of blind men, he who has one eye is king" (popular Brazilian saying). This proverb may help us to understand what Paul meant when he urged the Philippians to imitate him. The proverb means that even though no one has everything, having something is better than having nothing. What Paul meant to say was that the Philippians should not follow the example of non-Christians who were bound to a sensual manner of life. Instead, they should imitate the lifestyles of Paul and others who lived as citizens of the heavenly state. Remember that, since the church was so new, many Christians didn't really know how to behave. Paul merely urged the Philippians to look at him and other Christian leaders—rather than the pagans—for direction on how to lead their lives.

P R A I S E :

P E T I T I O N :

O God in Zion, we wait before you in silent praise, and thus fulfill our vow. And because you answer prayer, all mankind will come to you with their requests. (Ps. 65:1)

Christian Klansmen

FOR I have told you often before, and I say it again now with tears in my eyes, there are many who walk along the Christian road who are really enemies of the cross of Christ. Their future is eternal loss, for their god is their appetite: they are proud of what they should be ashamed of; and all they think about is this life here on earth. (Philippians 3:18, 19)

What does the future hold for enemies of the cross of Christ?

Many members of the Ku Klux Klan attend church regularly and consider themselves Christians. They say they are for God, country, and the "American way of life." In their own perverse, twisted manner, they somehow justify their racist extremism, and work toward expelling everyone from America who is not Caucasian and Protestant. It never occurs to them that their message of hatred runs contrary to Christ's message of love. These people are good examples of what Paul calls the "enemies of the cross of Christ." Under the guise of Christianity, they commit atrocities against other created beings. "They are proud of what they should be ashamed of."

P R A I S E :

P E T I T I O N :

Don't be afraid, for I have ransomed you; I have called you by name; you are mine. (Isa. 43:1)

The Oakwood Madonna

BUT our homeland is in heaven, where our Savior the Lord Jesus Christ is; and we are looking forward to his return from there. When he comes back he will take these dying bodies of ours and change them into glorious bodies like his own, using the same mighty power that he will use to conquer all else everywhere. (Philippians 3:20, 21)

What will Christ do when he returns?

There is a legend about an artist who was searching for a piece of sandalwood that he could use to carve a Madonna. At last he gave up in despair, leaving the vision of his life unrealized. Then in a dream he was bidden to shape the figure from a block of oakwood which was destined for the fire. Obeying the command, he produced from the log of common firewood a masterpiece. In like manner, many people wait for great and brilliant opportunities for doing the good things, the beautiful things, of which they dream. Meanwhile, through all the plain, common days, the very opportunities they require for such deeds lie close to them in the simplest and most familiar passing events, and in the homeliest circumstances. They wait to find sandalwood out of which to carve Madonnas, while far more lovely Madonnas than they dream of are hidden in the common log of oak they spurn with their feet in the woodyard.

P R A I S E :

P E T I T I O N :

I have been driven many times to my knees by the overwhelming conviction that I had nowhere else to go. (A. Lincoln)

Da Vinci's Christ

DEAR brother Christians, I love you and long to see you, for you are my joy and my reward for my work. My beloved friends, stay true to the Lord.

And now I want to plead with those two dear women, Euodias and Syntyche. Please, please, with the Lord's help, quarrel no more—be friends again. And I ask you, my true teammate, to help these women, for they worked side by side with me in telling the Good News to others; and they worked with Clement, too, and the rest of my fellow workers whose names are written in the Book of Life. (Philippians 4:1-3)

What problem does Paul deal with here?

While Leonardo da Vinci was putting on canvas his great masterpiece which the world knows today as "The Last Supper," he became quite angry with a certain man. He lashed him with hot and bitter words and threatened him with vengeance. When the great painter returned to his canvas and began to paint the face of Jesus, he found himself so perturbed and disquieted that he could not compose himself for the delicate work before him. Not until he had sought out the man and asked him for forgiveness did he find himself in possession of that inner calm which enabled him to give to the Master's face the tender and delicate expression he knew it must have.

PRAISE:

PETITION:

I will . . . heal your wounds. (Jer. 30:17)

The Smiling Heart

ALWAYS be full of joy in the Lord; I say it again, rejoice! Let everyone see that you are unselfish and considerate in all you do. Remember that the Lord is coming soon. Don't worry about anything; instead, pray about everything; tell God your needs and don't forget to thank him for his answers. If you do this you will experience God's peace, which is far more wonderful than the human mind can understand. His peace will keep your thoughts and your hearts quiet and at rest as you trust in Christ Jesus. (Philippians 4:4-7)

What should Christians do instead of worrying about things?

It is unreasonable to expect everyone to be happy all the time. Everyone has problems of one sort or another. And it is difficult to have a big smile on your face when you're undergoing a crisis. With this in mind, it seems a bit silly of Paul to say, "Always be full of joy. . . ." But if we consider the context from which Paul was speaking, and if we read the rest of the phrase, it begins to make sense. The conditions at Philippi were certainly not joyful; the repetition of the command to rejoice suggests that the situation there was such as to make such an exhortation seem unreasonable. But Paul insists that Christians must always rejoice "in the Lord." The joy of knowing the Lord must always be at the center of a Christian's life. Our joy depends not on circumstances but on the Lord.

P R A I S E :

P E T I T I O N :

O Lord, hear me praying; listen to my plea, O God my King, for I will never pray to anyone but you. (Ps. 5:1, 2)

Paul's Psychology

AND now, brothers, as I close this letter let me say this one more thing: Fix your thoughts on what is true and good and right. Think about things that are pure and lovely, and dwell on the fine, good things in others. Think about all you can praise God for and be glad about. Keep putting into practice all you learned from me and saw me doing, and the God of peace will be with you. (Philippians 4:8, 9)

What should occupy the thoughts of Christians?

As evidenced by today's reading, Paul seems to have known a lot about Christian psychology (even though psychology wasn't actually declared a science until centuries later). Paul had the God-given knowledge that positive thoughts develop healthy minds, and that healthy minds are the key to general health. He encouraged the Philippians to think on what is true, good, right, pure, and lovely. French philosopher Rene Descartes said, "I think, therefore I am." Paul's variation of this seems to be, "As I think, so I am." Let us nurture godly thoughts, so that we may be godly.

P R A I S E :

P E T I T I O N :

He who knows how to commune with God can truly know himself.

Us and Them

HOW grateful I am and how I praise the Lord that you are helping me again. I know you have always been anxious to send what you could, but for a while you didn't have the chance. Not that I was ever in need, for I have learned how to get along happily whether I have much or little. I know how to live on almost nothing or with every-thing. I have learned the secret of contentment in every situation, whether it be a full stomach or hunger, plenty or want; for I can do everything God asks me to with the help of Christ who gives me the strength and power. (Philippians 4:10-13)

What secret has Paul learned?

Have you ever noticed that:

- When the other person loses his temper, he is a *hothead;* when you do, it is just *nerves?*
- When the other person is set in his ways, he is *obstinate;* when you are, it is just *firmness?*
- When the other person does not like your friend, he is *prejudiced;* when you don't like his, you are simply a *good judge* of human nature?
- When the other person takes a long time to do things, he is *lazy;* when you do, you are *deliberate?*
- When the other person spends a lot of money, he is a *spendthrift;* when you do, you are *generous?*
- When the other person is mild-mannered, he is *weak;* when you are, you are being *gracious?* (From *The King's Highway*)

P R A I S E :

P E T I T I O N :

Ask, and you will be given what you ask for. Seek, and you will find. Knock, and the door will be opened. (Matt. 7:7)

Christian Thieves

BUT even so, you have done right in helping me in my present difficulty.

As you well know, when I first brought the Gospel to you and then went on my way, leaving Macedonia, only you Philippians became my partners in giving and receiving. No other church did this. Even when I was over in Thessalonica you sent help twice. But though I appreciate your gifts, what makes me happiest is the well-earned reward you will have because of your kindness. (Philippians 4:14-17)

Paul is happy about the Philippians' willingness to financially support him and the churches. But what makes him even happier?

Once a minister was trying to convince a certain man of his responsibility to be obedient to God's Word. When asked if he had ever been baptized, the man replied, "No, sir, I haven't. But why should I? The thief who died with Christ was not baptized, and he went to heaven." When the preacher urged him to be more faithful in church attendance, the man answered, "Why should I? The dying thief didn't go to church, and he was saved." Finally the minister spoke to him about the matter of tithing and his duty to support the work of the local assembly with his financial gifts. To that the man responded, "That's not necessary. The dying thief went to heaven, and he never gave one cent to missions or the church." Turning away, the man of God said with disgust, "Mister, the only difference I can see between you and the thief on the cross is that he was a dying thief and you are a living one!"

PRAISE:

PETITION:

Those who have reason to be thankful should continually be singing praises to the Lord. (James 5:13)

Travelers' Checks

AT the moment I have all I need—more than I need! I am generously supplied with the gifts you sent me when Epaphroditus came. They are a sweet-smelling sacrifice that pleases God well. And it is he who will supply all your needs from his riches in glory, because of what Christ Jesus has done for us. (Philippians 4:18, 19)

Who will supply the Philippians' needs? Why?

Picture this imaginary situation: A woman is preparing for a one-month vacation in England. Upon the insistance of a friend, she exchanges all her traveling money for American Express travelers' checks. On the flight to London, she doesn't sleep a wink. She frets and worries that the travelers' checks will not be accepted in England, and that she will be stuck there with no money. The woman would be worrying needlessly, you say. American Express travelers' checks are accepted universally. But what about the person who bears the "checks" of God's promises, yet goes fearing all the way, worried about whether he'll have the necessities of life? Isn't he a greater fool than the woman? No fire, no loss, no theft can destroy God's checks. When he says, "I will never leave you or forsake you" and "My grace is sufficient for you," believe it! Don't dishonor God by withholding from him the confidence you would freely place in American Express.

P R A I S E :

P E T I T I O N :

He prays well who is so absorbed with God that he does not realize he is praying. (F. de Sales)

Final Song

NOW unto God our Father be glory forever and ever. Amen.

Sincerely,
Paul

P.S.

Say "hello" for me to all the Christians there; the brothers with me send their greetings too. And all the other Christians here want to be remembered to you, especially those who work in Caesar's palace. The blessings of our Lord Jesus Christ be upon your spirits. (Philippians 4:20-23)

Who besides Paul sends their greetings to the Philippian Christians?

Some of life's most difficult moments come when we must say good-bye to a loved one. Many artists have devoted much time to rhapsodizing the grief of good-byes. There are many songs such as "The Last Farewell"; many movies such as *The Good-bye Girl;* many books such as *Farewell, My Lovely.* As Shakespeare writes in *Romeo and Juliet,* "Parting is such sweet sorrow." As Paul closes this epistle to the Philippians, we sense something of his reluctance to once again say good-bye. He doesn't know whether he'll ever be able to see them or communicate with them again. As usual, though, his optimism shines through with the moving closing line, "The blessings of our Lord Jesus Christ be upon your spirits."

P R A I S E :

P E T I T I O N :

O God, you have declared me perfect in your eyes; you have always cared for me in my distress; now hear me as I call again. (Ps. 4:1)

August C O L O S S I A N S

Young Christians who go to secular colleges often have their faith shaken to the roots. The discovery of new philosophies and ideologies, as well as new relationships with non-Christians, can place a strain on one's Christianity. A deep recommitment and rediscovery of Christian truth is often necessary to make it through. ■ As Paul writes this epistle, the Colossian church has been infiltrated with teaching foreign to the Christian faith. His intent is to set the church straight. He sets forth clearly and passionately the correct view of Christianity.

Love Letters

FROM: Paul, chosen by God to be Jesus Christ's messenger, and from Brother Timothy.

To: The faithful Christian brothers—God's people—in the city of Colosse. May God our Father shower you with blessings and fill you with his great peace. (Colossians 1:1, 2)

For what function did God choose Paul?

The longest letter ever written was 3,200 feet long (over three-fifths of a mile). It was written on an adding-machine roll over a period of a month in 1954. It was sent by a New York woman to her sweetheart in Asia during the Korean Conflict. Although none of Paul's letters is quite so long, he was, nevertheless, very prolific. In our Bible alone, we have thirteen letters from his pen. And no doubt there were many others that were not included in the Bible. Letter-writing is a good way of showing concern for someone. This was true in Paul's day as well as in the present. But Paul showed much more than human concern in his letters; his ardent love for the cause of Christ and for God's people is evident in every one of them.

PRAISE:

PETITION:

I will instruct you [says the Lord] and guide you along the best pathway for your life; I will advise you and watch your progress. (Ps. 32:8)

Beyond Imagination

WHENEVER we pray for you we always begin by giving thanks to
God the Father of our Lord Jesus Christ, for we have heard how much
you trust the Lord, and how much you love his people. And you are
looking forward to the joys of heaven, and have been ever since the
Gospel first was preached to you. The same Good News that came to
you is going out all over the world and changing lives everywhere,
just as it changed yours that very first day you heard it and understood about God's great kindness to sinners. (Colossians 1:3-6)

What two things had Paul heard about the Colossians?

What will heaven be like? With our earthly ideas about what is pleasant and
unpleasant, luxurious and shoddy, glorious and commonplace, or comfortable
and uncomfortable, we could each come up with our own image of heaven.
Some imagine it as a place of "streets of gold" and great wealth. Others think
it will be a place of overwhelming beauty. Others see it as a center for truth and
worship. Heaven will probably be all of this, and much more. Human minds
cannot even begin to imagine its glory.   **B**ut even though their powers of
imagination were limited, the Colossian Christians were eagerly anticipating
the joys of heaven. Paul was pleased to hear that their anticipation was based
on true faith in the Lord Jesus Christ.

P R A I S E :

P E T I T I O N :

When you pray, I will listen. (Jer. 29:12)

Slaves of Christ

EPAPHRAS, our much-loved fellow worker, was the one who brought you this Good News. He is Jesus Christ's faithful slave, here to help us in your place. And he is the one who has told us about the great love for others which the Holy Spirit has given you. (Colossians 1:7, 8)

Who told Paul about the Colossians' great love for others?

In modern times, slavery has practically vanished from the face of the earth. The principle that all men are equal has spread to nearly all nations, and most people now view slavery as something primitive, something to be abhorred. Some people would say that forms of slavery still exist today. They say that the "new slaves" include such groups as the blacks in South Africa, the "untouchable" caste in India, and the oppressed masses in the communist countries. There may be something to this, but there is no doubt that the past practices of slave-trading and slave-keeping have virtually disappeared. Even though the concept of slavery seems detestable to us, as Christians we should voluntarily surrender every aspect of our lives to Christ, becoming his slaves. In today's reading, Paul refers to the evangelist Epaphras as "Jesus Christ's faithful slave." Paul could have paid this man no higher compliment.

P R A I S E :

P E T I T I O N :

Power with God will be the gauge of real power with men.

Union/Communion

SO ever since we first heard about you we have kept on praying and asking God to help you understand what he wants you to do; asking him to make you wise about spiritual things; and asking that the way you live will always please the Lord and honor him, so that you will always be doing good, kind things for others, while all the time you are learning to know God better and better. (Colossians 1:9, 10)

What prayer requests did Paul make on behalf of the Colossians?

Some Christians have been saved for twenty or thirty years, but are no farther along in their spiritual lives than when they first began. By faith we stand justified in God's sight—this is *union* with God. But our *communion* and fellowship depend on our daily walk. Our union is once for all and cannot be broken, but our communion can be broken by carelessness and sin, and must be restored by confession and repentance. Christ left us two ordinances: baptism and the Lord's Supper. Baptism speaks of union once and for all, never to be repeated. But the Lord's Supper is to be observed often. Union is God's free gift; communion is our responsibility. "If we are living in the light of God's presence, just as Christ does, then we have wonderful fellowship [communion] with each other" (1 John 1:7). (From *Our Daily Bread*)

PRAISE:

PETITION:

God . . . will show you how to escape temptation's power so that you can bear up patiently against it. (1 Cor. 10:13)

Moved by Strength

WE are praying, too, that you will be filled with his mighty, glorious strength so that you can keep going no matter what happens—always full of the joy of the Lord, and always thankful to the Father who has made us fit to share all the wonderful things that belong to those who live in the Kingdom of light. (Colossians 1:11, 12)

Why did Paul pray that the Colossians would be filled with God's strength?

A retired musician lived alone in an old house. She loved her piano more than anything on earth, though she could no longer play it as well as she once could. One morning a short circuit in the basement caused a pile of old newspapers to begin burning. Within minutes the entire basement was ablaze. The old woman noticed the fire as it started burning through the kitchen floor. Alarmed, she rushed to the living room. She lifted the piano, carried it across the room, down a short flight of stairs, and out the front door of the house. When the excitement was over and the house had burned to the ground, a fireman asked her how the piano had gotten to the front lawn. The woman answered sheepishly, "I carried it out myself!" Later her doctors confirmed that a sudden surge in adrenaline had given her the incredible strength to move the 2,000-pound piano, her most prized possession. As Christians, we have a much greater reservoir of strength. Through prayer, we have access to the power of the Almighty God, who can move mountains and oceans. Let us be "always thankful to the Father who has made us fit to share all the wonderful things."

PRAISE:

PETITION:

The Lord says, "Because he loves me, I will rescue him; I will make him great because he trusts in my name." (Ps. 91:14)

The Birth of Death

FOR he has rescued us out of the darkness and gloom of Satan's kingdom and brought us into the Kingdom of his dear Son, who bought our freedom with his blood and forgave us all our sins. (Colossians 1:13, 14)

From what has God rescued us?

God created a perfect world. Before the sin of Adam and Eve, the natural order was in perfect harmony with the will of God. But when the first couple ate of the forbidden fruit, the curse of Satan fell upon the universe. Certain forms of life became destructive and predatory. Weather patterns shifted into potential killers. Volcanoes began to spew forth lava, and earthquakes became commonplace. Man's nature changed from inclination toward God to inclination toward sin. Illnesses developed, pain was born, and the final curse of death spread across the land. This was the fruit of Satan.   Believers know that one day this curse shall be reversed and thrown, along with Lucifer, into the lake of fire. Paul tells the Colossians that deliverance from an eternity in hell is possible. Jesus "bought our freedom with his blood." All we must do is believe him and follow him; he gives us comfort and joy on earth, and an eternity in heaven.

PRAISE:

PETITION:

True godliness is just as true, steady, persevering in faith as it is in prayer. When faith ceases to pray, it ceases to live.

Christ Is God Is Christ

CHRIST is the exact likeness of the unseen God. He existed before God made anything at all, and, in fact, Christ himself is the Creator who made everything in heaven and earth, the things we can see and the things we can't; the spirit world with its kings and kingdoms, its rulers and authorities; all were made by Christ for his own use and glory. He was before all else began and it is his power that holds everything together. (Colossians 1:15-17)

Describe the relationship between God the Father and God the Son.

Christ is more than just the Son of God. He is God himself. *Jesus Christ* created the universe. *Jesus Christ* breathed life into the lungs of man. *Jesus Christ* gave Moses the Ten Commandments. And so on. We often think of the three members of the Trinity as being completely separate from each other. But there is only one God, not three. The nature of the one God is such that it encompasses three "persons"—the Father, the Son, and the Holy Spirit. The mystery of the Trinity shall remain a mystery until we all reach heaven.   In today's reading, Paul is trying to get the Colossians to understand that Christ is not merely God's ambassador to earth. By giving them examples and illustrations, he declares that Jesus *is* God.

PRAISE:

PETITION:

The God of peace will soon crush Satan under your feet. (Rom. 16:20)

Head and Body

HE is the Head of the body made up of his people—that is, his Church—which he began; and he is the Leader of all those who arise from the dead, so that he is first in everything; for God wanted all of himself to be in his Son. (Colossians 1:18, 19)

To what does Paul compare Christ and the church?

Robots have many applications in modern industry. They are used in manufacturing everything from Mustangs to microchips. The experts predict that soon "domestic" robots will hit the market. They will vacuum the carpet, do the laundry, and wash the dishes.   The most sophisticated robots are made of a computer and sensitive mechanical parts. As you might imagine, the computer does all the "thinking," and the mechanical parts do all the doing. Without the moving parts, the computer would sit useless. And without the computer—the head—the mechanical parts would remain motionless.   Just as robots are composed of thinking and working parts, God's kingdom is composed of Christ—the Head—and the church—the body of believers. In order for the Kingdom of God to effectively grow, both elements must work together in perfect harmony. As the church, it is our duty to fulfill whatever Christ commands.

P R A I S E :

P E T I T I O N :

Be earnest, thoughtful men of prayer. (1 Pet. 4:7)

The Gospel in a Nutshell

IT was through what his Son did that God cleared a path for every-thing to come to him—all things in heaven and on earth—for Christ's death on the cross has made peace with God for all by his blood. This includes you who were once so far away from God. You were his enemies and hated him and were separated from him by your evil thoughts and actions, yet now he has brought you back as his friends. He has done this through the death on the cross of his own human body, and now as a result Christ has brought you into the very presence of God, and you are standing there before him with nothing left against you—nothing left that he could even chide you for; the only condition is that you fully believe the Truth, standing in it steadfast and firm, strong in the Lord, convinced of the Good News that Jesus died for you, and never shifting from trusting him to save you. This is the wonderful news that came to each of you and is now spreading all over the world. And I, Paul, have the joy of telling it to others. (Colossians 1:20-23)

How did Christ make peace between unbelievers and God?

Paul's God-given responsibility was to preach the gospel. He had the gift of persuasion—he could relate the Good News clearly and convincingly. Suppose someone were to ask you to explain the gospel. What would you say? In the space below, write a paragraph summarizing the plan of salvation.

_____

_____

_____

_____

PRAISE: _____

PETITION: _____

The quickest way to get on your feet is to get on your knees.

The Fruit Vendor's Fruits

BUT part of my work is to suffer for you; and I am glad, for I am helping to finish up the remainder of Christ's sufferings for his body, the Church.

God has sent me to help his Church and to tell his secret plan to you Gentiles. He has kept this secret for centuries and generations past, but now at last it has pleased him to tell it to those who love him and live for him, and the riches and glory of his plan are for you Gentiles too. And this is the secret: *that Christ in your hearts is your only hope of glory.* (Colossians 1:24-27)

What is God's secret?

There was once a quiet little man, a vendor of fruits and vegetables, who regularly passed the door of a minister. One day the man dropped a small notebook as he passed. The minister retrieved it and was about to return it when his eye was caught by the words on the first page. The inscription at the top read, "The Remainder of Christ's Sufferings." Under the heading were notations such as these: "The following were absent from Sunday school; be sure to visit them"; "Ask about the sick baby"; "Leave fruit for the blind lady"; "Speak a word of cheer to the old crippled man." And so on. The humble fruit peddler humbly took the book from the hand of the minister. "You see," he said, "this is my book of reminders." Pointing to the first page, he continued, "This is my reason for doing these things. It keeps my soul out of the dust, for as I do these things for Christ's children, I know I am ministering unto him."

PRAISE :

PETITION :

He feels pity for the weak and needy, and will rescue them. (Ps. 72:13)

Danger Ahead

SO everywhere we go we talk about Christ to all who will listen, warning them and teaching them as well as we know how. We want to be able to present each one to God, perfect because of what Christ has done for each of them. This is my work, and I can do it only because Christ's mighty energy is at work within me. (Colossians 1:28, 29)

According to this passage, what is Paul's work?

Jonathan Edwards was the most famous preacher of his time. As most ministers of that era, he spent more time pounding the pulpit with hellfire-and-brimstone sermons than he did talking about the love and mercy of God. His most famous sermon is "Sinners in the Hands of an Angry God," in which he said God is dangling man as a spider from a string of web over a raging lake of fire. In our day, most ministers avoid such scare tactics in preaching the gospel. They prefer a more "civilized" approach. But the fact remains that all nonbelievers are on their way to hell. We read in today's Scripture that Paul saw nothing wrong with warning people of the real danger ahead.

PRAISE:

PETITION:

Those who believe in him will never be disappointed. (Rom. 9:33)

Little Pictures

I wish you could know how much I have struggled in prayer for you and for the church at Laodicea, and for my many other friends who have never known me personally. This is what I have asked of God for you: that you will be encouraged and knit together by strong ties of love, and that you will have the rich experience of knowing Christ with real certainty and clear understanding. *For God's secret plan, now at last made known, is Christ himself.* In him lie hidden all the mighty, untapped treasures of wisdom and knowledge. (Colossians 2:1-3)

What is God's secret plan?

An old widow was living in poverty and want. A young man, hearing she was in need, went to visit her to see if he could be of any help. The old lady complained bitterly of her condition and remarked that her son in Australia was doing very well. Her friend inquired, "Doesn't he do anything to help you?" She replied, "No, nothing. He writes to me regularly once a month but he sends me only some little pictures with his letters." The young man asked to see the pictures she had received. To his surprise, he found each of them to be twenty-pound notes. The poor old lady did not realize the value of this foreign currency, but had imagined them to be mere pretty pictures. She had lived in poverty and want, whereas she could have had all the bodily comforts she desired and needed so much.   We smile at the foolishness of the old woman, but how many of us are like her, living as though we were paupers instead of sons and daughters of the King?

P R A I S E :

P E T I T I O N :

Prayer does not change God; it changes him who prays.

Modular Religion

I am saying this because I am afraid that someone may fool you with smooth talk. For though I am far away from you my heart is with you, happy because you are getting along so well, happy because of your strong faith in Christ. (Colossians 2:4, 5)

What are two reasons Paul is happy?

Millions of Japanese people are religious but have no single religion. Instead of adhering to the principles of one faith, these people choose elements from different religions—usually Shinto, Buddhism, and Christianity. They create their own home-brewed concoction of doctrines and standards of conduct. Theologians call such people syncretists.   Syncretism was also a problem in Colosse. At the time Paul was writing to the Christians there, many Colossians believed in elements from Gnosticism, paganism, and Judaic speculative philosophy. Some of these people thought it would be OK to throw in a dose of Christianity as well. Needless to say, Paul was adamantly against this; Christ is the only way to God, he said.   Paul was happy that the Colossian Christians had withstood the attacks of those who would fool them with the "smooth talk" of syncretism.

PRAISE:

PETITION:

Love him with all your heart and soul and mind and strength. (Mark 12:30)

The Gift

AND now just as you trusted Christ to save you, trust him, too, for each day's problems; live in vital union with him. Let your roots grow down into him and draw up nourishment from him. See that you go on growing in the Lord, and become strong and vigorous in the truth you were taught. Let your lives overflow with joy and thanksgiving for all he has done. (Colossians 2:6, 7)

We must trust Christ for our salvation. What else must we trust him for?

We can compare salvation to the blind receiving sight, the deaf receiving the sense of hearing, or the dead receiving life. But as Christians we have not merely received the gift of salvation from the hands of Christ. We have received Christ himself! Though we are eternally grateful to him for giving us salvation, peace, joy, love, wisdom, discernment, and other godly characteristics, we are most thankful to him for the gift of himself. The Son of God has been poured into us, and now resides within our hearts. It is too much for our finite minds to comprehend. All we can do is praise and worship him.

PRAISE:

PETITION:

You have done so much for me, O Lord. No wonder I am glad! I sing for joy. (Ps. 92:4)

Death by Improvement

DON'T let others spoil your faith and joy with their philosophies, their wrong and shallow answers built on men's thoughts and ideas, instead of on what Christ has said. (Colossians 2:8)

What is Paul's warning to the Colossians here?

A German woman was taken seriously ill and went to the hospital. Later that evening her husband inquired about her condition and was told she was improving. The next day he called again and was told she was still improving. This went on for some time. Finally, one night he received a phone call informing him that his wife had just died. Seeing the doctor the next day, the husband went up to him and said, "Well, doctor, what did she die of— improvements?" **I** know of a church that had the same problem. The first improvement was to get a new "theology minister." The next was to contract a highly-trained but godless quartet. Then the prayer meeting was changed into a weekly literary debating society. Finally, they decided to discontinue pulpit prayers—the minister saying that God knew far better than he what the people needed. **T**he church has since died. If someone would want to put up a tombstone over its grave, I'd suggest a truthful and appropriate epitaph: "Died of Improvements."

P R A I S E :

P E T I T I O N :

Men in public office have heavy burdens to bear, and they wield far-reaching influence. Their decisions affect the church, the city, the nation. The hands of wicked men and corrupt officials can be stayed by our prayers.

Back from the Grave

FOR in Christ there is all of God in a human body; *so you have everything when you have Christ,* and you are filled with God through your union with Christ. He is the highest Ruler, with authority over every other power.

When you came to Christ he set you free from your evil desires, not by a bodily operation of circumcision but by a spiritual operation, the baptism of your souls. For in baptism you see how your old, evil nature died with him and was buried with him; and then you came up out of death with him into a new life because you trusted the Word of the mighty God who raised Christ from the dead. (Colossians 2:9-12)

How does Paul describe the believer's state before his salvation?

Over the years Hollywood has produced dozens of horror movies which depict all sorts of zombies, witches, vampires, and monsters coming back from the dead. Resurrection has been portrayed as a gruesome, harrowing experience. But these "resurrections" are fictitious. Christ is the only one to ever raise himself from the dead. For Christians, his resurrection stands as the most glorious miracle. It stands above all other miracles not only because of the supernatural wonder of life springing from death, but because of its implications. Christ died for all the sins of humanity. When he rose from the dead, he proved his eternal victory over the forces of evil. All true Christians have arisen with Christ from spiritual death. When we came to him, our old, evil natures perished. In their place, new, godly natures came to life within us. We are alive because Christ lives within us.

PRAISE:

PETITION:

Nothing will ever be able to separate us from the love of God demonstrated by our Lord Jesus Christ when he died for us. (Rom. 8:39)

God's Court

YOU were dead in sins, and your sinful desires were not yet cut away. Then he gave you a share in the very life of Christ, for he forgave all your sins, and blotted out the charges proved against you, the list of his commandments which you had not obeyed. He took this list of sins and destroyed it by nailing it to Christ's cross. In this way God took away Satan's power to accuse you of sin, and God openly displayed to the whole world Christ's triumph at the cross where your sins were all taken away. (Colossians 2:13-15)

How has God taken away Satan's power to accuse us of sin?

Our society expects the judicial system to arrest and convict all criminals. It wants to see all offenders duly punished. It believes that imprisoning wrongdoers will remove them from law-abiding society, "teach them a lesson they'll never forget," and deter other potential criminals. Pardons are usually very unpopular; society wants the full force of the law to fall upon those who do not adhere to it. Not so with God. Our Lord is always ready to pardon sinners. Even the most vile offender can be entirely forgiven if he repents and confesses his sins. There will be no relief in hell for those who reject God in this life. But God will "blot out the charges" of anyone who meets the conditions of his law. How great is his mercy!

PRAISE:

PETITION:

You can ask him for anything using my name, and I will do it, for this will bring praise to the Father because of what I, the Son, will do for you. (John 14:12, 13)

The Temptation of Law

SO don't let anyone criticize you for what you eat or drink, or for not celebrating Jewish holidays and feasts or new moon ceremonies or Sabbaths. For these were only temporary rules that ended when Christ came. They were only shadows of the real thing—of Christ himself. (Colossians 2:16, 17)

How does Paul describe Jewish laws here?

Christ came to free humanity from the law. But the fact is, we *like* the law. We don't really want to be free from it. We like the church to have long lists of rules and regulations, so that we can easily assess our spiritual condition. We can look at these lists and say, "Well, I don't drink, smoke, gamble, or commit adultery, so I must be a pretty fine Christian." Many people would feel uncomfortable, exposed, and vulnerable without rules. But Christ wants us to focus on him, not on rules. He wants our Christianity to be based upon Christlikeness, not upon legalism. The true Christian is filled with love, and this love motivates him to act in a Christlike manner. For him, man-made rules seem redundant and unnecessary. Let us look first to Christ, not to church constitutions.

PRAISE:

PETITION:

Prayer governs conduct and conduct makes character. Conduct is what we do; character is what we are. Conduct is the outward life; character is the life unseen, hidden within, yet evidenced by that which is seen.

Unconnected

DON'T let anyone declare you lost when you refuse to worship angels, as they say you must. They have seen a vision, they say, and know you should. These proud men (though they claim to be so humble) have a very clever imagination. But they are not connected to Christ, the Head to which all of us who are his body are joined; for we are joined together by his strong sinews and we grow only as we get our nourishment and strength from God. (Colossians 2:18, 19)

What is Paul's opinion of people who say angels are to be worshiped?

The people to which Paul referred were Gnostics (pronounced "NAW-sticks"). Although they claimed to be true Christians, their beliefs were as unsound and bizarre as those of any cult today. They believed angels should be worshiped and that salvation came through knowledge of one's true self as explained in a myth revealed by Jesus. They taught that Jesus was not really God, but that a God-Spirit entered him after his baptism and departed from him before his death on the cross.   Although the Gnostics' central figure was Christ, they were not Christians. As we read elsewhere in the New Testament, not everyone who cries out "Lord, Lord" will be saved. Paul says that these people "are not connected to Christ." We should beware of people who seem to believe in Christ but who have strange, unbiblical doctrines. In our day, groups such as the Jehovah's Witnesses, the Mormons, the Unification Church, and the Church of Christ Scientist are also unconnected to Christ.

PRAISE:

PETITION:

Truth rises from the earth and righteousness smiles down from heaven. (Ps. 85:11)

Two Friends

SINCE you died, as it were, with Christ and this has set you free from following the world's ideas of how to be saved—by doing good and obeying various rules—why do you keep right on following them anyway, still bound by such rules as not eating, tasting, or even touching certain foods? Such rules are mere human teachings, for food was made to be eaten and used up. These rules may seem good, for rules of this kind require strong devotion and are humiliating and hard on the body, but they have no effect when it comes to conquering a person's evil thoughts and desires. They only make him proud. (Colossians 2:20-23)

What is the ultimate effect of legalism upon the believer?

Two men sat in a forest, meditating on the mysteries of life. Their names were Faith and Intellect. One day God visited them and said, "My children, I want to give you the things you most desire. What do you choose?" Intellect responded, "Give me all knowledge of everything in the past, present, and future." Faith's request was more modest: "I want you to continue to guide me and give me each day that which is best for me." A few days later Faith dropped by to visit Intellect. Faith noticed a weary look on his friend's face. He asked, "Why do you look sad when you know everything in the universe?" "I am unhappy because there is no further goal toward which I can strive," said Intellect. "Among other things I have learned is this: Wisdom becomes folly when it seeks too much." (Adapted from *Show of Wisdom,* by J. Warnack)

P R A I S E :

P E T I T I O N :

Your heavenly Father will . . . give the Holy Spirit to those who ask for him. (Luke 11:13)

The X-Rated Heaven

SINCE you became alive again, so to speak, when Christ arose from the dead, now set your sights on the rich treasures and joys of heaven where he sits beside God in the place of honor and power. Let heaven fill your thoughts; don't spend your time worrying about things down here. You should have as little desire for this world as a dead person does. Your real life is in heaven with Christ and God. And when Christ who is our real life comes back again, you will shine with him and share in all his glories. (Colossians 3:1-4)

What can Christians expect upon the return of Jesus Christ?

What is heaven? To Muslims, it is a place where all followers of Mohammad and Allah will go after death. There they will satisfy all their physical, mental, moral, and spiritual desires, including desires that they had to suppress as mortals. In other words, they believe heaven will be a great orgy of indulgence and hedonism. Unfortunately, Muslims will never get a chance to see if their speculations are true, for there is no such place as an Islamic heaven. There is only one way to heaven—Jesus Christ. The heaven we read about in the Bible is a place where the glory of God dwells, and where we'll be able to worship him forever.

PRAISE:

PETITION:

In prayer, God stoops to kiss man, to bless man, and to aid man in everything that God can devise or man can need.

Plaster Incarnations

AWAY then with sinful, earthly things; deaden the evil desires lurking within you; have nothing to do with sexual sin, impurity, lust and shameful desires; don't worship the good things of life, for that is idolatry. God's terrible anger is upon those who do such things. You used to do them when your life was still part of this world. (Colossians 3:5-7)

What is God's reaction to man's idolatry?

The Roman Catholic Church allows its parishioners to purchase and display figurines and statues of Jesus, Mary, the apostles, and the saints. The church condones the use of such products, saying that they provide the people with visual reminders of the lives of these people. Many evangelicals have criticized this Roman Catholic position, saying that it encourages people to idolize and worship man-made images, in violation of the second Commandment. Although these items were not meant to be idolized, it is man's nature to put faith in the tangible things of earthly life. Paul urges us, once again, to set our sights and lay up our treasures in a higher place.

PRAISE:

PETITION:

If anyone is thirsty, let him come to me and drink. (John 7:37)

Prank of Tramps

NOW is the time to cast off and throw away all these rotten garments of anger, hatred, cursing, and dirty language.

Don't tell lies to each other; it was your old life with all its wickedness that did that sort of thing; now it is dead and gone. You are living a brand new kind of life that is continually learning more and more of what is right, and trying constantly to be more and more like Christ who created this new life within you. In this new life one's nationality or race or education or social position is unimportant; such things mean nothing. Whether a person has Christ is what matters, and he is equally available to all. (Colossians 3:8-11)

What does Paul say about man's ethnic and educational background?

The Rev. Stephen Merritt one day gave a free dinner at his rescue mission. After sharing a good banquet with a large group of homeless men, he picked up his hat to leave. He discovered that some of the skid-row characters in a prankish mood had filled it with bacon rinds and other scraps from the table. He was furious for a moment, and in a towering rage stepped onto a chair and delivered a scorching denunciation of their action. He stormed at the tramps and berated them for their ingratitude. Then suddenly these words from Scripture flashed in his mind: "Love is not easily provoked." Merritt lived too near to God to be led astray for long. The Holy Spirit rebuked him. He hung his head for a moment and then apologized in humility, telling the men he knew he had grieved the Lord by becoming angry. To show his goodwill, he invited them all back to another dinner the following night. His true humility and spirituality were rewarded, for at that time nearly forty men accepted the Savior.

P R A I S E :

P E T I T I O N :

In your kindness, spare my life; then I can continue to obey you. (Ps. 119:88)

Oil Change

SINCE you have been chosen by God who has given you this new kind of life, and because of his deep love and concern for you, you should practice tenderhearted mercy and kindness to others. Don't worry about making a good impression on them but be ready to suffer quietly and patiently. Be gentle and ready to forgive; never hold grudges. Remember, the Lord forgave you, so you must forgive others.

Most of all, let love guide your life, for then the whole church will stay together in perfect harmony. (Colossians 3:12-14)

According to today's reading, what principle should guide our lives?

There was once an old man who carried a can of oil with him wherever he went. When he passed through a door that squeaked, he'd pour a little oil on the hinges. If a gate was hard to open, he'd oil the latch. He passed through life lubricating doors, windows, and gates, making it easier for people who came after him. People called him eccentric and weird, but they appreciated his spirit of helpfulness. There are many lives that creak and grate harshly as they live day by day. They need lubricating with the oil of gladness, gentleness, or thoughtfulness. Do you have your own "can of oil"?

PRAISE:

PETITION:

Prayer is the most perfect and most divine action of which a rational soul is capable. (A. Baker)

Empty Songs

LET the peace of heart which comes from Christ be always present in your hearts and lives, for this is your responsibility and privilege as members of his body. And always be thankful.

Remember what Christ taught and let his words enrich your lives and make you wise; teach them to each other and sing them out in psalms and hymns and spiritual songs, singing to the Lord with thankful hearts. And whatever you do or say, let it be as a representative of the Lord Jesus, and come with him into the presence of God the Father to give him your thanks. (Colossians 3:15-17)

What should be the attitude of our hearts as we sing to the Lord?

During church services we often sing, " 'Tis the Blessed Hour of Prayer," and then we allow our thoughts to wander aimlessly while others pray. We plead with enthusiasm, "Bring Them In," and later complain about the constant call for Sunday school bus drivers. We sing "For the Beauty of the Earth," then litter that earth with garbage and debris. We raise our voices to ask, "Is It the Crowning Day?" and proceed to live as though we had never heard of the Savior's return. We sing the hymn, "Holy Bible, Book Divine," but spend most of our time reading newspapers and magazines. We declare in song, "I Love to Tell the Story," and can't remember the last time we spoke a word for Christ. We sing, "One Step at a Time," and immediately begin to worry about tomorrow!   We are encouraged in the Scriptures to sing. Whether hymns of praise, worship, adoration, or dedication, these songs should emanate from the heart. They must never be mere hypocritical vocalizations.

PRAISE:

PETITION:

Is anyone among you suffering? He should keep on praying about it. (James 5:13)

Father Love

YOU wives, submit yourselves to your husbands, for that is what the Lord has planned for you. And you husbands must be loving and kind to your wives and not bitter against them, nor harsh.

You children must always obey your fathers and mothers, for that pleases the Lord. Fathers, don't scold your children so much that they become discouraged and quit trying. (Colossians 3:18-21)

What is Paul's advice for harmonious family life?

In *The Myth of the Greener Grass,* J. Allan Petersen says that most sermons preached on this passage—and the parallel passage in Ephesians 5—concentrate on the wife's duty to submit to her husband. Petersen says that not nearly enough attention is paid to the husband's duty—to love his wife and children. In this context, *to love* doesn't mean merely to bring home flowers for the wife and toys for the kids. A husband must love as Christ loved the church. He must be a model and an example for his family, always doing and being first what he expects them to do and be. It is not too early to begin preparing for marriage, even if you haven't yet found the right mate. By concentrating on what the Word says about marriage, even now you can begin cultivating attitudes of godly submission, love, and obedience.

P R A I S E :

P E T I T I O N :

When I, the Messiah, return, how many will I find who have faith [and are praying]? (Luke 18:8)

The Emancipation

YOU slaves must always obey your earthly masters, not only trying to please them when they are watching you but all the time; obey them willingly because of your love for the Lord and because you want to please him. Work hard and cheerfully at all you do, just as though you were working for the Lord and not merely for your masters, remembering that it is the Lord Christ who is going to pay you, giving you your full portion of all he owns. He is the one you are really working for. And if you don't do your best for him, he will pay you in a way that you won't like—for he has no special favorites who can get away with shirking.

You slave owners must be just and fair to all your slaves. Always remember that you, too, have a Master in heaven who is closely watching you. (Colossians 3:22—4:1)

Who is the slaves' real master?

Slavery was an accepted but deplorable relationship in both Old Testament and New Testament times. As is always the case where slavery exists, some humans were considered inferior to other humans. This attitude was condemned by God. When writing the passage above, Paul could easily have prefaced his remarks with something like this: "God didn't create some men inferior to others. He does not condone slavery. But since this condition *does* exist here, here's how slaves and masters should behave toward one another. . . ." We read in Galatians 3:28 that Christ unified both classes in the social order of his kingdom: "We are no longer Jews or Greeks or slaves or free men or even merely men or women, but we are all the same—we are Christians; we are one in Christ Jesus."

P R A I S E :

P E T I T I O N :

Men are never nearer heaven, nearer God, never more Godlike, and never in deeper sympathy with Jesus Christ, than when they are praying.

Unanswered Prayers

DON'T be weary in prayer; keep at it; watch for God's answers and remember to be thankful when they come. Don't forget to pray for us too, that God will give us many chances to preach the Good News of Christ for which I am here in jail. Pray that I will be bold enough to tell it freely and fully, and make it plain, as, of course, I should.

Make the most of your chances to tell others the Good News. Be wise in all your contacts with them. Let your conversation be gracious as well as sensible, for then you will have the right answer for everyone. (Colossians 4:2-6)

What is Paul's advice to Christians who want to tell others the Good News?

If you have been using the "Prayer Diary" in this devotional book, you have no doubt seen a few answers to your requests. But there are undoubtedly a few of your prayers that have not yet been answered. In the space below, write in what you consider to be your unanswered prayers. Concentrate on them today, praising God for his faithfulness. As Paul says, "Don't be weary in prayer."

_____

_____

_____

P R A I S E :

P E T I T I O N :

[The Lord says,] "When he calls on me I will answer; I will be with him in trouble, and rescue him and honor him." (Ps. 91:15)

Group Photo

TYCHICUS, our much loved brother, will tell you how I am getting along. He is a hard worker and serves the Lord with me. I have sent him on this special trip just to see how you are, and to comfort and encourage you. I am also sending Onesimus, a faithful and much loved brother, one of your own people. He and Tychicus will give you all the latest news. (Colossians 4:7-9)

How does Paul describe Tychicus?

Someone has compared Christians to a group of porcupines on a cold winter's night. They need the warmth of each other to keep away the cold of the night and to protect themselves from predators, but the minute they get too close together they begin to jab one another and are forced to move apart. It is refreshing to come to the close of this epistle and to see the picture of companionship as it ought to be for Christians. Paul names many of his close associates in the closing verses of Colossians. Someone has suggested that it is just like Paul to enclose a "group photo" in his letter to the church at Colosse.

P R A I S E :

P E T I T I O N :

Keep a constant watch. (Luke 21:36)

The Colossian Leader

ARISTARCHUS, who is with me here as a prisoner, sends you his love, and so does Mark, a relative of Barnabas. And as I said before, give Mark a hearty welcome if he comes your way. Jesus Justus also sends his love. These are the only Jewish Christians working with me here, and what a comfort they have been!

Epaphras, from your city, a servant of Christ Jesus, sends you his love. He is always earnestly praying for you, asking God to make you strong and perfect and to help you know his will in everything you do. I can assure you that he has worked hard for you with his prayers, and also for the Christians in Laodicea and Hierapolis. (Colossians 4:10-13)

Epaphras worked with Christians in Colosse and in two other cities. What were they?

Epaphras (a short form of the name Epaphroditus) was admired and respected by Paul. He had worked under great difficulty to establish the Christian church in Colosse, a center apparently never visited by Paul. Epaphras was so concerned about the growing heresy in Colosse that he personally delivered a report about it to the imprisoned Paul. It was this report that prompted the writing of the epistle to the Colossians. Paul has referred to Epaphras as "our much-loved fellow worker" (Col. 1:7). We should strive to be more like this admirable servant of Christ, working hard for others with our prayers.

P R A I S E :

P E T I T I O N :

Prayer tests the reality and sincerity of our faith, and saves it from being superficial.

God in Paul

DEAR doctor Luke sends his love, and so does Demas.

Please give my greeting to the Christian friends at Laodicea, and to Nymphas, and to those who meet in his home. By the way, after you have read this letter will you pass it on to the church at Laodicea? And read the letter I wrote to them. And say to Archippus, "Be sure that you do all the Lord has told you to."

Here is my own greeting in my own handwriting: Remember me here in jail. May God's blessings surround you. (Colossians 4:14-18)

Did Paul use a scribe in writing Colossians?

Some of Paul's greatest writing was done as he was rotting away in prison. He was in chains. His health was threatened by the damp, unsanitary environment. And he was under the constant danger of more heinous punishment. Yet he considered his remaining time on earth so important that he spent it writing epistles to churches and friends. And he even witnessed to fellow prisoners and guards.   There is no doubt that Paul's strength in the face of adversity came directly from God. As we contemplate the life of Paul, we should ask God for his all encompassing presence in our lives as well.

PRAISE:

PETITION:

Anyone who calls upon the name of the Lord will be saved. (Rom. 10:13)

September 1 TIMOTHY

The Vietnam War is widely believed to have been the most futile war the U.S. was ever involved in. The war brought about no satisfactory solutions to the problems of Vietnam and its neighbors. It has often been called a senseless, unjustified war. ■ First Timothy is a sort of battle manual for a worthwhile war—the conflict between good and evil. It was written from a veteran (Paul) to a rookie (Timothy). In this epistle Paul provides detailed instructions regarding how to fight against sin and immorality. Paul urges Timothy to "fight on for God."

World Savior

FROM: Paul, a missionary of Jesus Christ, sent out by the direct command of God our Savior and by Jesus Christ our Lord—our only hope.

To: Timothy.

Timothy, you are like a son to me in the things of the Lord. May God our Father and Jesus Christ our Lord show you his kindness and mercy and give you great peace of heart and mind. (1 Timothy 1:1, 2)

Do you think Paul and Timothy enjoyed a close relationship? How can you tell?

As he begins this epistle, Paul refers to God as "our Savior." This reference doesn't strike the average reader today as being out of the ordinary. To Timothy, though, it was quite radical. Nero, the Roman emperor at this time, had called himself the world savior. Most men would never have dreamed of calling anyone else a savior, for fear of punishment from government authorities. But Paul points to God as the only one worthy of the title of Savior.   Many people today are looking for other sources of salvation. It will never be found apart from Jesus Christ.

PRAISE:

PETITION:

Prayer is the peace of our spirit. (J. Taylor)

No Vacancy

AS I said when I left for Macedonia, please stay there in Ephesus and try to stop the men who are teaching such wrong doctrine. Put an end to their myths and fables, and their idea of being saved by finding favor with an endless chain of angels leading up to God—wild ideas that stir up questions and arguments instead of helping people accept God's plan of faith. (Colossians 1:3, 4)

What was one of the "wild ideas" that Paul urged Timothy to attack?

When the slow-moving clerk in a small store was not around one morning, a customer asked, "Where's Eddie?" "Eddie don't work here no more," replied the store owner. "Do you have anyone in mind for the vacancy?" inquired the customer, thinking of his sixteen-year-old son. "Nope," came the brisk reply. "Eddie didn't leave no vacancy." It is interesting to note that Paul spoke most often about Timothy's "work." Timothy was a young man with ambition, and he was devoted to the Lord. It could never be said of him that he was afraid of hard labor. Paul realized this about his colleague; in the epistles of 1 and 2 Timothy, Paul bestows upon him monumental responsibilities. How much work are we ready to accept? We should strive to become less like Eddie and more like Timothy.

P R A I S E :

P E T I T I O N :

When the outlook is bad, try the uplook.

The Cost of Love

WHAT I am eager for is that all the Christians there will be filled with love that comes from pure hearts, and that their minds will be clean and their faith strong.

But these teachers have missed this whole idea and spend their time arguing and talking foolishness. They want to become famous as teachers of the laws of Moses when they haven't the slightest idea what those laws really show us. (1 Timothy 1:5-7)

What does Paul describe as the ultimate goal of the false teachers?

Although the term "free love" is no longer as commonplace as it was in the sixties and seventies, the attitude it described still exists. Many teens see nothing wrong with having sex before marriage. They see sex as just another consumable pleasure.   Paul's statement about love in today's reading ought to be a great help in answering the proponents of free love. He says love is not free. It must be purchased with a pure heart, a good conscience, and a sincere faith.

P R A I S E :

P E T I T I O N :

He gives power to the tired and worn out, and strength to the weak. (Isa. 40:29)

The Man in the Suit

THOSE laws are good when used as God intended. But they were not made for us, whom God has saved; they are for sinners who hate God, have rebellious hearts, curse and swear, attack their fathers and mothers, and murder. Yes, these laws are made to identify as sinners all who are immoral and impure: homosexuals, kidnappers, liars, and all others who do things that contradict the glorious Good News of our blessed God, whose messenger I am. (1 Timothy 1:8-11)

For whom were God's laws made?

A communist was speaking to a group of people in Columbus Circle, New York. In praising the so-called virtues of his ideology, he said, "Communism can put a new suit on a man!" One Christian in the crowd quickly retorted, "Yes, but only Christ can put a new man in the suit!" The "glorious Good News" is the only way to live above sin. As nothing else, it frees us from the punishment that the law demands.

P R A I S E :

P E T I T I O N :

God is at work within you, helping you want to obey him, and then helping you do what he wants. (Phil. 2:13)

Law of the Boot

HOW thankful I am to Christ Jesus our Lord for choosing me as one of his messengers, and giving me the strength to be faithful to him, even though I used to scoff at the name of Christ. I hunted down his people, harming them in every way I could. But God had mercy on me because I didn't know what I was doing, for I didn't know Christ at that time. Oh, how kind our Lord was, for he showed me how to trust him and become full of the love of Christ Jesus. (1 Timothy 1:12-14)

What had Paul done to Christians before he himself met Christ?

During the early eighties the city of Chicago was faced with a big problem. Thousands of parking violators weren't paying their tickets. These people—called "scofflaws," because they scoffed at the law—would simply ignore the tickets issued to them by police officers. Some scofflaws had accumulated several hundred violations. In a major crackdown, the city decided to begin using an ingenious device known as the "Denver boot" to apprehend repeat offenders. The heavy steel "boot" could be locked onto an automobile's wheel, making it impossible to move the car without having the police come to remove the device. The police department really gave scofflaws a "boot" where it counted! Paul confesses here that he had constantly scoffed at the name and message of Christ Jesus before finally being "apprehended" in his Damascus-road experience. He learned—the hard way—to trust and love the Lord.

P R A I S E :

P E T I T I O N :

Fellowship with God as an activity will issue in fellowship with God as an attitude. (G. C. Morgan)

The Shack of the Past

HOW true it is, and how I long that everyone should know it, that Christ Jesus came into the world to save sinners—and I was the greatest of them all. But God had mercy on me so that Christ Jesus could use me as an example to show everyone how patient he is with even the worst sinners, so that others will realize that they, too, can have everlasting life. Glory and honor to God forever and ever. He is the King of the ages, the unseen one who never dies; he alone is God, and full of wisdom. Amen. (1 Timothy 1:15-17)

What was God's reason for being merciful to Paul?

Loretta Lynn, the country-music superstar, lives on a sprawling farm in the South. Her house is a gigantic white mansion, and she has many maids and groundskeepers. In one corner of the farm stands an old, dilapidated shack, the abandoned dwelling place of some unfortunate soul of the past. Lynn has insisted that the shack be preserved intact. She often strolls to it and, entering it, contemplates her childhood. The shack reminds her of where she was brought up, of the miserable living conditions which instilled in her the still-present quest for survival. The old shack serves to make her truly thankful for what she now has.   In today's passage, we catch Paul glancing back over his past. As he recalled his former days, he could not help but burst forth with praise to the heavenly Father.

P R A I S E :

P E T I T I O N :

He will answer all my prayers. (Ps. 6:9)

Leisure Army

NOW, Timothy, my son, here is my command to you: Fight well in the Lord's battles, just as the Lord told us through his prophets that you would. Cling tightly to your faith in Christ and always keep your conscience clear, doing what you know is right. For some people have disobeyed their consciences and have deliberately done what they knew was wrong. It isn't surprising that soon they lost their faith in Christ after defying God like that. Hymenaeus and Alexander are two examples of this. I had to give them over to Satan to punish them until they could learn not to bring shame to the name of Christ. (1 Timothy 1:18-20)

What happened soon after "some people" disobeyed their consciences?

Imagine an army in preparation for battle. The soldiers have long hair, are dressed in sombreros and sandals, and are carrying unloaded BB guns. The commanding officers ride mopeds and hang gliders. The tanks are painted bright yellow and are out of gas. This army is fit for a party, but definitely not fit for battle. They'd be better off at home.   Just as a military army requires a great degree of discipline and training, soldiers in the Lord's army need to be well prepared. We must train through regular Bible study, prayer, and fellowship with other Christians. Battle against the powers of darkness is no picnic; we must be thoroughly fit for spiritual warfare.

PRAISE:

PETITION:

I will call upon the Lord, who is worthy to be praised. (2 Sam. 22:4)

Prayer and Protest

HERE are my directions: Pray much for others; plead for God's mercy upon them; give thanks for all he is going to do for them. Pray in this way for kings and all others who are in authority over us, or are in places of high responsibility, so that we can live in peace and quietness, spending our time in godly living and thinking much about the Lord. (1 Timothy 2:1, 2)

Why should we pray for those in authority over us?

In *A Christian Manifesto* (Crossway, 1982), Francis Schaeffer urges Christians to take a stand for what they believe. He says we should not passively sit by while the government legislates its own morality on issues such as abortion, pornography, and prayer in public schools. After examining the Bible as well as church history, Schaeffer says it is the Christian's responsibility to defend matters of the faith. Not even civil disobedience and physical violence should be ruled out, he says.   Not all Christians would resort to disobeying the law, though, even in the times of moral crisis when the church is threatened. Some Christians believe they should be peacemakers and peacekeepers. But regardless of one's stand on this, one thing is clear: We must never cease praying for those in authority over us. Even though some people in authority are ungodly, we should remember that the ultimate fate of mankind is in God's hands.

P R A I S E :

P E T I T I O N :

Some people talk so much about the philosophy of prayer that there is no time for the practice of it.

The Bridge to God

THIS is good and pleases God our Savior, for he longs for all to be saved and to understand this truth: *That God is on one side and all the people on the other side, and Christ Jesus, himself man, is between them to bring them together, by giving his life for all mankind.*

This is the message which at the proper time God gave to the world. And I have been chosen—this is the absolute truth—as God's minister and missionary to teach this truth to the Gentiles, and to show them God's plan of salvation through faith.

So I want men everywhere to pray with holy hands lifted up to God, free from sin and anger and resentment. (1 Timothy 2:3-8)

What truth does God long for every man to understand?

A mediator is one who stands between two opposing parties, reconciling their differences. Jesus is the mediator who stands between God and man. By his blood shed on Calvary, Christ has broken down the wall of hostility between Jews and Gentiles, God and man. All Christians have direct and immediate access to the Father through Christ, not through any human middleman. There is no other mediator; thus, there is no hope without the mediation of Christ. This Bible passage eliminated the previously considered possibility of mediation by angels, saints, priests, or relatives of Jesus. Jesus is the only way to God. (From *Lindsell Study Bible,* Tyndale)

P R A I S E :

P E T I T I O N :

The Lord will give you an abundance of good things. . . . He will bless everything you do. (Deut. 28:11, 12)

Sin of Imagination

AND the women should be the same way, quiet and sensible in manner and clothing. Christian women should be noticed for being kind and good, not for the way they fix their hair or because of their jewels or fancy clothes. (1 Timothy 2:9, 10)

For what should Christian women be noticed?

A middle-aged woman approached the minister after the morning worship service, and said she wanted to confess a sin. "I am guilty of the terrible sin of pride," she said. "This morning before we came to church I spent over two hours in front of the mirror admiring my beauty." The minister replied, "You are innocent of the sin of pride, but guilty of the sin of having a terrible imagination!" To Christian women, there should be things that are more important than cosmetics, perfume, hair curlers, jewelry, and fashionable clothing. Let us remember to arrange our priorities the way God would.

PRAISE: _____

PETITION: _____

Fear not, for I am with you. Do not be dismayed. I am your God. I will strengthen you; I will help you; I will uphold you with my victorious right hand. (Isa. 41:10)

Women in Church

WOMEN should listen and learn quietly and humbly.

I never let women teach men or lord it over them. Let them be silent in your church meetings. Why? Because God made Adam first, and afterwards he made Eve. And it was not Adam who was fooled by Satan, but Eve, and sin was the result. So God sent pain and suffering to women when their children are born, but he will save their souls if they trust in him, living quiet, good, and loving lives. (1 Timothy 2:11-15)

According to Paul, how should women live their lives?

Things have obviously changed since Paul's day. We now have women in leadership roles throughout the ranks of the church. Our culture is different from that of the Middle East during New Testament times. It is now acceptable for women to speak, teach, and preach in the church. Answer these questions: What two reasons does Paul give for women to remain silent in the church? How did God punish women for causing sin to be brought into the world? How can women be saved?

PRAISE:

PETITION:

O loving and kind God, have mercy. Have pity upon me and take away the awful stain of my transgressions. Oh, wash me, cleanse me from this guilt. Let me be pure again. (Ps. 51:1, 2)

A Life Behind the Pulpit

IT is a true saying that if a man wants to be a pastor he has a good ambition. For a pastor must be a good man whose life cannot be spoken against. He must have only one wife, and he must be hard working and thoughtful, orderly, and full of good deeds. He must enjoy having guests in his home, and must be a good Bible teacher. He must not be a drinker or quarrelsome, but he must be gentle and kind, and not be one who loves money. He must have a well-behaved family, with children who obey quickly and quietly. For if a man can't make his own little family behave, how can he help the whole church? (1 Timothy 3:1-5)

Why is it important for a pastor to have a well-behaved family?

Have you ever considered entering full-time ministry? The task may seem awesome, especially in light of the qualifications Paul sets forth in today's reading. Among other things, becoming a minister means years of hard study, low pay for life, and living under the scrutiny of a congregation. But the rewards are great. A life of dedication to God's work can be more satisfying than any other earthly career. If you've never considered a lifetime in ministry, do so now. Review your strengths and weaknesses, and your commitment to Christ. What sort of ministry would interest you?

PRAISE:

PETITION:

If there was ever a time that we need to pray, it's now. More can be done by prayer than anything else. Prayer is our greatest weapon. (B. Graham)

Entrance Requirements

THE pastor must not be a new Christian, because he might be proud of being chosen so soon, and pride comes before a fall. (Satan's downfall is an example.) Also, he must be well spoken of by people outside the church—those who aren't Christians—so that Satan can't trap him with many accusations, and leave him without freedom to lead his flock. (1 Timothy 3:6, 7)

What does Paul illustrate in referring to Satan's downfall?

Why ought a pastor to be well spoken of by people who don't attend church? After all, the pastor will be leading his congregation, not the unchurched. Paul's rationale here is that a man who is not respected by all people will not be a good evangelist, for no one will wish to listen to him. Furthermore, there may be some truth behind their accusations, truth that would later prove fatal to the prospective pastor's ministry. **O**nce again we see that the qualifications for becoming a pastor are rigid. But there is great exhilaration in leading a flock to spiritual maturity, and in leading people to Christ. And the greatest reward of all comes on the Judgment Day. On that day, God may say to us, "Well done, my good and faithful servants."

P R A I S E :

P E T I T I O N :

Ask God for anything in line with the Holy Spirit's wishes. Plead with him, remind him of your needs, and keep praying earnestly for all Christians everywhere. (Eph. 6:18)

The Faithful Gopher

THE deacons must be the same sort of good, steady men as the pastors. They must not be heavy drinkers and must not be greedy for money. They must be earnest, wholehearted followers of Christ who is the hidden Source of their faith. Before they are asked to be deacons they should be given other jobs in the church as a test of their character and ability, and if they do well, then they may be chosen as deacons.

Their wives must be thoughtful, not heavy drinkers, not gossipers, but faithful in everything they do. Deacons should have only one wife and they should have happy, obedient families. Those who do well as deacons will be well rewarded both by respect from others and also by developing their own confidence and bold trust in the Lord. (1 Timothy 3:8-13)

What are a good deacon's earthly rewards?

A young graduate had been the editor of the college newspaper for the past two years. Now he was looking for full-time employment. A pair of magazine publishers in the area needed a new editor. They were familiar with the graduate's work, having seen the school paper periodically during the school year. They decided to give him a try. They hired him as a "gopher" ("*go for* this, *go for* that"). After a few months the publishers confirmed that he was meticulous and faithful even with the most insignificant, demeaning jobs. They were convinced he'd make a good editor, and soon promoted him. **P**aul seemed to believe in the concept of testing people's commitment before granting the real thing. He says that prospective deacons should first be given other jobs as a test of their character and ability. Let us remember to always be faithful even in the smallest responsibilities. Our dedication may pay off someday.

P R A I S E :

P E T I T I O N :

Don't be afraid, for the Lord will go before you and will be with you; he will not fail nor forsake you. (Deut. 31:8)

Jesus II

I am writing these things to you now, even though I hope to be with you soon, so that if I don't come for awhile you will know what kind of men you should choose as officers for the church of the living God, which contains and holds high the truth of God.

It is quite true that the way to live a godly life is not an easy matter. But the answer lies in Christ, who came to earth as a man, was proved spotless and pure in his Spirit, was served by angels, was preached among the nations, was accepted by men everywhere and was received up again to his glory in heaven. (1 Timothy 3:14-16)

How can we live godly lives?

Long ago, a Frenchman decided to start a new religious cult. He started by proclaiming himself to be God. When he couldn't get any worshipers, he complained to Napoleon. He asked the great general what he could do to get followers. Napoleon answered, "Get yourself crucified and three days later rise from the dead!" Napoleon's tongue-in-cheek advice was impossible for any man to follow. Only God could do such a thing. How thankful we should be that Christ resurrected from the dead and that he will soon return for his people. Praise the one true God!

PRAISE:

PETITION:

Prayer is the means by which our desires can be redirected and aligned with the will of God.

Fictitious Facts

BUT the Holy Spirit tells us clearly that in the last times some in the church will turn away from Christ and become eager followers of teachers with devil-inspired ideas. These teachers will tell lies with straight faces and do it so often that their consciences won't even bother them. (1 Timothy 4: 1, 2)

What will happen to some church people during the last times?

In 1861, the French Academy of Science published a brochure aimed at discrediting the Bible. The pamphlet set forth fifty-one "scientific facts" that controverted the Word of God. To the dismay of the Academy, it was soon discovered that some of the "facts" were quite erroneous. And today there is not a scientist in the world who believes even one of the fifty-one statements. Once again the Bible has withstood the attacks of man.

P R A I S E :

P E T I T I O N :

Create in me a new clean heart, O God, filled with clean thoughts and right desires. (Ps. 51:10)

You Are What You Eat

THEY will say it is wrong to be married and wrong to eat meat, even though God gave these things to well-taught Christians to enjoy and be thankful for. For everything God made is good, and we may eat it gladly if we are thankful for it, and if we ask God to bless it, for it is made good by the Word of God and prayer.

If you explain this to the others you will be doing your duty as a worthy pastor who is fed by faith and by the true teaching you have followed. (1 Timothy 4:3-6)

Is it wrong for Christians to eat certain foods? Explain.

Nutritionists often use the phrase, "You are what you eat" to stress the importance of good eating habits. Of course, the phrase does not mean your body is literally composed of bread, lettuce, orange juice, beef, tomatoes, and yogurt. It refers to the general principle that if we eat well-balanced meals, we are apt to be more healthy than those who don't.   As Paul says in today's Scripture passage, "Everything God made is good, and we may eat it gladly if we are thankful for it." But we must also keep another verse in mind: "Your body is the temple of the Holy Ghost" (1 Cor. 6:19, KJV). Although we may eat all foods, we should eat with moderation and nutritional sense. As Christians, we should exercise discipline in all areas of life, including eating and drinking.

PRAISE:

PETITION:

The Lord is a strong fortress. The godly run to him and are safe. (Prov. 18:10)

Trusting, Suffering

DON'T waste time arguing over foolish ideas and silly myths and legends. Spend your time and energy in the exercise of keeping spiritually fit. Bodily exercise is all right, but spiritual exercise is much more important and is a tonic for all you do. So exercise yourself spiritually and practice being a better Christian, because that will help you not only now in this life, but in the next life too. This is the truth and everyone should accept it. We work hard and suffer much in order that people will believe it, for our hope is in the living God who died for all, and particularly for those who have accepted his salvation. (1 Timothy 4:7-10)

Why do Paul and his companions "work hard and suffer much"?

It is true that those who trust, and who translate their trust into action, will often have to suffer for the cause of Christ. But the reverse is also true. Christians who undergo suffering usually learn to develop deeper trust. British evangelist George Müller once said that the only way to learn strong faith is to endure great trials. In our hour of weakness we are forced to turn to God. This is not to say we should actively seek out ways we can suffer. We should never abandon God, no matter how well off we are in this life, for we will always need him when things are not going so well.

P R A I S E :

P E T I T I O N :

Our short prayers in public owe their point and efficiency to the long ones in private that have preceded them.

Pastoral Prayer

TEACH these things and make sure everyone learns them well. Don't let anyone think little of you because you are young. Be their ideal; let them follow the way you teach and live; be a pattern for them in your love, your faith, and your clean thoughts. Until I get there, read and explain the Scriptures to the church; preach God's Word.

Be sure to use the abilities God has given you through his prophets when the elders of the church laid their hands upon your head. Put these abilities to work; throw yourself into your tasks so that everyone may notice your improvement and progress. Keep a close watch on all you do and think. Stay true to what is right and God will bless you and use you to help others. (1 Timothy 4:11-16)

According to Paul, what are the conditions for God's blessings?

The pastoral tasks mentioned in today's reading are just a few of the requirements of a minister. Pastors' responsibilities are great, and they need your support and prayer. Fill in the blanks below, then pray for each person on the list. Perhaps now would be a good time to send your pastor a note of encouragement or appreciation.

Pastor: _____

Spouse: _____

Child: _____

Child: _____

Child: _____

P R A I S E :

P E T I T I O N :

Prayer prepares the soul for action. (D. Mercier)

No Respect

NEVER speak sharply to an older man, but plead with him respectful-
ly just as though he were your own father. Talk to the younger men as
you would to much loved brothers. Treat the older women as mothers,
and the girls as your sisters, thinking only pure thoughts about them.
(1 Timothy 5:1, 2)

How should we treat older men? younger men? older women? girls?

Americans find it funny to poke fun at, satirize, and openly ridicule other
people. Unlike the humor of many countries, humor in the U.S. is characterized
by "attacks" on others. Large crowds gather to roar at the antics of speakers
who "roast" an "honored guest." Family members rarely miss an opportunity to
give each other a "friendly jab." Making people look silly is as American as
apple pie; it is done by everyone, from grandmotherly types to the most
seasoned comics.   While much of this humor is harmless, one cannot help
but think that some of it might result in a downgraded view of one's fellow
man. As Christians, our attitude toward others should be characterized by love
and respect. Even our humor should reflect that.

PRAISE:

PETITION:

How I pray that you will heed my prayers, O Lord my God! Listen to
my prayer that I am praying to you now. (2 Chron. 6:19)

The Missing God-Shelf

THE church should take loving care of women whose husbands have died, if they don't have anyone else to help them. But if they have children or grandchildren, these are the ones who should take the responsibility, for kindness should begin at home, supporting needy parents. This is something that pleases God very much.

The church should care for widows who are poor and alone in the world, if they are looking to God for his help and spending much time in prayer; but not if they are spending their time running around gossiping, seeking only pleasure and thus ruining their souls. This should be your church rule so that the Christians will know and do what is right.

But anyone who won't care for his own relatives when they need help, especially those living in his own family, has no right to say he is a Christian. Such a person is worse than the heathen. (1 Timothy 5:3-8)

Who is primarily responsible for the widows?

A Japanese girl who studied at an American college spent her Christmas vacation in the home of one of her American classmates. She had enjoyed her stay in America so far, but had not yet seen something she longed to see: the inside of a true Christian home, as this one was reported to be. She was treated royally and had a delightful time. As she was about to leave, the mother of the Christian family said, "How do you like the way we Americans live?" **"O**h," said the girl, "I love it! Your home is beautiful; yet, there is one thing I miss." A faraway look came into her eyes as she continued, "It all seems very strange to me. I have been with you to your church, and have seen you worship there, but I have missed God in your home! You know, in Buddhist Japan we have a 'God-shelf' in every home, so we can worship right there in the house. Excuse me, but don't you Americans worship God in your home?" Her host was shamefaced. It was true that they had not established a "family altar" of any kind. They had not learned to show "piety at home."

P R A I S E :

P E T I T I O N :

God commands us to come boldly to the throne of grace. God is glorified by large asking.

Good Works

A widow who wants to become one of the special church workers should be at least sixty years old and have been married only once. She must be well thought of by everyone because of the good she has done. Has she brought up her children well? Has she been kind to strangers as well as to other Christians? Has she helped those who are sick and hurt? Is she always ready to show kindness?

The younger widows should not become members of this special group because after awhile they are likely to disregard their vow to Christ and marry again. And so they will stand condemned because they broke their first promise. Besides, they are likely to be lazy and spend their time gossiping around from house to house, getting into other people's business. So I think it is better for these younger widows to marry again and have children, and take care of their own homes; then no one will be able to say anything against them.

Let me remind you again that a widow's relatives must take care of her, and not leave this to the church to do. Then the church can spend its money for the care of widows who are all alone and have nowhere else to turn. (1 Timothy 5:9-14, 16)

What qualifications must a widow have who wants to become a special church worker?

Ephesians 2:8 says, "Because of his kindness you have been saved through trusting Christ." This passage and many others in the New Testament make it clear that there is nothing man can do to deserve salvation. Man is saved by God's grace alone; he is not redeemed by good works. It seems, however, as though everything we've read in the past few days points to the fact that we were saved *for* good works. Once we have become God's children, he expects us to extend his kindness, love, and mercy to those in need. "It is God himself who has made us what we are and given us new lives from Christ Jesus; and long ages ago he planned that we should spend these lives in helping others" (Eph. 2:10).

P R A I S E :

P E T I T I O N :

O Lord God of Israel, there is no god like you in all of heaven and earth. You are the God who keeps his kind promises to all those who obey you, and who are anxious to do your will. (2 Chron. 6:14)

Living with Care

PASTORS who do their work well should be paid well and should be highly appreciated, especially those who work hard at both preaching and teaching. For the Scriptures say, "Never tie up the mouth of an ox when it is treading out the grain—let him eat as he goes along!" And in another place, "Those who work deserve their pay!"

Don't listen to complaints against the pastor unless there are two or three witnesses to accuse him. If he has really sinned, then he should be rebuked in front of the whole church so that no one else will follow his example. (1 Timothy 5:17-20)

What does Paul say about a pastor's salary?

The President of the United States has to be extremely careful of everything he says, in public or otherwise. He must choose his words with great heed, so as to minimize the chances for misinterpretation. He must also live a pure, blameless life. Even a speeding ticket could be blown into a national scandal. Those in the public eye are particularly susceptible to criticism and accusations from the ranks below. Many such accusations soon prove to be groundless. Paul wisely recommends that all complaints against the pastor be disregarded unless there is substantial evidence to prove him guilty.

P R A I S E :

P E T I T I O N :

God always deals in secret with the soul he intends to use in public.

Sound on Sin

I solemnly command you in the presence of God and the Lord Jesus Christ and of the holy angels to do this whether the pastor is a special friend of yours or not. All must be treated exactly the same. Never be in a hurry about choosing a pastor; you may overlook his sins and it will look as if you approve of them. Be sure that you yourself stay away from all sin. (By the way, this doesn't mean you should completely give up drinking wine. You ought to take a little sometimes as medicine for your stomach because you are sick so often.)

Remember that some men, even pastors, lead sinful lives and everyone knows it. In such situations you can do something about it. But in other cases only the judgment day will reveal the terrible truth. In the same way, everyone knows how much good some pastors do, but sometimes their good deeds aren't known until long afterward. (1 Timothy 5:21-25)

What danger lies in overlooking the sins of a prospective pastor?

The great Scottish preacher, Dr. Alexander Whyte, was once discussing with a church member what points should be considered in choosing a new minister. Dr. Whyte ended by saying with great earnestness, "Be sure he is sound on sin." The Scottish preacher had the insight to know that one's theology of sin is indicative of the caliber of one's Christianity. Bishop Handley Moule of England once said that "every heresy shows some connection with inadequate views of the exceeding sinfulness of sin."

P R A I S E :

P E T I T I O N :

I will pray morning, noon, and night, pleading aloud with God; and he will hear and answer. (Ps. 55:17)

Strength of Servanthood

CHRISTIAN slaves should work hard for their owners and respect them; never let it be said that Christ's people are poor workers. Don't let the name of God or his teaching be laughed at because of this. If their owner is a Christian, that is no excuse for slowing down; rather they should work all the harder because a brother in the faith is being helped by their efforts.

Teach these truths, Timothy, and encourage all to obey them. (1 Timothy 6:1, 2)

Should a Christian's slaves be expected to work as hard as a non-Christian's?

An important business executive employed a sickly, frail man as his chief assistant. A friend asked the executive how he could rely so heavily on such a weak creature. He replied, "There is a constant flow of women and men passing through this office. They all want something from me. They all want to know how I can help them get to 'the top.' Harry, on the other hand, wants only to serve me. That's why I keep him near."   When we serve because we want to, then and only then are we true servants.

PRAISE :

PETITION :

Don't be weary in prayer; keep at it; watch for God's answers and remember to be thankful when they come. (Col. 4:2)

The Slowest Pace

SOME may deny these things, but they are the sound, wholesome teachings of the Lord Jesus Christ and are the foundation for a godly life. Anyone who says anything different is both proud and stupid. He is quibbling over the meaning of Christ's words and stirring up arguments ending in jealousy and anger, which only lead to name-calling, accusations, and evil suspicions. These arguers—their minds warped by sin—don't know how to tell the truth; to them the Good News is just a means of making money. Keep away from them. (1 Timothy 6:3-5)

Does Paul advise Timothy to try to change the minds of the "arguers"? Explain.

It was a clear day on the campground, and a boy was feeding an apple to his pony. A passerby was moved by the sight, and walked over to talk to him. "Can your pony run fast?" asked the man, trying to start a conversation. "No, sir. He's not a fast runner," replied the boy. The man patted the pony on the back and asked, "Can he do anything good?" The boy thought for a moment, then his eyes brightened. "Yes sir. He can stand fast!" Steadfastness is one of the forgotten virtues. But in this day of many false teachers and preachers, we need Christians who stand fast in the truth.

P R A I S E :

P E T I T I O N :

Grant us grace, Almighty Father, so to pray as to deserve to be heard. (J. Austen)

Tithing to Self

DO you want to be truly rich? You already are if you are happy and good. After all, we didn't bring any money with us when we came into the world, and we can't carry away a single penny when we die. So we should be well satisfied without money if we have enough food and clothing. But people who long to be rich soon begin to do all kinds of wrong things to get money, things that hurt them and make them evil-minded and finally send them to hell itself. For the love of money is the first step toward all kinds of sin. Some people have even turned away from God because of their love for it, and as a result have pierced themselves with many sorrows. (1 Timothy 6:6-10)

What happens to most people who long to be rich?

One of the owners of a famous brand of heavy construction equipment was very wealthy. His company was expanding into many overseas markets, and soon he found himself rolling in millions of dollars. Being a Christian, he didn't feel right about keeping all his money. Ultimately he decided to tithe, but not to God. He tithed to himself! That's right: He kept only ten percent of his income, giving the rest to the cause of Christ. In spite of the enticement of riches, this man had retained a righteous perspective. He decided that his love for God was much greater than his love for earthly possessions.

_P R A I S E :_

_P E T I T I O N :_

Truly, if you have faith, and don't doubt, . . . you can even say to this Mount of Olives, "Move over into the ocean," and it will. (Matt. 21:21)

The Sacrifice of Victory

OH, Timothy, you are God's man. Run from all these evil things and work instead at what is right and good, learning to trust him and love others, and to be patient and gentle. Fight on for God. Hold tightly to the eternal life which God has given you, and which you have confessed with such a ringing confession before many witnesses.

I command you before God who gives life to all, and before Christ Jesus who gave a fearless testimony before Pontius Pilate, that you fulfill all he has told you to do, so that no one can find fault with you from now until our Lord Jesus Christ returns. For in due season Christ will be revealed from heaven by the blessed and only Almighty God, the King of kings and Lord of lords, who alone can never die, who lives in light so terrible that no human being can approach him. No mere man has ever seen him, nor ever will. Unto him be honor and everlasting power and dominion forever and ever. Amen. (1 Timothy 6:11-16)

When will Christ be revealed from heaven?

When the armies of Napoleon Bonaparte went to fight a battle, the great general would quickly note the location of the battlefield's most strategic location. He would then thrust all his forces and resources into conquering and keeping that position, no matter what the sacrifice to his troops. To claim spiritual conquests, soldiers in God's army must be alert and prepared to do the same. Noted leader Gordon B. Watt once said: "The point of obstruction must be found out, and prayer focused upon it. The mind must be convicted. The will must be stirred into right action. On the obstruction, whatever it may be, as it is revealed through waiting upon God, prayer must be concentrated."

P R A I S E :

P E T I T I O N :

He will teach the ways that are right and best to those who humbly turn to him. (Ps. 25:9)

Price: One Soul

TELL those who are rich not to be proud and not to trust in their money, which will soon be gone, but their pride and trust should be in the living God who always richly gives us all we need for our enjoyment. Tell them to use their money to do good. They should be rich in good works and should give happily to those in need, always being ready to share with others whatever God has given them. By doing this they will be storing up real treasure for themselves in heaven—it is the only safe investment for eternity! And they will be living a fruitful Christian life down here as well. (1 Timothy 6:17-19)

How can we store up real treasures for ourselves in heaven?

Riding past the estate of a wealthy man who had recently died, a man asked a friend who'd known the deceased, "How much was the estate worth?" "I don't know what it was worth," replied the friend, "but I do know what he paid for it. It cost him his soul." The estate owner had been approached time and time again about his eternal welfare, but he was always too busy laying up treasures on earth to be bothered with the riches of heaven. His reply was always, "I'll take care of those matters later; after a while, but not now." But the "after a while" never came for him, for he died without warning of a heart attack. "For what shall it profit a man if he gain the whole world and lose his own soul?" (Mark 8:36, KJV).

P R A I S E :

P E T I T I O N :

Prayer is love raised to its greatest power. (R. McCracken)

Avoiding Arguments

OH, Timothy, don't fail to do these things that God entrusted to you. Keep out of foolish arguments with those who boast of their "knowledge" and thus prove their lack of it. Some of these people have missed the most important thing in life—they don't know God. May God's mercy be upon you. (1 Timothy 6:20, 21)

According to Paul, what is the most important thing in life?

A righteous layman in an evangelical church began to notice that certain church rules were being overemphasized. Teens were told to never attend the theater or listen to popular music. Men and women were discouraged from reading any secular magazines. The church board proposed establishing a dress code for Sunday morning service. The layman protested this swing toward legalism, but his words fell on deaf ears. He was labeled a troublemaker. Soon he realized that it did no good to argue, and that he should either conform or leave. Paul's advice to him would have been to "keep out of foolish arguments," and to go someplace where people truly know and love the Lord.

P R A I S E :

P E T I T I O N :

He listened! He heard my prayer! He paid attention to it! (Ps. 66:19)

October 2 TIMOTHY

In August 1983, Philippine politician Benigno Aquino, Jr. was gunned down as soon as he stepped off the plane at the Manila International Airport. Aquino, leader of the opposition party, had known the trip to his homeland would be dangerous. Just a few hours before leaving for the Philippines he told reporters that he might be killed. But he went ahead anyway, confident that his presence at home was necessary for the good of the land. ■ In 2 Timothy, Paul says he senses that the end is near for him. He says, "I won't be around . . . much longer." Yet he remains firm in his commitments until the end. The advice and instructions of this epistle proved priceless to Timothy.

LA,Philippines, Aug.21(AP)- Security men carry the body of a man
enator Benigno Aquino Jr. moments after shots rang out at the Ma
rport as the opposition politician returned Sunday after three-y
d self-exile in the United States. Body lying down is unidentifi
Radiophoto)(ah11700str-Ben Malumay)1983

Doorway to Eternity

FROM: Paul, Jesus Christ's missionary, sent out by God to tell men and women everywhere about the eternal life he has promised them through faith in Jesus Christ.

To: Timothy, my dear son. May God the Father and Christ Jesus our Lord shower you with his kindness, mercy and peace. (2 Timothy 1:1, 2)

What does Paul call Timothy here? What does that indicate about their relationship?

There is a huge cathedral in Milan, Italy. It is noted for its beautiful front doorway. To the right of the door is sculpted a wreath of roses. Underneath it are the words, "All that pleases us is only for a moment." On the left-hand side there is a sculptured cross of thorns and the inscription, "All that troubles us is only for a moment." Over the magnificent doorway are the words, "Nothing is important but that which is eternal."

P R A I S E :

P E T I T I O N :

Lord, teach us a prayer to recite. (Luke 11:1)

The Strength of Prayer

HOW I thank God for you, Timothy. I pray for you every day, and many times during the long nights I beg my God to bless you richly. He is my fathers' God, and mine, and my only purpose in life is to please him.

How I long to see you again. How happy I would be, for I remember your tears as we left each other.

I know how much you trust the Lord, just as your mother Eunice and your grandmother Lois do; and I feel sure you are still trusting him as much as ever. (2 Timothy 1:3-5)

Does Paul seem certain that Timothy is still following the Lord?

Through all the epistles of Paul we notice the priority that he places on prayer. He is always telling people of his prayers for them. And he always urges the people to spend more time in prayer. Prayer without ceasing—day and night— is the one answer to the victorious Christian life. We should live our lives in an attitude of prayer. The one concern of the devil is to keep the saints from praying. He fears nothing from prayerless Bible studies, prayerless works, and prayerless living. Satan laughs at our toils and mocks our wisdom, but he trembles when we pray.

PRAISE:

PETITION:

The man who bows the lowest in the presence of God stands the straightest in the presence of sin.

Lower Lights

THIS being so, I want to remind you to stir into flame the strength and boldness that is in you, that entered into you when I laid my hands upon your head and blessed you. For the Holy Spirit, God's gift, does not want you to be afraid of people, but to be wise and strong, and to love them and enjoy being with them. (2 Timothy 1:6, 7)

What had entered Timothy when Paul blessed him?

The well-known hymn "Let the Lower Lights Be Burning" was inspired by the wreck of a passenger ship off the harbor of Cleveland. The few survivors of the tragedy related that the ship was unable to make port in the storm because the electricity had failed in the lower harbor. Although the lights were burning in the upper harbor, the crew needed the lower lights to safely see their way to port.   Christ is the upper light which has never faded, but the world can only see the "lower lights"—the lives of Christians. The spirit of fear and discouragement sometimes causes our lights to flicker. In today's reading, we see that Paul told Timothy that the Holy Spirit did not want him to be afraid. We should fight the spirit of fear with the Spirit of God.

PRAISE:

PETITION:

I will comfort you there as a little one is comforted by its mother. (Isa. 66:13)

The Grim Companion

IF you will stir up this inner power, you will never be afraid to tell others about our Lord, or to let them know that I am your friend even though I am here in jail for Christ's sake. You will be ready to suffer with me for the Lord, for he will give you strength in suffering. (2 Timothy 1:8)

What will happen if Timothy stirs up the power within him?

God never promised us a life free from pain and suffering. Because of the downfall of man and the subsequent curse that settled upon the earth, none of us is immune to misery of one sort or another. Suffering will be our constant companion until the return of Christ.   God could choose to relieve us from the agonies and anxieties of this world. But to do so would be to reclaim a bit of the free will he gave to man at the time of creation. In order for his plan to be perfect, we must wait until the end of the age to be totally restored to him.   In the meantime, we are promised the courage and strength necessary to withstand suffering. God will give us what we need to endure the hard times.

P R A I S E :

P E T I T I O N :

I will hide in God, who is my rock and my refuge. He is my shield and my salvation, my refuge and high tower. (2 Sam. 22:3)

Godly Desires

IT is he who saved us and chose us for his holy work, not because we deserved it but because that was his plan long before the world began—to show his love and kindness to us through Christ. (2 Timothy 1:9)

When did God formulate the plan of salvation?

Often we feel uneasy about turning our lives over to God and saying, "OK, God. My life's all yours. Do with it whatever you want." We tend to think that if we take this step, God certainly will take advantage of it by making us marry someone we dislike or sending us to work in subhuman conditions where all our talents will be wasted. **N**othing could be further from the truth. God is at work even within the desires of his children. He wants to direct us to happiness and fulfillment. We should listen to his voice and heed his promptings. **H**ow do we know if our desires are godly? If they don't contradict Scripture, and if they make perfect sense to you, your family, and your Christian friends, they certainly deserve close attention. God often shows us his will for us by stirring certain goals and wishes deep within us. Do you know what "holy work" God has chosen you for? How do you know, or how can you find out?

P R A I S E :

P E T I T I O N :

Those who trust in the Lord are steady as Mount Zion, unmoved by any circumstance. (Ps. 125:1)

Sin Junkies

AND now he has made all of this plain to us by the coming of our Savior Jesus Christ, who broke the power of death and showed us the way of everlasting life through trusting him. And God has chosen me to be his missionary, to preach to the Gentiles and teach them.

That is why I am suffering here in jail and I am certainly not ashamed of it, for I know the one in whom I trust, and I am sure that he is able to safely guard all that I have given him until the day of his return. (2 Timothy 1:10-12)

To what ministry had God called Paul?

A woman discovered with alarm that the Federal Drug Administration planned to ban her favorite sleeping pill. The government agency said the pill was habit-forming and unsafe. The woman was incensed; she wrote a long letter to her senator. "I know that this pill is not habit-forming," she wrote. "I have been taking it every night for twenty-five years and I still am not addicted!" Sin and self-deception often blind our spiritual eyes, chaining us to the miseries of lies and illusion. As Paul says in today's reading, God's plan has been made plain to us by the coming of Jesus. Yet many still choose to hide themselves from this fact, clutching vainly to humanistic ideologies.

P R A I S E :

P E T I T I O N :

The only way to do much for God is to ask much of God.

Murder in the Sky

HOLD tightly to the pattern of truth I taught you, especially concerning the faith and love Christ Jesus offers you. Guard well the splendid, God-given ability you received as a gift from the Holy Spirit who lives within you. (2 Timothy 1:13, 14)

What had Paul taught Timothy?

On September 1, 1983, a Korean Air Lines jet flying from Alaska to South Korea strayed over USSR airspace and was brutally shot down by the Soviets. All 269 civilians aboard were killed. The whole world joined together in protesting its moral outrage over the massacre. The facts were clear and the evidence overwhelming: The Soviets had purposefully downed an unarmed civilian airliner. Yet the Soviets at first denied the shooting; later they admitted to shooting at what they thought was a spy plane. Then they blamed the entire incident on U.S. "propagandists." The Soviet pattern of lies continued, heightening the world's fury over the crime. In a special meeting of the United Nations Security Council, the South Korean ambassador delivered an impassioned speech. He reviewed all the Soviets' lies and half-truths, pointing out contradictions and absurdities. He soundly denounced the Soviet position, accusing it of being utterly "unrelated to truth." Lenin said that all is moral that advances the cause of communism. What a sad "morality" that approves of murder and vicious lies. On the other hand, godly morality always promotes righteousness, love, and dignity. Godly morality leads to the "pattern of truth" Paul discusses here.

P R A I S E :

P E T I T I O N :

The God of heaven will help us. (Neh. 2:20)

Turning the Tables

AS you know, all the Christians who came here from Asia have deserted me; even Phygellus and Hermogenes are gone. May the Lord bless Onesiphorus and all his family, because he visited me and encouraged me often. His visits revived me like a breath of fresh air, and he was never ashamed of my being in jail. In fact, when he came to Rome he searched everywhere trying to find me, and finally did. May the Lord give him a special blessing at the day of Christ's return. And you know better than I can tell you how much he helped me at Ephesus. (2 Timothy 1:15-18)

Why is Paul thankful for Onesiphorus and his family?

Milton Nascimento, a black boy growing up in central Brazil, once went to a country club on the outskirts of town. For a few cents, the club admitted children who wanted to spend the afternoon swimming in the pool. But when Milton approached the ticket-taker, he was told to go home, because black people were not to be admitted.   Milton grew up to become one of the most famous singers in Brazil. His voice became known to jazz lovers around the world. On one occasion his hometown wanted to honor Nascimento. They named the town's central plaza after him, and prepared a great banquet for him at the very country club that, years before, had turned him away. But he didn't show up at the banquet; by his absence he protested the treatment he and others of his race were getting. As the press got wind of the story, the club owners were keenly embarrassed by their racist policies.   The exploitative, patronizing club owners altered their policies whenever it was to their advantage. Fair-weather "friends" such as these are a dime a dozen. True friends, such as Onesiphorus, are hard to find. But "there is a *friend* who sticks closer than a brother" (Prov. 18:24).

P R A I S E :

P E T I T I O N :

I will walk among you and be your God, and you shall be my people. (Lev. 26:12)

Pass It On

OH, Timothy, my son, be strong with the strength Christ Jesus gives you. For you must teach others those things you and many others have heard me speak about. Teach these great truths to trustworthy men who will, in turn, pass them on to others. (2 Timothy 2:1, 2)

To whom must Timothy teach the "great truths"?

A minister was sitting in church with a row of boys during a vacation Bible school program. Suddenly the little boy sitting beside him gave him a sharp jab in the ribs. As the minister was regaining his breath and composure, he heard the small voice beside him whisper, "Pass it on!"　Later the minister said that, since he was sitting on the aisle, he could not pass it on. But he had learned a small lesson about being faithful. What one boy at the other end of the pew had started was diligently passed down the line until the last person got "the message."　That's our responsibility as Christians—"Pass it on!"

P R A I S E :

P E T I T I O N :

Prayer is the key that opens to us the treasures of God's mercies and blessings.

First Priority

TAKE your share of suffering as a good soldier of Jesus Christ, just as I do, and as Christ's soldier do not let yourself become tied up in worldly affairs, for then you cannot satisfy the one who has enlisted you in his army. (2 Timothy 2:3, 4)

To what does Paul compare Christ's followers?

John Wanamaker of the famed Wanamaker department stores was once asked to become the Postmaster General for the United States Postal Service. He agreed to take the position on one condition: that he be free to carry on his work as a superintendent of a large Philadelphia Sunday school. Although his position with the Sunday school seemed to men to be much less critical than the position he'd been offered, Wanamaker knew how to keep his priorities straight. He knew that the furtherance of the gospel is much more important than the material success of any man. Wanamaker was involved with the affairs of the world, but he wasn't tied up in them.

P R A I S E :

P E T I T I O N :

For he rescues you from every trap, and protects you from the fatal plague. (Ps. 91:3)

Disqualified

FOLLOW the Lord's rules for doing his work, just as an athlete either follows the rules or is disqualified and wins no prize. (2 Timothy 2:5)

What must we do to win the "prize" of heaven?

Jim Thorpe was one of the greatest American athletes ever. During the 1912 Olympic Games, he became the first person to win both the decathlon and pentathlon. Later, though, it was discovered that he had been ineligible to compete in the games. Officials charged that he had previously played professional baseball, receiving wages for his efforts. Since the Olympics is strictly for amateurs, Thorpe was stripped of his medals. We must remember that no matter how sincere and diligent we may be, if we do not keep the rules, our efforts will be of no avail. In order to win the "prize"—heaven—we must follow the Lord's rules.

PRAISE:

PETITION:

The Lord [said], "I myself will go with you and give you success." (Exod. 33:14)

Soldiers, Athletes, Farmers

WORK hard, like a farmer who gets paid well if he raises a large crop. Think over these three illustrations, and may the Lord help you to understand how they apply to you. (2 Timothy 2:6, 7)

What does Paul ask Timothy to do with the three illustrations?

In today's reading, Paul presents a third analogy: Christians are like farmers. On the last two days he compared Christians to soldiers and athletes. Can you remember what he said about these? Draw a line from each vocation below (left-hand column) to the appropriate attribute (right-hand column). Each vocation has two attributes.

1. Good soldiers	A. Are paid well at the end of a good season.
	B. Work hard.
2. Good athletes	C. Take their share of suffering.
	D. Follow the Lord's rules.
3. Good farmers	E. Don't become involved in worldly affairs.
	F. Stand no risk of disqualification.

Answers: 1. C, E 2. D, F 3. A, B

P R A I S E :

P E T I T I O N :

Promises are like the unsown seed, but the soil and culture of prayer are necessary to germinate and culture the seed.

One Plus One Equals One

DON'T ever forget the wonderful fact that Jesus Christ was a Man, born into King David's family; and that he was God, as shown by the fact that he rose again from the dead. (2 Timothy 2:8)

What does Paul offer as proof of Christ's divinity?

Contrary to what some Christians believe, Jesus was not half man and half God. He could not be divided into human and divine parts. During his thirty-three years on earth, he was *all* man and *all* God. In every aspect of his human existence—mental, emotional, physical, spiritual, and social—he was a *man*. He even referred to himself as the "Son of Man." Yet his entire being was divine; this accounts for his sinless life, his perfect ministry, and his miracles.   To say that Christ was all man and all God is to defy a common law of mathematics. As we understand arithmetic, $1 + 1 = 2$. In Christ's case, however, $1 + 1 = 1$. This is a great mystery. We will probably never understand it. But we must realize that the God who created all men, as well as all laws of science, lies beyond the scope of human comprehension.

P R A I S E :

P E T I T I O N :

Hallelujah! Yes, praise the Lord! Sing him a new song. Sing his praises, all his people. (Ps. 149:1)

The Death-Defying Book

IT is because I have preached these great truths that I am in trouble here and have been put in jail like a criminal. But the Word of God is not chained, even though I am. I am more than willing to suffer if that will bring salvation and eternal glory in Christ Jesus to those God has chosen. (2 Timothy 2:9, 10)

For what will Paul gladly suffer?

Over the centuries the Bible has undergone thousands of crises, translations, bans, printings, and burnings. The history of the Bible is replete with accounts of great conflicts between people bent on destroying it and people dedicated to circulating it as widely as possible. Many people have given their lives for the sake of the Bible. Their efforts and sacrifices have not been in vain, for the Scriptures have survived intact. As Paul said, "The Word of God is not chained, even though I am." Today there are more Bibles in the world than ever before.   Although men have died for the Bible, the Bible has not died out. It never will. The sheer strength of its truth is more powerful than any human effort to destroy it.

PRAISE:

PETITION:

You can pray for anything, and if you believe, you have it; it's yours! (Mark 11:24)

Christ's Faithfulness

I am comforted by this truth, that when we suffer and die for Christ it only means that we will begin living with him in heaven. And if we think that our present service for him is hard, just remember that some day we are going to sit with him and rule with him. But if we give up when we suffer, and turn against Christ, then he must turn against us. Even when we are too weak to have any faith left, he remains faithful to us and will help us, for he cannot disown us who are part of himself, and he will always carry out his promises to us. (2 Timothy 2:11-13)

How does Christ treat Christians who are too weak to have any faith left?

Because we are human, our emotions and moods are in a constant state of flux. Even our faith in God is often affected by the tides of disposition. We sometimes find ourselves thinking that God doesn't really exist, or that if he does, he certainly doesn't care about us. But regardless of our state of mind, Christ will always remain faithful to his followers. Consider Peter, for example. Even though this apostle reached such a low point in his faith that he denied the Lord three times, Christ remained faithful to him. Peter was not only forgiven for his transgressions, but was allowed to become a great Christian leader—two of his books appear in the New Testament! As Paul says in today's reading, "Even when we are too weak to have any faith left, he remains faithful to us."

PRAISE:

PETITION:

If my people will humble themselves and pray, and search for me, and turn from their wicked ways, I will hear them from heaven and forgive their sins and heal their land. (2 Chron. 7:14)

Evangelism by Argument

REMIND your people of these great facts, and command them in the name of the Lord not to argue over unimportant things. Such arguments are confusing and useless, and even harmful. Work hard so God can say to you, "Well done." Be a good workman, one who does not need to be ashamed when God examines your work. Know what his Word says and means. (2 Timothy 2:14, 15)

What does Paul exhort us to become?

John is a sophomore anthropology major at a state university. He is a Christian and feels that he should witness by comparing science to the Bible. He has done a lot of research in the fields of creationism and evolution. John often gets into heated debates with atheist acquaintances, and thus feels he is witnessing to the lost. He thinks that if he convinces these people that evolution is false and creationism is true, they will automatically become Christians. Although John is a dedicated Christian, his efforts at evangelism are misdirected. Paul would call John's argumentative approach "confusing and useless, even harmful." Evangelism through analysis and scientific exposition usually proves fruitless. In order to bring people to Christ, we need only to show them the Savior, through our words and actions.

P R A I S E :

P E T I T I O N :

I love the Lord because he hears my prayers and answers them. Because he bends down and listens, I will pray as long as I breathe. (Ps. 116:1, 2)

Playing on the Edge

STEER clear of foolish discussions which lead people into the sin of anger with each other. Things will be said that will burn and hurt for a long time to come. Hymenaeus and Philetus, in their love of argument, are men like that. They have left the path of truth, preaching the lie that the resurrection of the dead has already occurred; and they have weakened the faith of some who believe them. (2 Timothy 2:16-18)

What heresy were Hymenaeus and Philetus preaching?

A family in California had a large mud puddle in their backyard during a particularly rainy summer. The children were told not to play in it. On one afternoon one of the little boys went outside and sat at the edge of the puddle. He played there for nearly an hour, never entering the puddle but nonetheless covering himself with mud. Although he did not directly disobey his parents, he got just as filthy as he would have by entering the puddle. **P**aul says we should steer clear of foolish discussions which are not sinful themselves, but which easily lead to the sin of anger. Playing with sin and error always leads to the filth of ungodliness.

P R A I S E :

P E T I T I O N :

I am with you and I will save you, says the Lord. (Jer. 30:11)

A Piece of the Rock

BUT God's truth stands firm like a great rock, and nothing can shake it. It is a foundation stone with these words written on it: "The Lord knows those who are really his," and "A person who calls himself a Christian should not be doing things that are wrong." (2 Timothy 2:19)

Paul compares God's truth to two items. What are they?

A major insurance company has adopted as its logo an artist's conception of the Rock of Gibraltar, the great geological formation on the southern coast of Spain. Its slogan, designed to entice prospective clients, is: "Get a piece of the rock." We associate great rocks and mountains with the qualities of steadfastness and endurance. On this changing earth, however, even mountains are not permanent. They can be carved away by water, blasted with dynamite, or even moved by the continental-drift phenomenon. **W**hen Paul compares God's truth to a "great rock," he means that the qualities of permanence we generally associate with such geological formations are inherent in God's truth. Unlike anything in his creation, God's truth is *absolutely* unchangeable.

P R A I S E :

P E T I T I O N :

Our prayers must mean something to us if they are to mean anything to God. (M. D. Babcock)

Paper Plates and China

IN a wealthy home there are dishes made of gold and silver as well as some made from wood and clay. The expensive dishes are used for guests, and the cheap ones are used in the kitchen or to put garbage in. If you stay away from sin you will be like one of these dishes made of the purest gold—the very best in the house—so that Christ himself can use you for his highest purposes. (2 Timothy 2:20, 21)

Using Paul's analogy, how can we be like dishes made of purest gold?

Paul has drawn an exquisite comparison in this passage. In his analogy, both kinds of dishes—expensive and cheap—are nevertheless *dishes*. They have basically the same form, but are of different quality. Likewise, there are "expensive" and "cheap" Christians. Both types are heaven-bound children of God, but the "cheap" ones are coming along just for the ride, while the "expensive" ones are serving God well through their beauty and function.   In the household of God's kingdom, we should strive to purge our lives of all sinful impurities. We ought to become less like paper plates and more like fine dishes of china and gold.

P R A I S E :

P E T I T I O N :

The Lord [said], "I will make my goodness pass before you." (Exod. 33:19)

Burning Oil

RUN from anything that gives you the evil thoughts that young men often have, but stay close to anything that makes you want to do right. Have faith and love, and enjoy the companionship of those who love the Lord and have pure hearts. (2 Timothy 2:22)

To whom should we become companions?

An oil lamp was once asked, "Aren't you afraid that your wick will quickly be consumed in flames?" "No, I don't fear that," replied the lamp, "because the flame doesn't consume me even though it burns on me. I only bear the oil that saturates my texture. I am only the ladder upon which the oil climbs. It is not I, but the oil in me that burns and furnishes the light." Vessels that are empty of self and full of oil provide the most light. Our lives should be saturated with the grace of our Lord, so that all those around us will sense his light.

P R A I S E :

P E T I T I O N :

O Lord, please hear my prayer! Heed the prayers of those of us who delight to honor you. (Neh. 1:11)

Fishing Tips

AGAIN I say, don't get involved in foolish arguments which only upset people and make them angry. God's people must not be quarrelsome; they must be gentle, patient teachers of those who are wrong. Be humble when you are trying to teach those who are mixed up concerning the truth. For if you talk meekly and courteously to them they are more likely, with God's help, to turn away from their wrong ideas and believe what is true. Then they will come to their senses and escape from Satan's trap of slavery to sin which he uses to catch them whenever he likes, and then they can begin doing the will of God. (2 Timothy 2:23-26)

What attitude should Christians adopt when teaching those who are "mixed up concerning the truth"?

An old trout fisherman was giving a few pointers to a group of novices. He said, "Most people who try trout fishing catch nothing at all. That's because they don't do their homework. There are rules you've got to follow. First, keep yourself out of sight. Second, use the right kind of bait. And third, have patience." These rules also apply to "fishing for men." When we are attempting to evangelize people, we should focus on Christ rather than ourselves. We should also use the right elements to attract them to the faith. Most important, we should be patient, allowing the Holy Spirit to speak to them in his own way.

PRAISE:

PETITION:

Oh, come, let us sing to the Lord! Give a joyous shout in honor of the Rock of our salvation! (Ps. 95:1)

Human Religion

YOU may as well know this too, Timothy, that in the last days it is going to be very difficult to be a Christian. For people will love only themselves and their money; they will be proud and boastful, sneering at God, disobedient to their parents, ungrateful to them, and thoroughly bad. They will be hardheaded and never give in to others; they will be constant liars and troublemakers and will think nothing of immorality. They will be rough and cruel, and sneer at those who try to be good. They will betray their friends; they will be hotheaded, puffed up with pride, and prefer good times to worshiping God. They will go to church, yes, but they won't really believe anything they hear. Don't be taken in by people like that. (2 Timothy 3:1-5)

What will the last days be like for Christians?

In his book *The Decline and Fall of the Roman Empire* (Modern Library, 1932), Edward Gibbon describes the Roman response to the religions of the day: "The various modes of worship which prevailed in the Roman world were all considered by the people as equally true, by the philosophers as equally false, and by the [government officials] as equally useful."   This is a picture of our nation today. Millions of Americans believe that in religion, "to each his own." Most intellectuals believe religions are literally false but socially valuable. And many politicians still use religious-sounding language, in order to get more votes.   It is time we understand that Christianity is not a mere social institution. It is a relationship with the Savior.

P R A I S E :

P E T I T I O N :

None is so needy as man, and none is so able and anxious to supply every need as God.

Smarter Sinners

THEY are the kind who craftily sneak into other people's homes and make friendships with silly, sin-burdened women and teach them their new doctrines. Women of that kind are forever following new teachers, but they never understand the truth. And these teachers fight truth just as Jannes and Jambres fought against Moses. They have dirty minds, warped and twisted, and have turned against the Christian faith.

But they won't get away with all this forever. Some day their deceit will be well known to everyone, as was the sin of Jannes and Jambres. (2 Timothy 3:6-9)

What kind of people are "forever following new teachers"?

Many people today believe that society's problems can be solved by education. They say that if people were properly educated—in the home as well as in school—there would be little or no crime, social injustice, or human rights violations. These people forget that sin originates not in the mind, but in the heart. Righteousness comes from cleansing the soul, not from training the mind. As C. S. Lewis has said, "Education only makes a man a more clever devil."

P R A I S E :

P E T I T I O N :

The people of the world shall know I am the Lord. (Ezek. 36:23)

Strange Medicine

BUT you know from watching me that I am not that kind of person. You know what I believe and the way I live and what I want. You know my faith in Christ and how I have suffered. You know my love for you, and my patience. You know how many troubles I have had as a result of my preaching the Good News. You know about all that was done to me while I was visiting in Antioch, Iconium and Lystra, but the Lord delivered me. Yes, and those who decide to please Christ Jesus by living godly lives will suffer at the hands of those who hate him. (2 Timothy 3:10-12)

What will happen to those who decide to please Christ Jesus by living godly lives?

Charles Ferrell, a taxi driver in Georgia, was suddenly stricken with blindness. His doctors said he would never regain his sight. During the next winter, he suffered from a severe case of intestinal flu. A few days later, he was suddenly able to see again. His doctors explained that for some reason, the strange chemical reaction created by the flu had caused his optic nerve to be restored. At first this intestinal flu appeared to be just another affliction. But it soon proved to be greatly beneficial. We rarely see any good in pain and suffering, but often the Lord has a purpose in mind.

P R A I S E :

P E T I T I O N :

Sometimes . . . God answers our prayers in the way our parents do, who reply to the pleas of their children with "Not just now" or "I'll have to think about that for a little while." (R. M. Pearson)

The Flying Fake

IN fact, evil men and false teachers will become worse and worse, deceiving many, they themselves having been deceived by Satan.

But you must keep on believing the things you have been taught. You know they are true for you know that you can trust those of us who have taught you. (2 Timothy 3:13, 14)

Who has deceived the evil men and false teachers?

A few years ago an airline pilot was arrested. He had been flying a large passenger plane for several years without a license. Using forged documents, he had been employed by a major airline. He had been piloting a jet across the U. S. regularly, though he was not qualified. Imagine how concerned the passengers would have been if they had known their lives were in the hands of an impostor. As Christians, we ought to be concerned that we do not entrust our spiritual lives to those who do not exhibit the reality of Christ. We should be on guard against false doctrines and false teachers, for they abound in the world today.

PRAISE:

PETITION:

Pardon our iniquity and our sins, and accept us as your own. (Exod. 34:9)

Unblemished Light

YOU know how, when you were a small child, you were taught the holy Scriptures; and it is these that make you wise to accept God's salvation by trusting in Christ Jesus. The whole Bible was given to us by inspiration from God and is useful to teach us what is true and to make us realize what is wrong in our lives; it straightens us out and helps us do what is right. It is God's way of making us well prepared at every point, fully equipped to do good to everyone. (2 Timothy 3:15-17)

According to this passage, how is the Bible useful to us?

Charles Spurgeon once told the story of two young boys—one good and one bad. The bad boy went out one night to throw mud at the moon. The good boy, knowing the bad boy's intentions, followed him out with a pail of water to wash it off. As the boys threw mud and water into the air, what do you suppose was happening to the moon? Nothing, of course; it was unaffected by the boys' foolish actions. Spurgeon compared the moon in this story to the Scriptures. The Bible continues to be the shining light it has always been, unaffected by the attacks and attitudes of men.

PRAISE:

PETITION:

Because they trust in him, he helps them and delivers them from the plots of evil men. (Ps. 37:40)

Introductions

AND so I solemnly urge you before God and before Christ Jesus—who will some day judge the living and the dead when he appears to set up his Kingdom—to preach the Word of God urgently at all times, whenever you get the chance, in season and out, when it is convenient and when it is not. Correct and rebuke your people when they need it, encourage them to do right, and all the time be feeding them patiently with God's Word. (2 Timothy 4:1, 2)

How should Timothy minister to his people?

Paul commanded Timothy to preach the Word of God urgently at all times. This command applies not only to professional ministers of the gospel, but to all Christians. We are all responsible for fulfilling the task of evangelism. List eight of your non-Christian acquaintances in the left-hand column below. In the spaces to the right, write how you plan to introduce each person to the gospel. Remember that we need to tell others about Christ "when it is convenient and when it is not."

1. _____   _____
2. _____   _____
3. _____   _____
4. _____   _____
5. _____   _____
6. _____   _____
7. _____   _____
8. _____   _____

P R A I S E :

P E T I T I O N :

If you would have God hear you when you pray, you must hear him when he speaks. (T. Brooks)

Weak Foundations

FOR there is going to come a time when people won't listen to the truth, but will go around looking for teachers who will tell them just what they want to hear. They won't listen to what the Bible says but will blithely follow their own misguided ideas.

Stand steady, and don't be afraid of suffering for the Lord. Bring others to Christ. Leave nothing undone that you ought to do. (2 Timothy 4:3-5)

What does Paul command Timothy to do?

A village in England was known for its salt mines. One day a major portion of the village collapsed into the ground. The salt mines had been dug under the city, completely destroying the foundations upon which it had once stood. Paul said a time will come when people will not listen to the truth. They will look for leaders who will tell them only what they want to hear. These people will build their lives upon fables and untruths. In the end, they too will collapse, for their foundations will have been weakened. A life built on fables cannot endure the test of time.

P R A I S E :

P E T I T I O N :

Whenever we pray for you we always begin by giving thanks to God the Father of our Lord Jesus Christ. (Col. 1:3)

Aliens

I say this because I won't be around to help you very much longer. My time has almost run out. Very soon now I will be on my way to heaven. I have fought long and hard for my Lord, and through it all I have kept true to him. And now the time has come for me to stop fighting and rest. In heaven a crown is waiting for me which the Lord, the righteous Judge, will give me on that great day of his return. And not just to me, but to all those whose lives show that they are eagerly looking forward to his coming back again. (2 Timothy 4:6-8)

How much longer does Paul believe he'll be living on earth?

One of Larry Norman's records is titled, "Only Visiting This Planet." On it he sings about the temporary nature of Christians on earth. He says we are aliens on this planet, and that our true home is heaven. In the days prior to his death, Paul looked forward with great anticipation to the day when he would finally receive his crown of glory. As he looked back over the years since his Damascus Road experience, he could confidently state that he was ready to die. He had "fought long and hard" for the Lord, and had kept true to him. We should live as Paul did, serving faithfully and anticipating Christ's return.

P R A I S E :

P E T I T I O N :

He who prays without confidence cannot hope that his prayers will be granted. (Fenelon)

Defecting to Sin

PLEASE come as soon as you can, for Demas has left me. He loved the good things of this life and went to Thessalonica. Crescens has gone to Galatia, Titus to Dalmatia. Only Luke is with me. Bring Mark with you when you come, for I need him. (Tychicus is gone too, as I sent him to Ephesus.) When you come, be sure to bring the coat I left at Troas with Brother Carpus, and also the books, but especially the parchments. (2 Timothy 4:9-13)

Timothy is preparing to visit Paul. What does Paul ask him to bring?

Paul was disappointed about the defection of one of his converts. Demas had forsaken Christ for the "good things of this life." He had been overcome by ambition and materialism, and had lost sight of the eternal treasures of heaven.   There are many things in this life that appeal to us. No matter how close we are to Christ, it is difficult to ignore the enticements that the world has to offer. How can we be sure not to be caught in the trap Demas fell into? What concrete advice would you give to those who love "the good things of this life"?

PRAISE:

PETITION:

Hallelujah! Yes, praise the Lord! How good it is to sing his praises! How delightful, and how right! (Ps. 147:1)

Light Beyond the Shadow

ALEXANDER the coppersmith has done me much harm. The Lord will punish him, but be careful of him, for he fought against everything we said.

The first time I was brought before the judge no one was here to help me. Everyone had run away. I hope that they will not be blamed for it. But the Lord stood with me and gave me the opportunity to boldly preach a whole sermon for all the world to hear. And he saved me from being thrown to the lions. Yes, and the Lord will always deliver me from all evil and will bring me into his heavenly Kingdom. To God be the glory forever and ever. Amen.

Please say "hello" for me to Priscilla and Aquila and those living at the home of Onesiphorus. Erastus stayed at Corinth, and I left Trophimus sick at Miletus.

Do try to be here before winter. Eubulus sends you greetings, and so do Pudens, Linus, Claudia, and all the others. May the Lord Jesus Christ be with your spirit. (2 Timothy 4:14-22)

What blessing does Paul give Timothy in concluding this epistle?

Many Bible scholars believe that Paul wrote this letter to Timothy from the cell where he awaited execution. If this is so, it is remarkable to observe Paul's tranquil, confident state in the face of death. He had absolute certainty about what death would mean for him, and he was ecstatic at the prospect of heaven. Charles Spurgeon had this to say about Christians facing death: "The dying saint is not in a flurry. He keeps his old pace—he walks. The last days of a Christian are the most peaceful of his whole career; many a saint has reaped more joy and knowledge when he came to die than ever he knew while he lived. When there is a shadow, there must be light somewhere. The light of Jesus shining upon death throws a shadow across our path; let us therefore rejoice for the light beyond."

PRAISE:

PETITION:

He who has learned to pray has learned the greatest secret of a holy and happy life. (W. Law)

November *JAMES*

Nothing can equal the sense of fulfilment that comes as a result of helping those in need. Participating in social work is a way of showing personal compassion and expressing one's faith. ■ James has been called the "works book." More than any other New Testament book, it stresses the importance of good works in the life of a Christian. James says that if we have faith in Christ as Savior, that faith should be demonstrated through works of love and charity.

Pearl of Great Price

FROM: James, a servant of God and of the Lord Jesus Christ.

To: Jewish Christians scattered everywhere. Greetings! Dear brothers, is your life full of difficulties and temptations? Then be happy, for when the way is rough, your patience has a chance to grow. So let it grow, and don't try to squirm out of your problems. For when your patience is finally in full bloom, then you will be ready for anything, strong in character, full and complete. (James 1:1-4)

Why should we be happy when faced with difficulties and temptations?

The oyster is one of the most fascinating shellfish. Once in a while an irritating object, such as a grain of sand, gets under the mantle of its shell. It usually falls upon the soft flesh within. In order to relieve the irritation, the oyster coats the grain with a smooth substance. Layer upon layer is added until at last the bothersome speck has become a pearl of great value. Pearls, then, are simply victories over irritation.   We should react to our difficulties in a similar way. If we would treat our misfortunes with patience, we would soon develop our own pearl of great price—strength of character.

P R A I S E :

P E T I T I O N :

Oh, give thanks to the Lord and pray to him. . . . Tell the peoples of the world about his mighty doings. (1 Chron. 16:8)

God's Way

IF you want to know what God wants you to do, ask him, and he will gladly tell you, for he is always ready to give a bountiful supply of wisdom to all who ask him; he will not resent it. But when you ask him, be sure that you really expect him to tell you, for a doubtful mind will be as unsettled as a wave of the sea that is driven and tossed by the wind; and every decision you then make will be uncertain, as you turn first this way, and then that. If you don't ask with faith, don't expect the Lord to give you any solid answer. (James 1:5-8)

Most of us want to know God's will for our lives. How does James recommend we do it?

A lot of writing has been done on the subject of discovering God's will. Some people say that God has an intricate plan mapped out for our lives—we should involve him in even our most trivial decisions. Others say that God's will has already been given to us through the Bible, and that it's up to us to make wise decisions based upon the Bible and upon our own common sense. Still others believe that God makes his will known through a combination of the Scriptures and specific guidance. Regardless of what we believe about discovering God's will, we should remember that he wants us to become godly children. Henry Jacobson points out that it is often our wish for God to change our circumstances; however, God prefers to change *us* to suit our circumstances.

PRAISE:

PETITION:

We never need to pray so earnestly as when we cannot lay hold of any pleasure in prayer. (Fenelon)

Acquired Disappointments

A Christian who doesn't amount to much in this world should be glad, for he is great in the Lord's sight. But a rich man should be glad that his riches mean nothing to the Lord, for he will soon be gone, like a flower that has lost its beauty and fades away, withered—killed by the scorching summer sun. So it is with rich men. They will soon die and leave behind all their busy activities. (James 1:9-11)

Who is great in the Lord's sight?

People who set their minds on material things are equally disappointed whether they get them or not. Let's take a typical case: Two teenage boys want stereo tape decks for their cars. One is not allowed to purchase the equipment—he is frustrated and disappointed right away. The other is given a tape deck. He is happy with it for a while, but when he hears of a quadrophonic, digital tape deck that can outperform his model, he suddenly becomes disappointed with what he has. Sooner or later most people come to the realization that happiness does not lie in material possessions. Wise Christians know the source of happiness—they serve Christ on earth and store their treasures in heaven.

PRAISE:

PETITION:

I am offering you my deliverance; not in the distant future, but right now! I am ready to save you. (Isa. 46:13)

The Refiner

HAPPY is the man who doesn't give in and do wrong when he is tempted, for afterwards he will get as his reward the crown of life that God has promised those who love him. (James 1:12)

What reward will be presented to the person who doesn't give in to temptation?

Charles Colson says that God's great concern with his children is not to make them comfortable, but to develop in them a character like that of Christ.   The refiner of silver melts the precious metal in large vats. As impurities rise to the top, he removes them. He waits until the molten silver reflects his image before it is taken from the fire. Likewise, the Lord permits trials and problems to simmer in our lives; only after the impurity of sin is removed can people see the image of the Refiner in us.

P R A I S E :

P E T I T I O N :

Come and I will forgive you. (Mal. 3:7)

The Glittering Lure

AND remember, when someone wants to do wrong it is never God who is tempting him, for God never wants to do wrong and never tempts anyone else to do it. Temptation is the pull of man's own evil thoughts and wishes. These evil thoughts lead to evil actions and afterwards to the death penalty from God. (James 1:13-15)

What is the source of temptation?

Just as the fisherman attracts the fish with a glittering lure and draws him with its dancing motion, so the lustful heart can attract us, even as we stand next to God, and draw us to sin by its seductive ways. Even though we read in today's passage that "temptation is the pull of man's own evil thoughts and wishes," we should remember that all sin comes from Satan. Let us strive to become careful and well prepared to meet Satan's onslaughts. Christians are to pray for strength against temptation. "Don't bring us into temptation, but deliver us from the Evil One" (Matt. 6:13).

PRAISE:

PETITION:

Lord, lead me as you promised me you would; otherwise my enemies will conquer me. Tell me clearly what to do, which way to turn. (Ps. 5:8)

The Artist

SO don't be misled, dear brothers.

But whatever is good and perfect comes to us from God, the Creator of all light, and he shines forever without change or shadow. And it was a happy day for him when he gave us our new lives, through the truth of his Word, and we became, as it were, the first children in his new family. (James 1:16-18)

How does James refer to the Lord in this passage?

The best art exposes truth in creative and moving ways. This is true of any art form, whether it be literature, painting, music, sculpture, dance, architecture, theater, or film. Art that portrays universal truth or beauty often assumes a timeless quality. That is why the work of artists such as Shakespeare, da Vinci, Bach, Michelangelo, El Greco, Sophocles, and Chaucer have held up through the centuries. It may be said that all true art orginates from God, since he is the Creator of the universe and the Father of truth and beauty.   The next time you see great art—whether it be in a book, a theater, a concert hall, or a museum—make a note of who the real Artist is.

PRAISE:

PETITION:

Every religion teaches that men ought to pray, but only the biblical faith promises that God will answer. (B. Graham)

Two Ears, One Mouth

DEAR brothers, don't ever forget that it is best to listen much, speak little, and not become angry; for anger doesn't make us good, as God demands that we must be.

So get rid of all that is wrong in your life, both inside and outside, and humbly be glad for the wonderful message we have received, for it is able to save our souls as it takes hold of our hearts. (James 1:19-21)

For what ought we to be glad? Why?

"It is better to keep silent and appear foolish than to open your mouth and remove all doubt." This humorous phrase, recently seen on a T-shirt, has an element of truth in it. James says in today's reading that it is best to listen much, speak little. The Book of Proverbs contains many references to the silence of the wise and the noisiness of the foolish. It has been said that God created us with two ears and one mouth so that we will listen twice as much as we talk!

PRAISE: *For our marriage / Chance to melt Dr.*
11-7-88 Patrick will get ET you - God willing Jerem

PETITION:

You will live in joy and peace. The mountains and hills, the trees of the field—all the world around you—will rejoice. (Isa. 55:12)

Suicide Bombers

AND remember, it is a message to obey, not just to listen to. So don't fool yourselves. For if a person just listens and doesn't obey, he is like a man looking at his face in a mirror; as soon as he walks away, he can't see himself anymore or remember what he looks like. But if anyone keeps looking steadily into God's law for free men, he will not only remember it but he will do what it says, and God will greatly bless him in everything he does. (James 1:22-25)

What must we do after listening to God's message?

During World War II one of the weapons most feared by the Allies was the Japanese suicide bomber. These bombers were small airplanes loaded with explosives and piloted by Japanese airmen who were ready to die for their nation. Upon sighting a target, such as an enemy aircraft carrier, the pilot would take careful aim, then fly his plane directly into the target. These suicide missions invariably caused extensive damage and destruction. Although their patriotic cause was suspect, these men were totally devoted to it.   As Christians, we can be just as devoted to a much greater cause—the truth of Christianity. We should be ready at any time to give our lives for our Savior, as he has given his life for us.

PRAISE:

PETITION:

Far be it from me that I should sin against the Lord by ending my prayers. (1 Sam. 12:23)

Showing Our Faith

ANYONE who says he is a Christian but doesn't control his sharp tongue is just fooling himself, and his religion isn't worth much. The Christian who is pure and without fault, from God the Father's point of view, is the one who takes care of orphans and widows, and who remains true to the Lord—not soiled and dirtied by his contacts with the world. (James 1:26, 27)

What kind of life characterizes the pure and faultless Christian?

James believed that salvation could be attained by faith alone. But he also believed that once people have become Christians, they should demonstrate that faith through good works. More than any other New Testament writer, James emphasized the importance of good works. In today's reading, for example, he says that pure and faultless Christians are those who take care of orphans and widows. Christians need to listen to what James is saying. We need to be more involved in helping the poor, the homeless, the ill, the oppressed, the suffering. We ought to show what our faith is. As the popular chorus goes: "And they'll know we are Christians by our love."

PRAISE:

PETITION:

He who rises from a prayer a better man has had his prayer answered.

Rich Friends/Poor Friends

DEAR brothers, how can you claim that you belong to the Lord Jesus Christ, the Lord of glory, if you show favoritism to rich people and look down on poor people?

If a man comes into your church dressed in expensive clothes and with valuable gold rings on his fingers, and at the same moment another man comes in who is poor and dressed in threadbare clothes, and you make a lot of fuss over the rich man and give him the best seat in the house and say to the poor man, "You can stand over there if you like, or else sit on the floor"—well, judging a man by his wealth shows that you are guided by wrong motives. (James 2:1-4)

What does James say about showing favoritism to the rich?

It is easy for us to read passages such as the one we've seen today, and heartily agree that it is wrong to show favoritism to the rich. It is also easy, however, to be guilty of such discrimination. Sometimes our partiality is unconscious. In the columns below, list three of your richest friends and three of your poorest friends:

Rich Friends   Poor Friends

_____   _____

_____   _____

_____   _____

Think about how you treat these people. Are you favoring one group over another (deliberately or otherwise)? If not, great; you are following James' advice. If so, ask the Lord to give you the right motives in developing personal friendships. "Men judge by outward appearance, but [the Lord looks] at a man's thoughts and intentions" (1 Sam. 16:7).

P R A I S E : _____

P E T I T I O N : _____

O Lord, do good to those who are good, whose hearts are right with the Lord. (Ps. 125:4)

The Riches of Poverty

LISTEN to me, dear brothers: God has chosen poor people to be rich in faith, and the Kingdom of Heaven is theirs, for that is the gift God has promised to all those who love him. And yet, of the two strangers, you have despised the poor man. Don't you realize that it is usually the rich men who pick on you and drag you into court? And all too often they are the ones who laugh at Jesus Christ, whose noble name you bear. (James 2:5-7)

What is the gift that God has promised to all those who love him?

Old John—one of the poorest members of a large church—had a vision one night. He dreamed that at midnight the next day the richest member of the church would die. Concerned for the welfare of the wealthiest church member—a deacon named George Hortega—Old John called him the next morning and told him about the dream. Hortega gathered his many friends around him and told them the news. That night he trembled with fright in his bed as his friends looked on. But midnight came and went. Then one o'clock, two o'clock, and Hortega was still quite healthy. The next morning he and his friends were shocked to discover that at midnight on the previous night, Old John had died. The richest church member had died after all. "God has chosen poor people to be rich in faith."

PRAISE:

PETITION:

The Lord is our Judge, our Lawgiver and our King; he will care for us and save us. (Isa. 33:22)

The First Rule

YES indeed, it is good when you truly obey our Lord's command, "You must love and help your neighbors just as much as you love and take care of yourself." But you are breaking this law of our Lord's when you favor the rich and fawn over them; it is sin.

And the person who keeps every law of God, but makes one little slip, is just as guilty as the person who has broken every law there is. For the God who said you must not marry a woman who already has a husband, also said you must not murder, so even though you have not broken the marriage laws by committing adultery, but have murdered someone, you have entirely broken God's laws and stand utterly guilty before him.

You will be judged on whether or not you are doing what Christ wants you to. So watch what you do and what you think; for there will be no mercy to those who have shown no mercy. But if you have been merciful, then God's mercy toward you will win out over his judgment against you. (James 2:8-13)

How will God treat people who have shown no mercy to others?

The command that James quotes at the beginning of today's Scripture reading is often called the Golden Rule. It has been said that this command covers all of the Ten Commandments. If we always obey the Golden Rule, we will never have to worry about breaking any of the Commandments. Think about it: If we have true, pure love for our neighbors and for God, there will never be an occasion when we will seriously consider murder, adultery, theft, lying, covetousness, disrespect for parents, etc. Love is the basis for every one of God's commands to us. In fact, God *is* love (1 John 4:16).

P R A I S E :

P E T I T I O N :

God hears no more than the heart speaks; and if the heart is dumb, God certainly will be deaf. (T. Brooks)

The Proof of Faith

DEAR brothers, what's the use of saying that you have faith and are Christians if you aren't proving it by helping others? Will *that* kind of faith save anyone? If you have a friend who is in need of food and clothing, and you say to him, "Well, good-bye and God bless you; stay warm and eat hearty," and then don't give him clothes or food, what good does that do?

So you see, it isn't enough just to have faith. You must also do good to prove that you have it. Faith that doesn't show itself by good works is no faith at all—it is dead and useless. (James 2:14-17)

What must we have besides faith?

A man who loves his wife goes out of his way to make her happy. He compliments her, helps her with household tasks, allows her to have as much freedom as she desires, and tells her of his love for her. The evidence of his love for his wife lies in such actions. Christians who truly have faith also show evidence of it. They praise and serve the Lord, they live holy lives, and they help those who are less fortunate. If Christians don't show any evidence of their faith, that faith is probably very weak, even nonexistent. James says that faith that doesn't show itself is as good as dead. We have to learn to translate our beliefs into behavior, our faith into charity and service.

PRAISE:

PETITION:

I will betroth you to me in faithfulness and love [says the Lord]. (Hos. 2:20)

Faith into Action

BUT someone may well argue, "You say the way to God is by faith alone, plus nothing; well, I say that good works are important too, for without good works you can't prove whether you have faith or not; but anyone can see that I have faith by the way I act."

Are there still some among you who hold that "only believing" is enough? Believing in one God? Well, remember that the demons believe this too—so strongly that they tremble in terror! Fool! When will you ever learn that "believing" is useless without *doing* what God wants you to? Faith that does not result in good deeds is not real faith. (James 2:18-20)

What does James say about faith that does not result in good deeds?

Intellectual assent means to believe something in your mind but not live it in your heart. Even the demons believe in God and Christ by intellectual assent. The difference between demons and Christians is that Christians back up their beliefs with action. What is the best way for *you* to transform your Christian beliefs into positive action for others? Think about this question for a minute, then write your answer in the space below. Resolve to start *acting out* your faith right away.

_____

_____

_____

_____

PRAISE: *For the joy of knowing God in our lives*

PETITION: *I will continue to lose weight & maintain*

I will be your God through all your lifetime, . . . I made you and I will care for you. I will carry you along and be your Savior. (Isa. 46:4)

The Copy Cat

DEAR brothers, don't be too eager to tell others their faults, for we all make many mistakes; and when we teachers of religion, who should know better, do wrong, our punishment will be greater than it would be for others. (James 3:1)

What will happen to teachers of religion who do wrong?

A few years ago a strikingly effective antismoking commercial appeared on television. It showed a four-year-old boy following his father. The little boy imitated everything Daddy did. Step by step he copied his father in admiration. As the man sat down to rest under a tree, his son positioned himself exactly like his father. And when the man reached for a cigarette, so did the boy. **We** are responsible not only for ourselves, but for those who follow us.

PRAISE:

PETITION:

Prayers of petition go into God's presence to bring something back, but prayers of praise go into his presence never to return.

The Power of the Tongue

IF anyone can control his tongue, it proves that he has perfect control over himself in every other way. We can make a large horse turn around and go wherever we want by means of a small bit in his mouth. And a tiny rudder makes a huge ship turn wherever the pilot wants it to go, even though the winds are strong. (James 3:2-4)

What is the hardest thing for a person to control?

The tongue is one of our most powerful weapons. With just a few words we can make people feel insecure, provoke anger or jealousy, devastate someone, or destroy a reputation. The uncontrolled tongue has provoked people to commit every sin imaginable, from white lies to brutal murder. Barclay has said that "the stroke of the whip marks on the flesh, but the stroke of the tongue breaks the bones. Many have fallen by the edge of the sword, but not so many as have fallen by the tongue." If we can show restraint in what we say, we can easily show restraint in other areas of our lives.

P R A I S E :

P E T I T I O N :

I want you to trust me in your times of trouble, so I can rescue you, and you can give me glory. (Ps. 50:15)

Verbal Arson

SO also the tongue is a small thing, but what enormous damage it can do. A great forest can be set on fire by one tiny spark. And the tongue is a flame of fire. It is full of wickedness, and poisons every part of the body. And the tongue is set on fire by hell itself, and can turn our whole lives into a blazing flame of destruction and disaster. (James 3:5, 6)

What has set the tongue of man on fire?

Arsonists set fire to buildings for various reasons. Some of them do it for motives of revenge or intimidation. Others secretly set fire to their own property in order to receive the insurance money. And some arsonists commit their crimes for the sheer pleasure of watching a huge structure go up in flames. Whatever their motives may be, arsonists are considered to be among the most reckless and despicable of criminals. People often die in blazes set by arsonists. These criminals show no respect for life or property. It is significant that James has compared the damage a fire can do to the destruction a tongue can wreak. When we use our tongues as weapons, we are guilty of verbal arson. James says the fire is set by hell itself.

P R A I S E :

P E T I T I O N :

Let not your heart be troubled. (John 14:1)

Taming the Tongue

MEN have trained, or can train, every kind of animal or bird that lives and every kind of reptile and fish, but no human being can tame the tongue. It is always ready to pour out its deadly poison. Sometimes it praises our heavenly Father, and sometimes it breaks out into curses against men who are made like God. And so blessing and cursing come pouring out of the same mouth. Dear brothers, surely this is not right! Does a spring of water bubble out first with fresh water and then with bitter water? Can you pick olives from a fig tree, or figs from a grape vine? No, and you can't draw fresh water from a salty pool. (James 3:7-12)

What sort of action does James condemn in this passage?

Living near Aurora, Ohio, I often saw the Sea World trainers at work with whales, sharks, and dolphins. These creatures had been trained so that they would obey every command. One trainer even went so far as to hand food to a killer whale.   At the circus an even greater act of discipline can be seen when the lion trainer opens the mouth of a huge cat and places his head between the powerful jaws of the lion.   Men have shown that they can train or control vicious animals, awesome forces of nature, and great machines. Yet few have learned to control their tongues.

P R A I S E :

P E T I T I O N :

He who does not know how to kneel never rises high.

Dog-Eat-Dog

IF you are wise, live a life of steady goodness, so that only good deeds will pour forth. And if you don't brag about them, then you will be truly wise! And by all means don't brag about being wise and good if you are bitter and jealous and selfish; that is the worst sort of lie. For jealousy and selfishness are not God's kind of wisdom. Such things are earthly, unspiritual, inspired by the devil. For wherever there is jealousy or selfish ambition, there will be disorder and every other kind of evil. (James 3:13-16)

What are not "God's kind of wisdom"?

"Dog-eat-dog" is an expression used to describe the climate in certain business offices where everyone is busily trying to get promoted to higher prestige, greater power, and a fatter salary. When people are ruled by jealousy and selfish ambition, they will tolerate no obstacles to their desired goals. People have been known to lie, cheat, misrepresent, steal, threaten, and even murder in their frantic climb to the "top." Jealousy and selfish ambition open the floodgates to every other sort of disorder and evil. The Christian should replace jealousy with contentment, and selfish ambition with a desire to follow God's will.

PRAISE:

PETITION:

Admit your faults to one another and pray for each other so that you may be healed. (James 5:16)

The Benefits of Wisdom

BUT the wisdom that comes from heaven is first of all pure and full of quiet gentleness. Then it is peace-loving and courteous. It allows discussion and is willing to yield to others; it is full of mercy and good deeds. It is wholehearted and straightforward and sincere. And those who are peacemakers will plant seeds of peace and reap a harvest of goodness. (James 3:17, 18)

What characterizes the wisdom that comes from heaven?

Today's reading gives us a good definition of the sort of wisdom God wishes each of us to cultivate. There is nothing more pleasing to God than a person who seeks to find true wisdom. In 1 Kings 3 we read about Solomon's request for wisdom. When the Lord offered him anything he wanted, Solomon said, "Give me an understanding mind so that I can govern your people well and know the difference between what is right and what is wrong." The Lord, pleased with Solomon's request, answered, "Because you have asked for wisdom in governing my people, and haven't asked for a long life or riches for yourself, or the defeat of your enemies—yes, I'll give you what you asked for! I will give you a wiser mind than anyone else has ever had or ever will have! And I will also give you what you didn't ask for—riches and honor! And no one in all the world will be as rich and famous as you for the rest of your life!"

P R A I S E :

P E T I T I O N :

When you draw close to God, God will draw close to you. (James 4:8)

The Deepening Spiral

WHAT is causing the quarrels and fights among you? Isn't it because there is a whole army of evil desires within you? You want what you don't have, so you kill to get it. You long for what others have, and can't afford it, so you start a fight to take it away from them. And yet the reason you don't have what you want is that you don't ask God for it. And even when you do ask you don't get it because your whole aim is wrong—you want only what will give *you* pleasure. (James 4:1-3)

Why don't we have what we want?

Because we are human, we have temptations and evil desires. If these unhealthy ambitions remain unchecked, they will lead to sinful ways of attaining them. This is how the ever-deepening spiral of sin begins. If our lives are ruled by our human passions, we will certainly be immersed in all sorts of sin. What's the solution? A good place to start is by rooting out evil temptations and desires. We should recognize these desires for what they are, and refuse to fulfill them. In their place we can cultivate healthy, godly desires. God has promised that he will help us to attain the good desires of our hearts. Our aim in life should be to do only what gives God pleasure.

PRAISE:

PETITION:

The Christian who says his prayers to men will not get answers from God.

Deadly Luxury

YOU are like an unfaithful wife who loves her husband's enemies. Don't you realize that making friends with God's enemies—the evil pleasures of this world—makes you an enemy of God? I say it again, that if your aim is to enjoy the evil pleasure of the unsaved world, you cannot also be a friend of God. Or what do you think the Scripture means when it says that the Holy Spirit, whom God has placed within us, watches over us with tender jealousy? But he gives us more and more strength to stand against all such evil longings. As the Scripture says, God gives strength to the humble, but sets himself against the proud and haughty.

So give yourselves humbly to God. Resist the devil and he will flee from you. And when you draw close to God, God will draw close to you. Wash your hands, you sinners, and let your hearts be filled with God alone to make them pure and true to him. Let there be tears for the wrong things you have done. Let there be sorrow and sincere grief. Let there be sadness instead of laughter, and gloom instead of joy. (James 4:4-9)

What will happen when Christians resist the devil?

A prominent Christian leader was asked why so few intellectuals and wealthy people choose to follow Christ. He responded that "the more a man learns and the more a man earns, the easier it is for him to trust in himself and fail to see his need of God." The self-sufficient "I," the pride of man, has kept many from God.   Jesus said that it is difficult for a rich person to enter the kingdom of heaven. This is not because the Lord despises the wealthy, but because the wealthy are often so padded in luxury that they are insensitive to the needs of their souls.

P R A I S E :

P E T I T I O N :

Come, everyone, and clap for joy! Shout triumphant praises to the Lord! (Ps. 47:1)

The Success of Serving

THEN when you realize your worthlessness before the Lord, he will lift you up, encourage and help you. (James 4:10)

What will happen when we realize our worthlessness before the Lord?

In Mark 9 we read that a group of disciples had traveled to Capernaum to meet Jesus: "When they were settled in the house where they were to stay [Jesus] asked them, 'What were you discussing out on the road?' "But they were ashamed to answer, for they had been arguing about which of them was the greatest! "He sat down and called them around him and said, 'Anyone wanting to be the greatest must be the least—the servant of all!' " Such is the irony of God's law. The first will be last and the last, first. Let us remember that, in God's eyes, those who serve faithfully are the most successful.

P R A I S E :

P E T I T I O N :

Can a mother forget her little child and not have love for her own son? Yet even if that should be, I will not forget you. (Isa. 49:15)

Target of Critcism

DON'T criticize and speak evil about each other, dear brothers. If you do, you will be fighting against God's law of loving one another, declaring it is wrong. But your job is not to decide whether this law is right or wrong, but to obey it. Only he who made the law can rightly judge among us. He alone decides to save us or destroy. So what right do you have to judge or criticize others? (James 4:11, 12)

Do we have any right to judge or criticize people? Explain your answer.

Michael had a bad habit. He was always criticizing people. He had negative things to say about everybody he knew. He never complimented anyone. Everyone was either too fat or too thin, too shy or too outgoing, too conservative or too liberal. When he read the newspaper, he criticized the writers for simplemindedness or obscurity. When he watched TV, he laughed at all the actors and newscasters. The reason Michael was so critical was to make his friends think he was witty, bright, and discerning. But ultimately he found that he had very few friends left. They had been turned off by his attitudes. They now avoided him, because they suspected that they too were targets of his criticism. We should not speak evil about each other in order to hurt someone or bolster our self-image. God alone stands as the judge. Our duty is simply to love each other as God loves us.

PRAISE:

PETITION:

Never achieve success without giving God the praise.

The Danger of Tomorrow

LOOK here, you people who say, "Today or tomorrow we are going to such and such a town, stay there a year, and open up a profitable business." How do you know what is going to happen tomorrow? For the length of your lives is as uncertain as the morning fog—now you see it; soon it is gone. What you ought to say is, "If the Lord wants us to, we shall live and do this or that." Otherwise you will be bragging about your own plans, and such self-confidence never pleases God.

Remember, too, that knowing what is right to do and then not doing it is sin. (James 4:13-17)

According to today's reading, what kind of attitude displeases the Lord?

People who always wait until "tomorrow" are often caught by surprise by the demands of today. People who procrastinate in paying bills often need to pay additional late charges. Those who procrastinate in writing letters sometimes lose the confidence and respect of friends. And people who put off spiritual concerns face the danger of eternal damnation.   Don Anderson says that "tomorrow cannot be found on God's calendar. Tomorrow is the locked door that shuts people out of heaven. Tomorrow is the nursemaid of perdition. Those who expect to repent tomorrow usually die today. Don't count on tomorrow."   "*Right now* God is ready to welcome you. *Today* he is ready to save you" (2 Cor. 6:2).

PRAISE:

PETITION:

I waited patiently for God to help me; then he listened and heard my cry. (Ps. 40:1)

Payday for the Greedy

LOOK here, you rich men, now is the time to cry and groan with anguished grief because of all the terrible troubles ahead of you. Your wealth is even now rotting away, and your fine clothes are becoming mere moth-eaten rags. The value of your gold and silver is dropping fast, yet it will stand as evidence against you, and eat your flesh like fire. That is what you have stored up for yourselves, to receive on that coming day of judgment. For listen! Hear the cries of the field workers whom you have cheated of their pay. Their cries have reached the ears of the Lord of Hosts.

You have spent your years here on earth having fun, satisfying your every whim, and now your fat hearts are ready for the slaughter. You have condemned and killed good men who had no power to defend themselves against you. (James 5:1-6)

What do godless rich people have to look forward to?

Because of the curse that has settled over the earth, all humans are subject to suffering. No one is exempt from oppression by men and the tyranny of circumstance. In considering this fact, American clergyman Harry Ironside pointed out that God is not an uninterested spectator to our suffering. He is deeply concerned about injustice and oppression. As of old, when he heard the cries of the slaves in Egypt when they sighed and groaned because of their unfair and wicked treatment by the taskmasters of Pharaoh, so he still takes heed of every injustice that the privileged and powerful inflict upon the poor and downtrodden.

P R A I S E :

P E T I T I O N :

What a wonderful God we have—he is the Father of our Lord Jesus Christ, the source of every mercy, and the one who so wonderfully comforts and strengthens us in our hardships and trials. (2 Cor. 1:3, 4)

The Homecoming

NOW as for you, dear brothers who are waiting for the Lord's return, be patient, like a farmer who waits until the autumn for his precious harvest to ripen. Yes, be patient. And take courage, for the coming of the Lord is near.

Don't grumble about each other, brothers. Are you yourselves above criticism? For see! The great Judge is coming. He is almost here. [Let him do whatever criticizing must be done.]

For examples of patience in suffering, look at the Lord's prophets. We know how happy they are now because they stayed true to him then, even though they suffered greatly for it. Job is an example of a man who continued to trust the Lord in sorrow; from his experiences we can see how the Lord's plan finally ended in good, for he is full of tenderness and mercy. (James 5:7-11)

To whom should we look for examples of patience in suffering?

Dr. J. Sidlow Baxter once told a story to illustrate our attitudes toward Christ's second coming: "A Scotsman and his two sons were returning from a fishing trip. The younger son said, 'I can see her now, my precious wife, waiting at home for me. She is indeed a faithful one.' The older son said, 'My wife will not only be waiting, but she will be perched on the windowsill watching for me to come home. That is what I call faithfulness.' The father then said, 'Sons, I can show you where your mother, bless her dear heart, will excel them both because of her age and experience. She will not only be waiting and watching for me to come home, but she will be fixing my dinner as well.'" We should be watching, waiting, and working until our Lord comes.

PRAISE:

PETITION:

If Christianity is to survive in a world filled with materialism, the church must have a revival of prayer. (B. Graham)

Yes or No

BUT most of all, dear brothers, do not swear either by heaven or earth or anything else; just say a simple yes or no, so that you will not sin and be condemned for it. (James 5:12)

What warning does James give the Jewish Christians in this passage?

Part of becoming a Christian means that we agree to follow Christ's laws. One of those laws is that we must always tell the truth (Exod. 20:16 says: "You must not lie."). So, all true Christians are committed to telling the truth. Thus, James says that it is not necessary for Christians to swear by someone or something when they make an affirmation or negation. To swear by an external person or object detracts from the solemn promise we've made before Christ to always tell the truth. For the Christian, a simple yes or no is enough.

PRAISE:

PETITION:

Always give thanks for everything to our God and Father in the name of our Lord Jesus Christ. (Eph. 5:20)

Praying for Healing

IS anyone among you suffering? He should keep on praying about it. And those who have reason to be thankful should continually be singing praises to the Lord.

Is anyone sick? He should call for the elders of the church and they should pray over him and pour a little oil upon him, calling on the Lord to heal him. And their prayer, if offered in faith, will heal him, for the Lord will make him well; and if his sickness was caused by some sin, the Lord will forgive him.

Admit your faults to one another and pray for each other so that you may be healed. The earnest prayer of a righteous man has great power and wonderful results. Elijah was as completely human as we are, and yet when he prayed earnestly that no rain would fall, none fell for the next three and one half years! Then he prayed again, this time that it *would* rain, and down it poured and the grass turned green and the gardens began to grow again. (James 5:13-18)

The Bible tells us we should confess our sins to Christ. To whom else should we admit our faults? Why?

In this passage James makes some specific promises regarding prayer for sickness. Reread the passage carefully, then fill in the blanks below.

If a sickness occurs in the church,

a. the one in need should _____;

b. the elders of the church should _____

_____;

c. and if the above conditions are met, the Lord will _____

_____, if it pleases him to do so.

PRAISE : _____

PETITION : _____

Each morning I will look to you in heaven and lay my requests before you, praying earnestly. (Ps. 5:3)

Back to God

DEAR brothers, if anyone has slipped away from God and no longer trusts the Lord and someone helps him understand the Truth again, that person who brings him back to God will have saved a wandering soul from death, bringing about the forgiveness of his many sins. (James 5:19, 20)

If a backslider doesn't return to God, what shall be his fate?

In the *Lindsell Study Bible* (Tyndale, 1980), Harold Lindsell says the following about this passage: "James is not talking about someone who has ceased to be a believer. Rather [he is referring] to someone who has slipped into error in his daily life, or in the practice of his faith. Just as we should be concerned for bodily healing so should we likewise be concerned for spiritual healing in the case of a backslider. All believers are their brothers' keepers, and believers should engage in this form of ministry. It will save the backsliders' souls [from] death."

PRAISE:

PETITION:

The more you pray, the more the Holy Spirit will lead you out into service.

December *1, 2, 3 JOHN*

Cults and false religions are flourishing around the world.
Groups such as the Unification Church, the Bahais, the
Children of God, and the Mormons are gaining new converts
by the thousands. Many such cults distort Christ's message to
accommodate their own ideologies and false teachings. ■ A
recurring theme in the three epistles of John is the danger of
false teachers and doctrines. John advises his friends and
fellow Christians to stay firm in the Word, never straying
from the teachings of Christ.

america
needs
♥
sun myung
moon

Paid Friend

CHRIST was alive when the world began, yet I myself have seen him with my own eyes and listened to him speak. I have touched him with my own hands. He is God's message of life. This one who is life from God has been shown to us and we guarantee that we have seen him; I am speaking of Christ, who is eternal Life. He was with the Father and then was shown to us. Again I say, we are telling you about what we ourselves have actually seen and heard, so that you may share the fellowship and the joys we have with the Father and with Jesus Christ his Son. And if you do as I say in this letter, then you, too, will be full of joy, and so will we. (1 John 1:1-4)

According to this passage, how long has Jesus Christ existed?

A famous British playwright was leaving Liverpool by ship. He noticed that the other passengers were waving to friends on the dock. Just before the ship was to leave, he rushed down to the dock and stopped a little boy. "Would you wave to me if I pay you?" he asked the boy. "Of course," he agreed. The writer gave him a few shillings, then ran back aboard and leaned over the rail. Sure enough, the boy was waving to him. The playwright disliked solitude and loneliness so much that he had gone so far as to create an artificial friend. To him, though, even the semblance of friendship was better than the crushing loneliness he felt. The key to assurance in life *is* fellowship. Fellowship with people locks out the grim feelings of loneliness. And fellowship with God keeps away the threat of eternal solitude. In this epistle, John wanted to make it clear to his readers that they could fellowship with God through Jesus Christ. He stressed the importance of love: Since Christians have experienced the love of God in their lives, they have no need to fear neither in this life nor in the life to come.

PRAISE:

PETITION:

Come, follow me. (Mark 10:21)

Light and Dark

THIS is the message God has given us to pass on to you: that God is Light and in him is no darkness at all. So if we say we are his friends, but go on living in spiritual darkness and sin, we are lying. But if we are living in the light of God's presence, just as Christ does, then we have wonderful fellowship and joy with each other, and the blood of Jesus his Son cleanses us from every sin. (1 John 1:5-7)

How can Christians have "wonderful fellowship and joy with each other"?

Few criminals commit their offenses under bright lights. Like cockroaches, they are most active in the dark. Law enforcement officials tell us that a good way of protecting our homes from burglary is to keep them well lit. Most businesses that operate during the night hours usually keep everything exposed to bright lights—even the sidewalks and parking lots.   Because light seems to discourage unrighteous behavior, we have come to associate light with goodness and darkness with evil. The Bible refers to Satan and his cohorts as the "powers of darkness." And God is often called "Light," because in him can be found no trace of the darkness of sin. The more we expose ourselves to God's light, the less we will be affected by the world's darkness.

PRAISE:

PETITION:

We can spend our time in prayer. (Acts 6:4)

How to Sin

IF we say that we have no sin, we are only fooling ourselves, and refusing to accept the truth. But if we confess our sins to him, he can be depended on to forgive us and to cleanse us from every wrong. [And it is perfectly proper for God to do this for us because Christ died to wash away our sins.] If we claim we have not sinned, we are lying and calling God a liar, *for he says we have sinned.*

My little children, I am telling you this so that you will stay away from sin. But if you sin, there is someone to plead for you before the Father. His name is Jesus Christ, the one who is all that is good and who pleases God completely. He is the one who took God's wrath against our sins upon himself, and brought us into fellowship with God; and he is the forgiveness for our sins, and not only ours but all the world's. (1 John 1:8—2:2).

If we claim that we have not sinned, what are we calling God? Why?

In the process of raising a family, there are many things that parents have to teach their children. The kids must learn to walk, talk, groom themselves, eat, and behave properly. But one thing that parents never have to teach their children is how to sin. All of us are born with a sinful nature; sinning comes as naturally to us as does breathing or blinking our eyes. John says that if we say we have no sin, we are fooling ourselves. To say we've never sinned is like saying we've never taken a breath. All humans, without exception, need Christ's forgiveness and cleansing power. He is the only one who can deliver us from sin's hold.

PRAISE:

PETITION:

To pray is to desire; but it is to desire what God would have us desire. (Fenelon)

More Is Less

AND how can we be sure that we belong to him? By looking within ourselves: are we really trying to do what he wants us to?

Someone may say, "I am a Christian; I am on my way to heaven; I belong to Christ." But if he doesn't do what Christ tells him to, he is a liar. But those who do what Christ tells them to will learn to love God more and more. That is the way to know whether or not you are a Christian. Anyone who says he is a Christian should live as Christ did. (1 John 2:3-6)

How can we be sure that we belong to Christ?

Many scholars have commented that the more they know, the more they find out how much they don't know. It is impossible for any man to know everything about everything. And the more information men obtain, the more obvious it becomes that there are still worlds of information beyond their grasp or capacity. But this fact rarely hinders man's quest for further knowledge and truth. So it is in the Christian life. We must constantly reevaluate our spiritual condition to see if we are truly following Christ. Previously unexplored areas of devotion and service must be probed. The Bible must be read and reread endlessly. We cannot rely on the knowledge that we once accepted Christ as Savior. If we are not growing, we are stagnating. It is necessary that we closely follow Christ's commands in our everyday lives.

PRAISE:

PETITION:

Keep alert and pray. Otherwise temptation will overpower you. (Matt. 26:41)

Revolution of Love

DEAR brothers, I am not writing out a new rule for you to obey, for it is an old one you have always had, right from the start. You have heard it all before. Yet it is always new, and works for you just as it did for Christ; and as we obey this commandment, *to love one another,* the darkness in our lives disappears and the new light of life in Christ shines in. (1 John 2:7, 8)

What happens when we obey Christ's commandment to "love one another"?

"Love one another."   Imagine what the consequences would be if all men obeyed this command. The factional fighting in the Middle East would stop. Central American guerillas and government troops would lay down their guns. Racial prejudice would cease. The troubled waters of international relations would be calmed. And there would be no more crime or hatred in the world.   "Love one another" sounds so simple. Yet, for it to be universally obeyed, there would have to be a revolution in the hearts of billions of people. This sort of revolution is what Christianity is all about. Christ came to tell the world that it is possible to replace hatred with love. It is our duty to spread Christian love, and to spread the *message* of his love. As all Christians know, the revolution of love will ultimately overthrow the tyranny of sin.

P R A I S E :

P E T I T I O N :

Exalt the Lord our God, and worship at his holy mountain in Jerusalem, for he is holy. (Ps. 99:9)

Temple of the Sun

ANYONE who says he is walking in the light of Christ but dislikes his fellow man, is still in darkness. But whoever loves his fellow man is "walking in the light" and can see his way without stumbling around in darkness and sin. For he who dislikes his brother is wandering in spiritual darkness and doesn't know where he is going, for the darkness had made him blind so that he cannot see the way. (1 John 2:9-11)

What does John say about people who claim to be Christians but dislike their fellow men?

An ancient legend has it that three architects brought to an oriental king their models for a proposed Temple of the Sun. The first model was of stone, finely chiseled and richly polished. As the king beheld it, he could only admire and praise the splendid work. The second model was of gold; the burnished walls reflected in every angle the image of the sun. The king was awed. The third architect presented a model made entirely of glass, so transparent that at first it was invisible. But as the sunlight poured through, it was immediately obvious that *this* was the true Temple of the Sun—it reflected not its own glory but revealed and received in every part the glorious object to whose honor it was to be dedicated.   This is the supreme object of the church: to reflect the glory of Christ.

P R A I S E :

P E T I T I O N :

God grant me the serenity to accept the things I cannot change, courage to change the things I can, and wisdom to know the difference. (R. Neibuhr)

In the Red

I am writing these things to all of you, my little children, because your sins have been forgiven in the name of Jesus our Savior. I am saying these things to you older men because you really know Christ, the one who has been alive from the beginning. And you young men, I am talking to you because you have won your battle with Satan. And I am writing to you younger boys and girls because you, too, have learned to know God our Father. (1 John 2:12, 13)

Why is John saying "these things" to the older men?

Suppose that ten years ago you went to the bank and made a deposit of one hundred dollars. Ever since, you have been drawing twenty-five dollars a month on that account. "That would be impossible," you say. "The account would have been overdrawn years ago." Precisely. This is why many Christians are operating "in the red"—spiritually speaking. Years ago they received Jesus into their hearts. They were soundly saved. But ever since then they have been drawing on a beginner's experience. They have known Christ nominally, but have not come to know him by experience. We should continue to make "deposits," investing time and devotion into our spiritual condition, if we are to truly enjoy the blessings of a Christ-centered life.

PRAISE:

PETITION:

Anything is possible if you have faith. (Mark 9:23)

Hand Washing

AND so I say to you fathers who know the eternal God, and to you young men who are strong, with God's Word in your hearts, and have won your struggle against Satan: Stop loving this evil world and all that it offers you, for when you love these things you show that you do not really love God; for all these worldly things, these evil desires—the craze for sex, the ambition to buy everything that appeals to you, and the pride that comes from wealth and importance—these are not from God. They are from this evil world itself. And this world is fading away, and these evil, forbidden things will go with it, but whoever keeps doing the will of God will live forever. (1 John 2:14-17)

What will happen to those who keep on doing the will of God?

A group of first-graders had just completed a tour of the hospital, and the nurse who had guided them asked them if they had any questions. Immediately a small hand went up. **"H**ow come the people who work here are always washing their hands?" a little boy asked. After laughter had subsided, the nurse answered wisely: "They are always washing their hands for two reasons. First, they love health; and second, they hate germs!" **I**n more than one area of life, love and hate go hand in hand. (Warren Wiersbe)

P R A I S E :

P E T I T I O N :

I will say, "These are my people," and they will say, "The Lord is our God." (Zech. 13:9)

Chains of Love

DEAR children, this world's last hour has come. You have heard about the Antichrist who is coming—the one who is against Christ—and already many such persons have appeared. This makes us all the more certain that the end of the world is near. These "against-Christ" people used to be members of our churches, but they never really belonged with us or else they would have stayed. When they left us it proved that they were not of us at all.

But you are not like that, for the Holy Spirit has come upon you, and you know the truth. So I am not writing to you as to those who need to know the truth, but I warn you as those who can discern the difference between true and false.

And who is the greatest liar? The one who says that Jesus is not Christ. Such a person is antichrist, for he does not believe in God the Father and in his Son. For a person who doesn't believe in Christ, God's Son, can't have God the Father either. But he who has Christ, God's Son, has God the Father also. (1 John 2:18-23)

What does John call the one who is against Christ?

A five-year-old boy became angry with his mother and decided to run away from home. He walked out of his house with a small suitcase in a wagon, and began to trudge around the block again and again. Finally, when it was beginning to grow dark, a policeman who had been watching the boy asked, "Why do you keep walking around the block?" The little boy answered, "I'm running away." **"Y**ou call that running away?" the policeman smiled. The boy burst into tears. He sobbed, "Well, what do you want me to do? I'm not allowed to cross the street!" **T**he boy obviously respected his parents and knew that they loved him. He couldn't really run away. **I**n today's reading, John says that the "against-Christ" people who left the church had never really belonged to the fellowship. They neither loved nor respected the local body of believers. He said, "When they left us it proved that they were not of us at all."

P R A I S E :

P E T I T I O N :

Prayer means warfare: Every time we pray we possess more of the enemy's ground.

Forever in Eternity

SO keep on believing what you have been taught from the beginning. If you do, you will always be in close fellowship with both God the Father and his Son. And he himself has promised us this: *eternal life*.

These remarks of mine about the Antichrist are pointed at those who would dearly love to blindfold you and lead you astray. But you have received the Holy Spirit and he lives within you, in your hearts, so that you don't need anyone to teach you what is right. For he teaches you all things, and he is the Truth, and no liar; and so, just as he has said, you must live in Christ, never to depart from him. (1 John 2:24-27)

What should the Jewish Christians keep on believing? What will be the outcome of their belief?

It is difficult to comprehend eternity. It seems to represent the opposite of everything we experience on earth. When people are born, they live for a few years then die. New homes soon become old homes, and eventually are torn down or abandoned. All manufactured items have a limited life expectancy. On earth, nothing lasts forever. Everything is affected by death, deterioration, change, or destruction. In eternity, this trend toward mutation and extinction will be turned around. God will "program" everything to last forever; not just for a mere million, trillion, or quadrillion years, but *forever!*

P R A I S E :

P E T I T I O N :

Sing out your praises to our God, our King, the King of all the earth. Sing thoughtful praises! (Ps. 47:6, 7)

Keeping in Contact

AND now, my little children, stay in happy fellowship with the Lord so that when he comes you will be sure that all is well, and will not have to be ashamed and shrink back from meeting him. Since we know that God is always good and does only right, we may rightly assume that all those who do right are his children. (1 John 2:28, 29)

On what may we base the assumption that all those who do right are God's children?

John advises us to remain in "happy fellowship" with the Lord. What are you doing to stay in contact with the Father? Look over the list below; each of these items is important to maintaining proper fellowship with God. Are you neglecting any areas of spiritual health?

Church attendance
Sunday school attendance
Daily devotions
Prayers of intercession
Prayers of thanksgiving and praise
Bible study
Bible reading
Fellowship with other Christians
Application of the Bible to daily life
Confession of sins

PRAISE:

PETITION:

If we confess our sins to him, he can be depended on to forgive us and to cleanse us from every wrong. (1 John 1:9)

Always Ready

SEE how very much our heavenly Father loves us, for he allows us to be called his children—think of it—and we really *are!* But since most people don't know God, naturally they don't understand that we are his children. Yes, dear friends, we are already God's children, right now, and we can't even imagine what it is going to be like later on. But we do know this, that when he comes we will be like him, as a result of seeing him as he really is. And everyone who really believes this will try to stay pure because Christ is pure. (1 John 3:1-3)

What does the Father allow us Christians to be called?

A tourist traveling through the northern part of Italy came to the castle Villa Asconati. The grounds looked so inviting that the tourist asked the gardener at the gate if he might walk through them. Nothing could have pleased the gardener more. Before he left, the tourist asked, "How long has it been since the owner of the castle was here?" **"A**bout twelve years," answered the gardener. **"D**oes he ever write?" **"N**o." **T**he tourist smiled kindly and said, "You certainly keep these grounds in excellent condition. They look as if you expected your master to come tomorrow." The gardener almost interrupted the visitor: "Today, sir. Today!" **W**e should also be ever prepared for the return of our Master. As John says in today's reading, we ought to "stay pure because Christ is pure."

P R A I S E :

P E T I T I O N :

It may be that your prayers are not answered because of your disobedience to God and lack of faith. (B. Graham)

Heavenly Temptation

BUT those who keep on sinning are against God, for every sin is done against the will of God. And you know that he became a man so that he could take away our sins, and that there is no sin in him, no missing of God's will at any time in any way. So if we stay close to him, obedient to him, we won't be sinning either; but as for those who keep on sinning, they should realize this: They sin because they have never really known him or become his. (1 John 3:4-6)

Why did God become a man?

Benedito had lost his job and he had no money for food. His children were beginning to feel real hunger, and his wife was frightened about their health. As he rode his bicycle back from his brother's house, where he'd been denied a personal loan, Benedito came across a wallet in the street. He stopped, picked it up, and looked inside. He found a driver's license, several credit cards, and seventy-five dollars in cash. A thought flashed through his mind: Could this have been God's answer to his prayers? Had the money been a gift from God? After pondering the question for a few minutes, he decided that no, God would not want him to steal someone's wallet, even if the money were to be spent for desperately-needed food. He decided that stealing, no matter what the circumstances, is a sin. So, he took the wallet to the nearest police station and handed it over. "Every sin is done against the will of God."

PRAISE:

PETITION:

Follow me now! Let those who are spiritually dead care for their own dead. (Matt. 8:22)

Born Again, Again

OH, dear children, don't let anyone deceive you about this: If you are constantly doing what is good, it is because you *are* good, even as he is. But if you keep on sinning, it shows that you belong to Satan, who since he first began to sin has kept steadily at it. But the Son of God came to destroy these works of the devil. The person who has been born into God's family does not make a practice of sinning, because now God's life is in him; so he can't keep on sinning, for this new life has been born into him and controls him—he has been *born again.*

So now we can tell who is a child of God and who belongs to Satan. Whoever is living a life of sin and doesn't love his brother shows that he is not in God's family. (1 John 3:7-10)

According to this passage, why did the Son of God come to earth?

The popular term "born again" was coined by Jesus himself. He first used it when telling Nicodemus, a non-Christian religious leader, about the only way to go to heaven. Jesus told Nicodemus that it was necessary for humans to die to themselves and be "born again" out of sin.   During the past few years we have used the phrase "born-again Christians" to define evangelicals. This phrase, however, is redundant. Anyone who is born again is a Christian, and all true Christians are born again. Saying "born-again Christian" is like saying "a rich wealthy man."   Now that we've taken care of proper usage (!), let's concentrate on meaning: John says that the person who has been born into God's family (born again) does not make a practice of sinning. As Christians, we ought to lead "newborn" lives of righteousness.

P R A I S E :

P E T I T I O N :

Fear not, . . . says the Lord, for I am with you. (Jer. 46:28)

The Great Lesson

FOR the message to us from the beginning has been that we should love one another.

We are not to be like Cain, who belonged to Satan and killed his brother. Why did he kill him? Because Cain had been doing wrong and he knew very well that his brother's life was better than his. So don't be surprised, dear friends, if the world hates you. (1 John 3:11-13)

Why did Cain kill Abel?

"We may learn the finest arts of life—music, painting, sculpture, poetry—or we may master the noblest sciences, or by means of reading, study, travel, and conversations with refined people, we may attain the best culture; but if in all this we do not learn love, and become more gentle in spirit and action, we have missed the prize of living. If in the midst of all our duties, cares, trials, joys, sorrows, we are not growing day by day in sweetness, gentleness, unselfishness, thoughtfulness, and in all the branches of love, we are not learning the great lesson set for us by our Master in this school of life." (J. R. Miller) Every word Jesus ever uttered originated from a love so profound that we cannot comprehend it. Love is at the root of all that is Christian.

P R A I S E :

P E T I T I O N :

Don't pray for tasks equal to your powers. Pray for powers equal to your tasks.

"Kind of Pregnant"

IF we love other Christians it proves that we have been delivered from hell and given eternal life. But a person who doesn't have love for others is headed for eternal death. Anyone who hates his Christian brother is really a murderer at heart; and you know that no one wanting to murder has eternal life within. We know what real love is from Christ's example in dying for us. And so we also ought to lay down our lives for our Christian brothers. (1 John 3:14-16)

What is the destiny of people who don't have love for others?

When a woman is expecting a baby, she is no less pregnant at two months than at eight months following conception. There are no such things as degrees of pregnancy. Phrases such as "kind of pregnant" or "very pregnant" are absurd. A woman is either pregnant or she is not. In today's passage, John communicates to the Jewish Christians that the same principle applies to the condition of sin. A man who hates his brother is no less a sinner than a man who kills his brother. There are no such things as degrees of sin. If we have Christ in our hearts, we are free from sin; if we have not accepted Christ, we are sinners. It's just as simple as that.

PRAISE:

PETITION:

Guide me with your laws so that I will not be overcome by evil. (Ps. 119:133)

Beggar on the Corner

BUT if someone who is supposed to be a Christian has money enough to live well, and sees a brother in need, and won't help him—how can God's love be within *him?* Little children, let us stop just *saying* we love people; let us *really* love them, and *show it* by our *actions.* Then we will know for sure, by our actions, that we are on God's side, and our consciences will be clear, even when we stand before the Lord. But if we have bad consciences and feel that we have done wrong, the Lord will surely feel it even more, for he knows everything we do. (1 John 3:17-20)

What should we do instead of merely *saying* we love people?

When we see a beggar on a street corner, it is hard to know what to do. If we don't give him any money, we feel a touch of guilt, as if we're neglecting Christ's command to help the unfortunate. But if we do give him some money, we can't help but wonder if he will squander it on alcohol or the lottery. There are alternatives, of course. If someone looks hungry, we can buy them groceries; that way we will be assured that the money has been well spent. Or we can donate our time and/or money to the church or parachurch organizations that specialize in helping the poor. But regardless of the method we choose for helping the unfortunate, the important thing is that we *do* it. The world will know we are Christians by our *love in action.*

PRAISE:

PETITION:

Our Lord alone is God; we have no other Savior. (2 Sam. 22:32)

Live Communication

BUT, dearly loved friends, if our consciences are clear, we can come to the Lord with perfect assurance and trust, and get whatever we ask for because we are obeying him and doing the things that please him. And this is what God says we must do: Believe on the name of his Son Jesus Christ, and love one another. Those who do what God says— they are living with God and he with them. We know this is true because the Holy Spirit he has given us tells us so. (1 John 3:21-24)

What does God say we must do?

In this passage John gives us one of the Bible's most marvelous promises. It is comforting to know that through prayer we can have direct two-way communication with God—we approach him with our praises and requests, and he answers through his Word, through guidance, and through miracles. Throughout the Scriptures we read of people who were not afraid to make specific requests to God: Abraham's servant prayed, Rebekah appeared; Moses cried out to God, the sea divided in two; Joshua prayed, Achan was discovered; Hannah prayed, Samuel was born; Daniel prayed, the lions were muzzled; Nehemiah prayed, the king's heart was softened; Jehoshaphat cried out to God, God turned away his foes.

P R A I S E :

P E T I T I O N :

Prayer is not conquering God's reluctance, but taking hold of God's willingness. (P. Brooks)

Believing Anything

DEARLY loved friends, don't always believe everything you hear just because someone says it is a message from God: test it first to see if it really is. For there are many false teachers around, and the way to find out if their message is from the Holy Spirit is to ask: Does it really agree that Jesus Christ, God's Son, actually became man with a human body? If so, then the message is from God. If not, the message is not from God but from one who is against Christ, like the "Antichrist" you have heard about who is going to come, and his attitude of enmity against Christ is already abroad in the world. (1 John 4:1-3)

Should we automatically believe people who say they are bringing us messages from God? Explain your answer.

Many people believe anything and everything they see in print. They assume that the writers, editors, and publishers are generally "decent" people, and that if they have put forth the effort to print something, chances are it will be accurate. There is also a tendency among people to believe that if a minister has attracted a large body of church members, he has been confirmed in his ministry and he is preaching the truth.   Such assumptions are dangerous. John appears to have been concerned with the gullibility of certain Jewish Christians who were falling for the heresies of false teachers. In this passage he prescribes a formula for testing to see whether a message is from God. He says we should ask: "Does [the message] really agree that Jesus Christ, God's Son, actually became man with a human body?"

PRAISE:

PETITION:

You are the world's light—a city on a hill, glowing in the night for all to see. (Matt. 5:14)

Fifty-five Kisses

DEAR friends, let us practice loving each other, for love comes from God and those who are loving and kind show that they are the children of God, and that they are getting to know him better. But if a person isn't loving and kind, it shows that he doesn't know God—for God is love.

God showed how much he loved us by sending his only Son into this wicked world to bring to us eternal life through his death. In this act we see what real love is: it is not our love for God, but his love for us when he sent his Son to satisfy God's anger against our sins. (1 John 4:7-10)

Why is it important for us to "practice loving each other"?

A distraught father once related the following story: "One year ago today I sat at my desk with a month's bills and accounts before me when my bright-faced, starry-eyed lad of twelve rushed in and impetuously announced, 'Hey, Dad, this is your birthday. You're fifty-five years old, and I'm going to give you fifty-five kisses, one for each year!' He began to peck away and I exclaimed, 'Andrew, don't do it now. Can't you see I'm busy?' **"H**is silence attracted my attention, and looking up, I saw his big blue eyes fill with tears. Apologetically, I said, 'Come on over and finish the kisses now.' But he did not hear me. **"T**wo months later Andrew drowned in a swimming accident. If I could only tell him now how much I regret those thoughtless words I spoke. It takes time to love one another. . . ."

PRAISE:

PETITION:

Always keep on praying. (1 Thess. 5:17)

Too Small to Love Back

WE need have no fear of someone who loves us perfectly; his perfect love for us eliminates all dread of what he might do to us. If we are afraid, it is for fear of what he might do to us, and shows that we are not fully convinced that he really loves us. So you see, our love for him comes as a result of his loving us first.

If anyone says "I love God," but keeps on hating his brother, he is a liar; for if he doesn't love his brother who is right there in front of him, how can he love God whom he has never seen? And God himself has said that one must love not only God, but his brother too. (1 John 4:18-21)

Our love for Christ comes as a result of what?

A mother was sewing while her little girl was busily occupied with her dolls and toys. After some time, the little girl came to her busy parent and wanted to be loved and caressed. "Why do you want me to hold you?" asked the mother. " 'Cause I love you," lisped the little girl. "What about your dolls and your toys? Don't you love them too?" said her mother teasingly. With amazing insight, the little girl answered, "Yes, but I love you more. I guess it's 'cause *you loved me when I was too small to love you back.*" Tears welled up in the mother's eyes as she contemplated God's great compassion for us. He loved us when we could not love him back.

PRAISE:

PETITION:

Let me see your kindness to me in the morning, for I am trusting you. Show me where to walk, for my prayer is sincere. (Ps. 143:8)

Radical Love

IF you believe that Jesus is the Christ—that he is God's Son and your Savior—then you are a child of God. And all who love the Father love his children too. So you can find out how much you love God's children—your brothers and sisters in the Lord—by how much you love and obey God. Loving God means doing what he tells us to do, and really, that isn't hard at all; for every child of God can obey him, defeating sin and evil pleasure by trusting Christ to help him.

But who could possibly fight and win this battle except by believing that Jesus is truly the Son of God? And we know he is, because God said so with a voice from heaven when Jesus was baptized, and again as he was facing death—yes, not only at his baptism but also as he faced death. And the Holy Spirit, forever truthful, says it too. So we have these three witnesses: the voice of the Holy Spirit in our hearts, the voice from heaven at Christ's baptism, and the voice before he died. And they all say the same thing: that Jesus Christ is the Son of God. (1 John 5:1-8)

According to today's reading, what does "loving God" mean?

In this passage, John sets forth a logical proposition. He says we can determine a person's relationship with Christ by observing him with the rest of God's family: If someone is a true Christian, he loves God. Anyone who loves God must also love his creation as well, which includes man. So, anyone who loves God must also love his fellow man.   One of the most difficult aspects of Christianity is the radical love it requires of its followers. Let us remember to always pray for an increasing capacity to love our neighbors.

PRAISE:

PETITION:

Praise is the blossom of prayer.

The Poor Rich Man

WE believe men who witness in our courts, and so surely we can believe whatever God declares. And God declares that Jesus is his Son. All who believe this know in their hearts that it is true. If anyone doesn't believe this, he is actually calling God a liar, because he doesn't believe what God has said about his Son.

And what is it that God has said? That he has given us eternal life, and that this life is in his Son. So whoever has God's Son has life; whoever does not have his Son, does not have life.

I have written this to you who believe in the Son of God so that you may know you have eternal life. (1 John 5:9-13)

Who does God declare Jesus to be?

A certain Muslim lived in a cottage on a hill. Every week as he returned from his itinerary of commerce, he rode his camel to a little stream. And every week as the camel stopped to drink, it nosed up the pebbles in order to make a deeper place for drinking. Again and again, the Muslim picked up the bright stones the animal uncovered and took them home with him, placing them on a shelf near his fireplace. **O**ne day a traveler told the Muslim of the easy comfort and riches that certain men in the city enjoyed; the traveler filled the Muslim's eyes and heart with discontent. So, he sold his cottage and wandered the earth looking for money. Finally he died in rags and poverty, and was buried. The man who bought the cottage found the stones and preserved them. One day a merchant came to his home and discovered that these well-preserved stones were diamonds. The owner of the diamonds immediately became a millionaire. The first man had great wealth, but being ignorant of it, sold it and traveled the world looking for it. The second man simply made use of what he had. **A**ll people have eternal life at their disposal. Some respond to this treasure like the first man, some like the second.

P R A I S E :

P E T I T I O N :

O Lord God of Israel, there is no god like you in heaven or earth, for you are loving and kind and you keep your promises to your people if they do their best to do your will. (1 Kings 8:22, 23)

The Greater Hand

IF you see a Christian sinning in a way that does not end in death, you should ask God to forgive him and God will give him life, unless he has sinned that one fatal sin. But there is that one sin which ends in death and if he has done that, there is no use praying for him. Every wrong is a sin, of course. I'm not talking about these ordinary sins; I am speaking of that one that ends in death.

No one who has become part of God's family makes a practice of sinning, for Christ, God's Son, holds him securely and the devil cannot get his hands on him. We know that we are children of God and that all the rest of the world around us is under Satan's power and control. (1 John 5:16-19)

Who is currently in power over our world?

When a little girl takes hold of her father's hand, he also takes hold of hers. Her safety in crossing the street doesn't depend on her hold, but on her father's. When we submit ourselves to Christ, confessing our sins to him and accepting him into our hearts, Jesus will hold us securely as we "cross the streets" of life. John makes the promise that the devil cannot so much as touch the person who has become a part of God's family. What a comfort to know that we don't have to depend on our own strength or vigilance. We have an active enemy, but we also have a watchful Guardian.

P R A I S E :

P E T I T I O N :

Praise the Lord. For the Lord our God, the Almighty, reigns. (Rev. 19:6)

Merry Christmas!

AND we know that Christ, God's Son, has come to help us understand and find the true God. And now we are in God because we are in Jesus Christ his Son, who is the only true God; and he is eternal Life.

Dear children, keep away from anything that might take God's place in your hearts. Amen. (1 John 5:20, 21)

What does John tell the Jewish Christians to keep away from?

Today is Christmas, the day when we celebrate the coming of God's Son to earth, the incarnation of God into a human body. Today is a day of rejoicing for all Christians—it reminds us of God's immeasurable love for his creation. John tells the Jewish Christians that Jesus came to earth to help us understand and find the true God. He came to free us from the law, and to show us the way of love.   Merry Christmas!

PRAISE:

PETITION:

Seven days without prayer makes one weak. (A. E. Bartlett)

Successful Kids

FROM: John, the old Elder of the church.

To: That dear woman Cyria, one of God's very own, and to her children whom I love so much, as does everyone else in the church. Since the Truth is in our hearts forever, God the Father and Jesus Christ his Son will bless us with great mercy and much peace, and with truth and love. How happy I am to find some of your children here, and to see that they are living as they should, following the Truth, obeying God's command.

And now I want to urgently remind you, dear friends, of the old rule God gave us right from the beginning, that Christians should love one another. If we love God, we will do whatever he tells us to. And he has told us from the very first to love each other. (2 John 1-6)

Which "old rule" of God does John reiterate here?

Charles Spurgeon once said that "it is very grievous to see how some professedly Christian parents are satisfied so long as their children display cleverness in learning or sharpness in business, although they show no signs of a renewed life. . . . Many who ought to know better think themselves superlatively blessed in their children if they become rich, if they marry well, if they enter profitable enterprises, or if they attain eminence in their profession. When a man's heart is really right with God and he himself has been saved from the wrath to come, it is certain that he is anxious about his children's souls and feels that nothing could give him greater joy than to hear that his children walk in truth."

P R A I S E :

P E T I T I O N :

Come before him with thankful hearts. Let us sing him psalms of praise. (Ps. 95:2)

God's Elite

WATCH out for the false leaders—and there are many of them around—who don't believe that Jesus Christ came to earth as a human being with a body like ours. Such people are against the truth and against Christ. Beware of being like them, and losing the prize that you and I have been working so hard to get. See to it that you win your full reward from the Lord. For if you wander beyond the teaching of Christ, you will leave God behind; while if you are loyal to Christ's teachings, you will have God too. Then you will have both the Father and the Son.

If anyone comes to teach you, and he doesn't believe what Christ taught, don't even invite him into your home. Don't encourage him in any way. If you do you will be a partner with him in his wickedness.

Well, I would like to say much more, but I don't want to say it in this letter, for I hope to come to see you soon and then we can talk over these things together and have a joyous time.

Greetings from the children of your sister—another choice child of God. (2 John 7-13)

What happens to believers who "wander beyond the teaching of Christ"?

Some people are surprised by the elitist mentality John apparently exhibited here when he said, "If anyone comes to teach you, and he doesn't believe what Christ taught, don't even invite him into your home." But *all* the great teachers of the Christian church were what one would call "narrowminded" today. They knew only one way to heaven.   Astronauts returning to the earth from the moon are also very "narrowminded." The spaceship must follow a certain limited path which permits little deviation. If they were to miss their entry slot by even one degree, they could end up lost in space or burned up completely. We should be careful with whom we align ourselves. When you tie two birds together, though they might have a total of four wings, they don't fly better. In fact, they don't fly at all.

PRAISE:

PETITION:

Pray much for others; plead for God's mercy upon them; give thanks for all he is going to do for them. (1 Tim. 2:1)

John's Notes

FROM: John, the Elder.
  To: Dear Gaius, whom I truly love.
  Dear friend, I am praying that all is well with you and that your body is as healthy as I know your soul is. Some of the brothers traveling by have made me very happy by telling me that your life stays clean and true, and that you are living by the standards of the Gospel. I could have no greater joy than to hear such things about my children. (3 John 1-4)

Is John happy about the reports he has received concerning Gaius? Explain.

It is interesting to compare the epistles of 2 John and 3 John. Both are brief enough to have been written on a single sheet of papyrus. Both deal with similar problems: the visit of itinerant teachers and what treatment should be afforded them. The second epistle of John was written to instruct Christians not to receive those who denied the incarnate Word of God. The third epistle was written to instruct them to receive those who have a good record and who love and walk in the truth. The positive instruction of the third letter is to complement the negative instruction of the second letter. Both letters are concerned with Christian truth and love and hospitality. The second letter is addressed to the local church. The third letter is addressed by name to one of the leading members of the local church—Gaius.

P R A I S E :

P E T I T I O N :

One can see God in everything, but we can see God best with our eyes closed.

Money Matters

DEAR friend, you are doing a good work for God in taking care of the traveling teachers and missionaries who are passing through. They have told the church here of your friendship and your loving deeds. I am glad when you send them on their way with a generous gift. For they are traveling for the Lord, and take neither food, clothing, shelter, nor money from those who are not Christians, even though they have preached to them. So we ourselves should take care of them in order that we may become partners with them in the Lord's work. (3 John 5-8)

Who should take care of the financial needs of itinerant evangelists?

In this passage we are reminded of Paul's gratitude to the Philippian church. Just as Paul commends the Philippians for their faithful financial support of the church, John praises Gaius for his faithfulness and generosity. John reminded Gaius that the church should not have to appeal to the world to support its cause. The heathen cannot support missions. That is why for Christians to give large sums of money to non-Christian charities is to rob the church of her only biblical means of support for her local and worldwide ministry. The unsaved in our cities will never support their own evangelization. We must do it ourselves!

PRAISE:

PETITION:

May the God of peace himself make you entirely pure and devoted to God. (1 Thess. 5:23)

Troublemaker

I sent a brief letter to the church about this, but proud Diotrephes, who loves to push himself forward as the leader of the Christians there, does not admit my authority over him and refuses to listen to me. When I come I will tell you some of the things he is doing and what wicked things he is saying about me and what insulting language he is using. He not only refuses to welcome the missionary travelers himself, but tells others not to, and when they do he tries to put them out of the church.

Dear friend, don't let this bad example influence you. Follow only what is good. Remember that those who do what is right prove that they are God's children; and those who continue in evil prove that they are far from God. (3 John 9-11)

Why is John disappointed in Diotrephes?

Diotrephes was one of John's greatest concerns. He was a troublemaker who constantly stirred up controversy and divisiveness. Dr. H. Ironside has said that "unfortunately, the spiritual descendants of Diotrephes are many. They may be found not only in the great denominations, but in the humblest Christian assemblies. They are self-seeking, self-important, self-elected 'bishops' and 'elders' who lord it over their brethren and arrogate to themselves the right to say who may or who may not be recognized." It is said that Dr. Lee Robertson wrote an article on Diotrephes in a denominational paper. Later the editor told him that twenty-five pastors had cancelled their subscriptions to the magazine to show their resentment against being personally attacked!

P R A I S E :

P E T I T I O N :

Be delighted with the Lord. Then he will give you all your heart's desires. (Ps. 37:4)

Your Future

BUT everyone, including Truth itself, speaks highly of Demetrius. I myself can say the same for him, and you know I speak the truth.

I have much to say but I don't want to write it, for I hope to see you soon and then we will have much to talk about together. So good-bye for now. Friends here send their love, and please give each of the folks there a special greeting from me. (3 John 12-14)

Who does John commend in this passage? Why?

As you come to the close of another year, look back over the events of the past twelve months. How have you changed? Which goals have you achieved or abandoned? Which new goals have you added? If you have spent the past months reading the daily devotionals of *In Transit,* you have probably done some thinking about your beliefs, your behavior, and your Christian walk. Do you sense that you have experienced spiritual growth? How? In the spaces below, list your five most important goals for the year to come:

1. _____
2. _____
3. _____
4. _____
5. _____

"In everything you do, put God first, and he will direct you and crown your efforts with success" (Prov. 3:6).

Man is the only created being who bows in humility and adoration.